Selected Letters

SELECTED WRITINGS
OF C.F.W. WALTHER

Selected Letters

† Roy A. Suelflow, Translator

Aug. R. Suelflow, Series Editor

Publishing House
St. Louis

Copyright © 1981
Concordia Publishing House
3558 South Jefferson
Saint Louis, Missouri 63118

Manufactured in the United States of America

1   2   3   4   5   6   7   8   9   10   WW   90   89   88   87   86   85   84   83   82   81

Library of Congress Cataloging in Publication Data

Walther, C. F. W. (Carl Ferdinand Wilhelm), 1811-1887.
    Selected letters.

    (Selected writings of C.F.W. Walther)
    1. Walther, C.F.W. (Carl Ferdinand Wilhelm), 1811-1887. 2. Lutheran Church—Clergy—Correspondence. 3. Clergy—United States—Correspondence. I. Title. II. Series: Walther, C. F. W. (Carl Ferdinand Wilhelm), 1811-1887. Selections. English. 1981.
BX8080.W3A4 1981   284.1'322'0924 [B]   81-3228
ISBN: 978-0-7586-1820-7   AACR2

Contents

Walther as Churchman: Administration of Synod and Interchurch Relationships

Walther the Schoolman

Introduction

It is an ambitious project to permit C. F. W. Walther (1811—87) to address English readers. Efforts to do so have occurred in the past from time to time. But this English edition constitutes one of the most significant contributions made to the study of the theology of Lutheranism in America within past years. The stereotype of Walther heretofore imposed upon him by those who were unable to read his German writings will now be significantly altered! It is to be regretted that a rich treasury of many other works from Walther's pen still await a future project.

Dr. Henry E. Jacobs (1844—1932), late president of Lutheran Theological Seminary in Philadelphia, Pa., said of Walther:

> He is as orthodox as John Gerhard, but as fervent as a pietist, as correct in form as a university or court preacher, and yet as popular as Luther himself. If the Lutheran Church will bring its doctrines again to the people, it must be as faithful and as definite in its doctrine and as interesting and thoroughly adapted to the times in form, as is the case in Walther. He is a model preacher in the Lutheran Church ("Dr. Walther as a Preacher, *Lutheran Church Review,* III [October 1889], 319).

In each of the volumes a special effort was made to select the most significant and relevant materials and to have Walther speak contemporary English. We have further endeavored, wherever possible, to quote from the American Edition of *Luther's Works* and to utilize the Revised Standard Version of the Bible for Scriptural references. Quotations from the Lutheran Confessions were keyed to the Tappert edition of the *Book of Concord.* It was helpful to be able to consult some resources which Walther had in his own library.

Walther was an exceedingly involved church leader. A founding father of The Lutheran Church—Missouri Synod, he served as its first president 1847—50 and 1864—78. He was Concordia Seminary's (St. Louis) foremost instructor from 1849 until his death in 1887, and served as its president 1850—87.

His concern for Lutheran unity is demonstrative. He conceived the "Free Conferences" in the aftermath of the confessional crisis in 1855. Later, in 1872, he was elected the first president of a new pan-Lutheran federation, the Evangelical Lutheran Synodical Conference.

The project to translate Walther into English received support from The Lutheran Church—Missouri Synod in 1962, when a special committee was formed. When funds were not available, the project was transferred to Concordia Publishing House. It has now become a pioneer in publishing both Luther's and Walther's select works in English.

Walther's classic *Law and Gospel,* generally considered one of the most important books produced within American Lutheranism, deserves a volume of its own. In it we see him as theological professor, with his students gathered around him.

Another volume acquaints us with Walther the preacher. He made a great impact on his hearers, and much of his sermonic and homiletical material was published in German during his lifetime and in the years following his death. In spite of this, several thousand sermon manuscripts still remain untouched.

In a further volume we see Walther the convention essayist. None of these essays, presented to Western District conventions between 1873 and 1886, with their ever-recurring theme "To God All Glory!" have seen the English light of day until now.

Of particular importance were Walther's writings on the church, and one of our volumes brings a condensation of these. *Church and Ministry* (1852), *The Proper Form* (1863), and *The True Visible Church* (1866) give the theological foundation for the Missouri Synod's strong emphasis on the congregation and on lay involvement.

We include a volume of Walther's correspondence. It lets us see him in his intense and complex relationships with many different people. Concordia Historical Institute, with funds provided by the Aid Association for Lutherans, has in recent years transcribed several hundred original *Fraktur* letters. Only a few have been published in English heretofore, and we too can bring only a selection.

Finally we take a look at Walther the editor—one of his most important functions. Through *Lehre und Wehre* (from which we bring articles never before presented in English) and *Der Lutheraner* Walther exerted a strong influence toward orthodox Lutheranism.

The translators of this edition hope that readers and users will develop a new appreciation for this 19th-century hero of faith, but above all, that Walther, as the preceptor of Luther in America, will direct the readers to the very cross of our Lord Jesus Christ, his and our only hope.

Aug. R. Suelflow, *Series Editor*

Translator's Preface

In the 1830s a small group of students at the University of Leipzig in Saxony, Germany, became convinced that the only hope for their personal salvation and for their church, long devastated by rationalism, lay in the rediscovery of their Christian roots in the Lutheran reformation. They were by no means the only Germans to experience a thoroughgoing religious awakening in those years. But they became the carriers of this religious awakening to America, where in a few years it was to take organizational form in the shape of The Lutheran Church—Missouri Synod. But this did not come to pass except through a most unusual sequence of developments. In these developments C. F. W. Walther played a very significant role.

Carl Ferdinand Wilhelm Walther (1811—87) was a man with unusual talents and ability who, like Carlyle's "heroes" or great men, appeared in history precisely at the time when his talents carried him to greatness on the cross-currents of history.

In his letters many facets of Walther's greatness are evident. His commitment to Biblical truth and to the Lutheran Confessions, his keen ability to apply this to pastoral problems, his Gospel-oriented approach— these are some of Walther's qualities evidenced in his letters. But he was also a devoted husband, a loving father, and a devoted and respected friend among his peers.

Walther produced an enormous amount of correspondence in an age when every letter was written in longhand in German script. At one time he mentioned that he was receiving five or six letters a day which required serious responses. At that rate he might have produced tens of thousands of letters. He had no way of keeping carbons, of course. Only in a very rare case or two does a copy of a letter survive which he had a student secretary make before mailing the original.

Walther's son-in-law, J. H. Niemann (1848—1910), began the first larger collection of Walther's letters, which Dr. Ludwig Fuerbringer (1864—1947) added to those he himself had been collecting, making over 500 in all. When the Concordia Historical Institute (CHI) was organized in the 1920s, this collection became the core of the Walther correspondence in the official archives of Synod. Other churchmen collected additional letters and deposited them with the CHI, unfortunately not always depositing the original but often handwritten copies made by unidentified individuals. The copies are often in very neat handwriting—much more legible than Walther's own hurried script—but the copyists did not always know the people or places mentioned, and thus there are serious problems with spellings with which a translator and editor has to cope.

The first serious attempt at publishing a collection of Walther's letters was by Dr. Ludwig Fuerbringer in his *Briefe von C. F. W. Walther an seine Freunde, Synodalgenossen und Familienglieder* (St. Louis: Concordia Publishing House, 1915—1916). This two-volume collection in German contained 225 letters, none of them later than 1871. Fuerbringer frequently deleted the names of people Walther was discussing. This makes it mandatory for a serious study to undertake time-consuming comparisons with the very-hard-to-read Gothic-script originals in the CHI. Fuerbringer's work is particularly valuable because he often made editorial notations or filled in complete names in cases where Walther used only initials—even on letters which Fuerbringer excluded from the published edition. Where a letter in this volume can be found in Fuerbringer's collection, we give the reference right under the heading. A number of Walther's letters in German can also be found in *Dr. C. F. W. Walther* by Martin Guenther (St. Louis: Concordia Publishing House, 1890), both in an appendix and scattered throughout the book.

Carl S. Meyer (1907—72) published two collections of Walther's letters in English. They are *Letters of C. F. W. Walther: A Selection* (Philadelphia: Fortress Press, 1969) and *Walther Speaks to the Church* (St. Louis: Concordia Publishing House, 1973).

Prof. Werner Karl Wadewitz of Concordia Senior College, Fort Wayne, Ind., some years ago undertook the massive task of transcribing into typescript all the letters of Walther in the CHI collection. This proved very helpful for this present project. But certain difficulties still remained, especially in the case where Wadewitz had only copies to work with and where the original copyist had copied names incorrectly. In some cases the task of annotating these letters proved to be extremely time-consuming.

We have made changes in Walther's paragraphing, breaking up the extremely long paragraphs he often wrote.

It is regretted that not more of Walther's letters could be included in this volume. Severe limitations of space permit us to bring only a sampling of letters showing Walther as a family man and friend, as a pastor, as a churchman, and as an educator and schoolman.

† Roy A. Suelflow

Walther in His Personal Letters

To His Brother Otto Hermann
Kloesterlein, Germany

Chursdorf, Germany, August 1833

Dear brother,[1]

Even though I haven't much time, yet since Wilhelm[2] is going back now, I must impart a few things to you in writing.

The most important of these for me is that last Thursday I received the citation for my examination. The *written* examinations are to take place on the 13th and 14th of September, the *oral* examination on the 19th of September. It is up to you whether you want to come on the 19th, which I indeed would appreciate very much. You will, however, take consideration of your circumstances; I do not demand a sacrifice.

Furthermore, with the citation I also received the text for my sermon and catechization, which I am to submit next Thursday. The text for the sermon is Acts 26:24-29. I am yet undecided between the two themes: I. The Preaching of the Word of God to Those Who Are Not Obedient to Its Effects

(Exposition:)
1) according to its nature
   a) uncompromising in regard to purity of doctrine
   b) but with consideration for the particular spiritual condition of the hearers when it comes to the choice of material and the manner of presentation.
2) according to its result
   a) either it is slandered as nonsense,
   b) or the working of grace is restricted

II. The Results of Witnessing to Jesus in Those Who Refuse to Be Obedient to the Power of the Divine Word.—The text for the catechization is 2 Thessalonians 3:10-11, with the prescribed theme: Faith in the Divine Support of Human Life Does Not Release Us from the Duty to Work for Our Support Ourselves.—Sound advice is now scarce: I cannot make any progress in working it out. Please back me up with your prayers. I rely on this.

You would like to have the recipe for those suffering from lung disease. It is as follows: Take fresh unsalted goat's butter, 6 spoonfuls; melt this and mix it with 3 spoonfuls of honey. Stir this well, until the butter is well mixed. Take one tablespoon twice daily, mornings before breakfast, and evenings shortly before retiring. Continue this for a few months. Avoid anything sour. Pray God for His blessing, and in a short time you will be cured from tuberculosis.

Have you read in the paper the proposal of Minister Dr. Mueller for the establishment of an ecclesiastical board which would in the future formulate the doctrine of the Saxon Church, with the prescription and the good advice to formulate it so "as it will be best received *by the educated people*"? It seems as if God would inflict a severe judgment on the Saxon Church. Under these conditions we would probably never be able to enter the ministry, at least not in Saxony, including Schoenburg. Who can bind himself to symbols like that without jeopardizing his salvation?

It seems that in the investigation of orthodox teachers they want to start with Keyl.[3] Already he has received a notice from the supreme council in which he is forbidden to teach the doctrine of the natural depravity of man and is accused of Manichean, Schwenkfeldian, and Donatistic errors. He is said to have led two people astray by his crass teachings about the impending punishment in hell. He was therefore put on trial. He is supposed to pay a fine of more than 80 thaler. He does not yet have an answer to his appeal to the highest secular Court of Appeals, in reference to the oath he took on the Symbolical Books at that same place where they tried to force him to retract that oath.

God be with you, even as He was with me yesterday when I preached in Chursdorf and in Langenberg. Let us praise Him, fear Him, and always plead for grace.

Greetings from many.

Farewell, and answer soon,

Your distressed brother,
[C.] F. W. [Walther]

To Emilie Buenger
Perry County, Mo.
(Fuerbringer, I, 1—3)[1]

St. Louis, Aug. 10, 1841

Dear, heartily beloved Emilie,[2]

As little as I have till now had the right to write to you, and particularly with such a greeting, yet I cannot do otherwise if I am to be honest with you. Nearly two years have gone by, as you will perhaps recall, since through your dear brother Fritz[3] I at least indicated from afar a precious, sublime wish of my heart which no one in the world but you can fulfill. But how wonderful have been the ways on which our heavenly Father has led me during the past two years! I do not need to tell you anything of this; my life has been an open book for you.[4] Only this much I must confess, that I often, with deep misery of soul, felt forced to believe that God's dark leadings were a sign that it was not His holy will to grant me the fulfillment of the dearest wish I have in this world.

However, also in me the promise of Psalm 103 has been fulfilled: "He will not always chide, nor will He keep His anger forever." God has turned His friendly countenance toward me once more, and trustfully I have therefore again laid my old wish down at the feet of my God and Savior. I have also today poured out my heart to your dear mother.[5] So you alone remain, whose yes or no will reveal to me the will of my gracious God.

Therefore I cannot wait any longer to express this my wish frankly also to you. It is this: Will you, dearest Emilie, become my life's companion? Can you return, at least in some degree, the love which, as I now confidently hope, God has enkindled in my heart for you? Do you believe that you can live with me happily, contentedly, and God-pleasingly in a union as intimate and inseparable unto death as the holy estate of matrimony is?

I do not believe that any explanations on my part are necessary, as if you first had to become acquainted with me. You know me, my character, my faith, my failings and weaknesses, my outward position; you know that you will find no temporal fortune, no honor before the world, no assured future with me. I can therefore only add my pledge that you will have in me a spouse who will love you dearly and by God's grace faithfully. I have no one whom I could ask to speak for me to you; I have therefore prayed the dear Lord Himself to be my Eliezer[6] and to direct your heart according to His holy will and to our mutual temporal and eternal welfare. Follow His guidance and then inform me by return messenger of your God-directed decision.

As communication between here and Perry County is often long interrupted, you will not, as I hope for your love, think ill of me for making the following suggestion. If you can, in God's name, say yes to my question, then we shall look upon your declaration as the completion of our betrothal, since your dear mother today and my good mother already in Germany in advance have given their parental consent thereto. I would therefore in this event not come to Perry County before our marriage. If this is agreeable to you, I should like to have the publication of the banns of marriage made in Frohna and here on the 13th, 14th and 15th Sundays after Trinity (5th, 12th, and 19th of September) and the marriage ensue perhaps on the Monday after the last date, namely Sept. 20, in the church at Frohna. The day of my arrival and that of your dear mother would be, if you accept my suggestion, God willing, on the 15th or 16th of September. The enclosed letter, addressed to my dear brother-in-law,[7] contains the request to publish the banns on the suggested days and to perform the marriage ceremony;[8] I beg you, therefore, not to deliver this letter to my dear brother-in-law before you can also announce to him that you have given me your dear yes.

I am almost surprised at myself for daring, in this first letter, to speak so freely of betrothal, of publishing the banns, of marriage, etc.; how much more will you perhaps be astonished! May you, however, recognize this as nothing else than my wholehearted confidence in you, that you will, even if you could not give me your hand, certainly grant me the privilege of having at least vividly imagined myself out of pure grace, without my merit or worthiness, in the position of seeing you as my God-given, dearly beloved bride!

Now, may all my wishing and hoping be commended to the Lord and to the guidance of His love and grace! May He give you a joyous decision and then make your heart firm, sure, and certain that you rest in His grace and under His holy benevolence; and if God brings us together, we will mutually serve Him day and night, without ceasing, faithfully, until death, by the power of His omnipotent grace in Christ Jesus, your and my Savior. Amen.

Please give my hearty greetings to dear Ernst[9] and Lyddie[10] and tell them that I hope to see them very soon if God wills.

Your daily intercessor with God,
Carl Ferdinand Wilhelm Walther

To Emilie Buenger

Perry County, Mo.
(Fuerbringer, I, 4—5)

St. Louis, Aug. 25, 1841

In Christ Jesus, my dearly beloved bride,

After a long, yearning wait, your[1] precious answer is finally in my hands. As I see with great joy from your answer, God has assured you of His gracious will, that we should together journey through this earthly life toward heaven. May His holy name be praised eternally! Let us now daily beseech our good and gracious God for His Holy Spirit that we may enter into the estate of marriage in His grace and fear. A chief purpose of matrimony is that thereby the Christian church is expanded and edified. Oh, join me in praying in the name of Jesus, that our Lord would grant grace that on the day of our wedding we may lay the first cornerstone for a little house-church (Romans 16:5). How I long to see our home as a true model for a genuinely Christian family, in which God dwells and all God's children are stirred up to praise our Father in heaven! (Matthew 5:16).

But the more I feel inadequate for this, the more I hope for from you, my precious Emilie. May God continue to adorn you with the true beauty of a bride of Christ, with humility, faith, confidence, praise of God, with a heavenly attitude and a joyful denial of all things earthly. Oh, how happy we will be then!

Last Sunday I delivered a short engagement address for the betrothal of our dear little Clementine,[2] in which I tried to visualize for her how God Himself is encouraging her and her bridegroom, who is a very respectable, Godfearing, and likeable man, at the very threshhold of their new life, with the words of Ps. 128: "You shall be happy, and it shall be well with you." You can well imagine that I was also thinking of *us,* and I hope that also in your heart the lively realization may increase as to how comforting it is that God Himself tells us in that Biblical betrothal and wedding hymn, Ps. 128, not "You poor people, you are bad off," but rather: "You shall be happy, and it shall be well with you." Let us therefore gladly cast all our cares on the Lord and cling to this precious Word of promise with firm confidence. Then God will also fulfill this promise for us, and we by His grace will be blessed not only in good days but also in bad.

It would be good for you now in this time of preparation if you could read something good about marriage, that estate which we shall so soon be entering. I would recommend the wedding sermons which that dear man of God, Dr. Luther, included in his Epistle sermons. My brother-in-law[3] has this volume. Besides this, the reading of the fine apocryphal Book of Tobit would certainly be helpful and enlightening for you.

It was a great joy for me that you accepted the proposed dates. I have nothing to change in this matter. Only one thing I have come to understand, and that is that it will not be practical to perform the ceremony in Frohna. Could we not possibly settle on the Dresden church? My brother-in-law has proposed the college, but I fear there would be too many disturbing memories.[4]

Because Mr. Schubert is in a sudden hurry to leave, I need to break off here.[5]

Cordially greet our dear Dr. Ernst and Lyddie[6] and please ask Ernst not to be angry with me because I am intending to take you away from him. Tell him that my heart's desire is that God might soon open a way for him that he could follow my example, and then he won't need to be concerned about being without a housekeeper.

Now, may God be with you, my heartily beloved bride! May He preserve your love for me, even as I will remain therein with the help of God even unto death.

Your
Ferdinand

To His Wife

St. Louis, Mo.
(Fuerbringer, I, 73—82)

Erlangen, Germany,[1] Oct. 11, 1851

My dear, precious wife,

Finally I am with my dear old friend Delitzsch,[2] as you see from the return address, and I make haste to send you a sign of life. My last letter, from Verden, has reached you by now, I hope. May our faithful God grant that also these lines may find you and our dear little ones well and healthy. As far as I am concerned, the Lord has graciously led me and my travel companion[3] on all our ways, and has sent His holy angel so that I did not dash my foot against a stone. In spite of the many mental and physical exertions, I have become constantly more energetic.

From Verden we traveled to Halle. There we looked up our dear Dr. Guericke[4] and stayed with him two days with great enjoyment. For in him we found the first believing theologian in Germany with whom we soon saw eye to eye on everything. He also expressed great joy to recognize and feel himself completely one with us. From Halle we made a diversion to Nordhausen, by request of our neighbor Mr. Rudloff,[5] to look up his relative there. We found the friendliest reception there. Rudloff's sister did not give any indication that she has become a really heartfelt believer, much less so her husband. But we observed with joy that their two daughters belong to the congregation of separated Lutherans in Nordhausen and attended services there whenever these are conducted by Pastor Wermelskirch of Erfurt. Please tell Rudloff that.

From Nordhausen we went back over Halle to Leipzig. Although there we learned to know many dear, believing men and were both spiritually and physically refreshed by them (although almost always through hard disputations), the biggest joy was accorded me by the

18

renewed acquaintance with Dr. Marbach[6] and his dear wife. During the first hour of our meeting our attitude to each other was restrained and full of evidence of mutual distrust, but we soon had a deep mutual exchange of ideas from which I learned that the Marbach family, although under totally different circumstances and under totally different divine guidance, has come to the same understanding and outlook as we Lutherans in America as far as matters of the church and Christianity are concerned. God be praised that with Marbach the old love has not only been rekindled but is burning in much brighter and purer flames than ever before. Although with the other believing scholars in Leipzig (Master Schneider, Professor Kahnis, Candidate von Zezschwitz,[7] and others) I had to fight a hard battle against the Loehe[8] errors, at Marbach's home I found a glad "Yea and Amen" to all our present convictions which I presented to them, with thanks and praise to God.

We also visited Mr. Doederlein's[9] father and brother here; they are all well. To my joy I saw that they had taken the believing and gifted preacher Ahlfeld (who of course ought to be more decisive on the doctrine of the church) as their pastor and thus, as I hope, are instructed and live in the true Gospel. From Leipzig I made a detour to Langenschursdorf.[10] You can well imagine how joy and nostalgia contended within my heart. My dear mother was no longer there, and of my father I found only his grave mound. But I thanked God that I again saw my sister with her large family.[11] It had just barely become known that I was there and the rooms were full of former acquaintances to see me and speak to me. One of the first was old mother Nagel.

Most of the time I spent in the Muldental, however, I had to use for conferences, which were held in Waldenburg. There I met the pastors Pasig and Wilhelm[12] from the city, Fuellkruss from Kaufungen, Kranichfeld from Wolkenburg, Niedner from Chursdorf, Gotsch from Ziegelheim, Spiegelhauer from Altstadt-Waldenburg, Meurer from Callenberg, Schnabel from Tettau, and a number of schoolteachers. May God grant that our witness here has not remained fruitless, for it was not a very hopeful situation among those gentlemen. We like Pasig, Schnabel, and Gotsch the best. The others gave evidence not only of great confusion in the pure evangelical doctrine, combined with great insolence, but they did not seem to be very zealous in their pastoral office. At least one hears nothing of any awakening to repentance, nor of any responses of hatred which might have arisen in their congregations through them.

I was in Kaufungen twice and found "Cousin" Fuellkruss[13] doing quite well. I also spoke with his mother for just a bit in Wolkenburg. Pastor Fuellkruss made me the proposition to urge his brother, the fiance of our

19

Emma,[14] to emigrate to America, but the brother was not inclined to leave the fatherland since he hoped to find a good position in Saxony. Pastor Fuellkruss explained to me that sympathy had pretty well disappeared for us in Germany after people heard about the free congregational constitutions and democratic principles of the American church. Fuellkruss, though the same old good-natured man, showed as far as doctrine is concerned the most stubborn resistance of all the pastors in the Muldental. I have to confess that I did not find again the old beautiful Muldental, where once such a mighty fire was going for the Lord.[15] Indeed under the umbrella of a believing church administration more and more believing pastors have been appointed but they are worn out, paralyzed, lukewarm, and lazy, and although the future of Germany looks very threatening, they dream only of improvement and glory, and their confident and reckless motto is "Peace, peace! There is no danger." After we had unburdened ourselves of the most earnest testimony, we departed with a heavy heart.

Our way took us back over Leipzig, where Marbach, obviously the most active of men, urgently prevailed on us and finally persuaded us to go also to Dresden to visit Harless. And I must say, though we did not expect much of Harless, yet we found the most open entree with this highly placed man. He received us like brothers, and soon it came out that our American Lutheran church with its doctrine and practice is the joy of his heart. In all the points discussed we were fully agreed. Harless was deeply interested in our experiences, and he gave us a letter of introduction to the queen of Bavaria, through whom he hoped to provide us with significant support for our college building plans. Harless explained to us, and he has already told others in Germany, that the German church needed a hand from the healthily blossoming church in America as well as vice versa. He complained that neither pastors nor congregations in Saxony were sufficiently utilizing the legal protection which was now available to Lutheran doctrine and practice because he had been called to head the state church.

In Dresden I also met Emma, who was invited by a letter to come there. As she stepped into the room, I thought I saw a younger Agnes.[16] She is an extremely lovely and, I believe, pious child. In the 10 hours we had together she wept many tears of joy and nostalgia. As much as she would like to be with us, she sees herself as exiled here, since her fiance will in no way leave Germany. She takes part in the Old Lutheran services in Goerlitz with her aunt. I tried to strengthen her in the faith and to exhort her to seriousness of life and of confession, as much as God gave me grace. Besides that I could not do anything. The description of Hennig Fuellkruss which I got unanimously from all sides moved me not to spend another day in order to speak to him. He is seeking a quiet and comfortable area of work for his "orthodoxy."

On the way from Dresden, after I had paid a short visit to my sister[17] in Kleinhartmannsdorf, I hurried to Leulitz, where I visited Herman Hasse[18] and his very dear wife, our cousin, whom I both found standing much nearer to our position than I had believed before; then I returned to Leipzig and from there traveled with Wyneken via Zwickau to Nuernberg. We arrived there last Sunday, Oct. 5, and were received in the most friendly way by Mr. Volk.

Here in Bavaria we found the Lutherans in great commotion. For there was a report that Pastor Loehe was about to separate himself from the state church, and this had really heated up the feelings of both pastors and people especially in this area of Bavaria. Early on Tuesday we drove to Neuendettelsau with Mr. Volk. Pastor Loehe received us heartily and fraternally. We very soon got to serious discussion on the prevailing differences between us. As to the outcome of this, I can only say this much at the present time: Many mutual reservations have been eliminated, and Loehe has now stated his position better than hitherto on several significant points; but we have not come to a complete understanding. Whether we will ever get to that, only God knows; my hope is rather weak in this respect. To many a person, if they had heard the discussions, it would have seemed as if all the differences were mere subtleties; but anyone who could look deeper would soon see that Loehe has a thoroughly different viewpoint on church and ministry in his total outlook compared to us, that is, to our Lutheran church. Pastors Wucherer in Noerdlingen, Stirner in Fuerth, Volk (another pastor), Fischer, Semm in Memmingen, the prep school professor Bauer in Nuernberg, the lawyer Hommel in Erlangen, and some other pastors whom I have gotten to know but whose names I have forgotten—these all side with Loehe. But even outside of Bavaria Loehe has a large following among the preachers, especially in Saxony, Prussia, and Hanover, although one could hardly find any two who would agree on doctrine, if one were to go into greater detail.

Only one thing one always finds among all the hollering about "Lutheran church," and that is a reluctance to sit at the feet of our old teachers in a childlike simple way, before one tries to ferret everything out of the Scriptures for oneself. There is *no* willingness to sit and hear the teachers who spoke to us the Word of God, to consider the outcome of their life, and to imitate their faith (Hebrews 13:7).

It is true, Germany is not the same anymore as it was 13 years ago when we left. All over one sees that the orthodox confession has formally found friends, but there is also the most frightful expansion of the kingdom of darkness and of enmity against God. Yet everywhere there are people who say they want to be strictly Lutheran. Even the church consistories in the main provinces of Protestant Germany declare the legal rights of the Lutheran confession to exist and state that it should again be legally protected. But there are few who faithfully utilize this time of visitation. There is no serious return to the Reformation. Some talk of nothing but the need for ongoing development; the others are lazy and want to wait till God does what He wants to do through them and for which He has called them. It seems indeed that the morning is dawning here, but under a heavy cloud of fog and rain.

But I want to return to my travel narrative. On Thursday, Oct. 9, there was a special conference of the Loehe followers (*Löheaner,* if I may speak thus) in Schwabach, where we were also present. Upon the initiative of this conference a rescript has been presented to the Supreme Consistory which would acknowledge the right of all strict Lutherans to appeal to the Lutheran Confessions. It is promised that the Lutheran Church of Bavaria is supposed to receive its proper constitution. Therefore Loehe and his followers resolved, and that with our complete and joyful assent, that they would remain in the state church complex and wait for improvement, with the proviso that one should publicly and formally reject all syncretistic altar fellowship, which one still finds in the state church, and also carry this separation through in a practical way.

In the response to the Supreme Consistory it says verbatim: "As much as we are willing to look to the Royal Supreme Consistory with confidence for the further development of our true Lutheran Church in Bavaria, even so decisively we have to declare to our superiors, that (1) we will not recognize any altar fellowship with the Reformed and with the United, (2) we cannot consider any pastor or other Christian who knowingly remains in such altar fellowship as truly Lutheran, and (3) we have to follow this conviction of ours in all our official practical relationships, as difficult and sorrowful as this may become for us here and there."

I hope this way will lead to a better goal than an overhasty separation from the state church. Indeed, the better we have come to know the German state churches, the more clearly we have come to see that what would now most offend one's conscience would not be remaining in them but separating from them, for in them the orthodox are only very little restricted and threatened in the conduct of their office. Even the practical application of their confession is no longer impossible, to say nothing of the confession itself. In any case, the decisively Lutheran preachers first have to see what will happen to them when they carry out their office in faithfulness to their church.

Wyneken has returned from Schwabach to Neuendettelsau to preach there tomorrow. I came here to Erlangen to complete my book.[19] Here in Bavaria the so-called strict Lutherans are divided into two sharply opposed camps, namely the Loehe people and the Erlangen people. The Nuernberg preachers hold with the latter. What the Loehe people *add* to the Confessions, when they allege that they make the latter's determinations more distinct and develop them further, that in almost the same measure the Erlangen people[20] *take away* from the Confessions, although both claim to be justified in doing what they do. In Erlangen I made the acquaintance of Professors Thomasius, Hofmann, Schmid, and Hoefling, who received me with unusual, unexpected love and friendliness. They all speak with one voice. Although on the doctrine of the church and church authority they agree with our position, yet they all deny that the office of the ministry is of immediate divine establishment. They rather see it as being developed from an ethical necessity and from a merely insinuated will of the Lord. I have already had many a hard brush with these scholarly gentlemen on that account, but up to now the only result has been that they moved slightly closer to us, yet without becoming fully one with us. On this point Delitzsch is in harmony with us, but on other points all the more differences have become evident. There is a mighty ferment here. God is obviously planning to do a great work here. May men through their unfaithfulness not dampen it or trifle it away!

Next Monday Wyneken will come here. He is well and healthy. We will probably stay here another 14 days and then return to Loehe to inaugurate a second discussion with him. May God grant victory! Please help us in praying for this to God. The blessing of our delegation for the church here as well as in America is evident. Many prejudices against our American church and its condition have been dropped, many hearts have again been won for it, and a refining fire has been kindled.

My dear Emilie, you see from this letter that it is indeed addressed first of all to you but that it is drawn up in such a way that it may interest others more than you, although I know that also in your heart there is concern and love for the church. So I would ask you to share this letter, which I am sending via the hands of Pastor Brohm,[21] with all the dear fellow pastors and brothers in the faith in St. Louis of whom you know that they will consider the news contained herein to be of importance. I must indeed ask them to be forbearing with my miserable scribbling and to consider how difficult it is to gather one's wits for letter writing with all the thousands of sense impressions that impinge on one's eyes and heart on this kind of a trip. Up to now I have not been able to bring Wyneken to the point where he would write the second official report for the *Lutheraner*, although it is his turn to do so. I hope that he will take care of this next week. Since I had time right now, I did not want to delay any longer with the writing of a personal letter. Soon I shall be writing more.

I do not have to reassure you how much I yearn for America and to be with you again, with my precious family and those fellow believers and fellow soldiers of the Lord closest to me. As much good as we see and enjoy here, it is still my wish to live in America and to die there and nowhere else, and this resolve has grown not weaker but ever stronger. As *much* as God has done here toward improvement, yet I have to say after observing many things in Germany that induce me to praise God: The *greatest* thing God has done for us is in America. Please greet all relatives and brothers and sisters in Christ over there with the greeting of my fervent love. On the 28th of November we intend to sail from Bremen if at all possible, for that is the last sailing from Germany to America before the onset of winter. Thus if everything goes according to my wish, we will celebrate the joyous Christmas holidays together with you and edify ourselves again in beholding the lovely Christ Child.

I commend you and our dear little ones, whom I ask you to kiss in my name, together with our dear Marie,[22] to the grace and protection of God our Savior. In the innermost, most tender love, always yours,

Your
Ferdinand

To Adolf Marbach
Leipzig, Germany
(Fuerbringer, I, 83—85)

St. Louis, July 1, 1853

Honored, faithful friend,[1]

Immediately after I returned from Germany I wanted to write you to express also in writing that the brief hours which I was permitted to experience with you and your dear wife were among the best, the most enjoyable, and the most unforgettable which we spent in Germany. But the thought that there was insufficient time for a really extensive letter always kept me from writing up to this time. But now a situation has arisen which compels me to write to you anyway, although I have only a few moments available. The occasion is the following. A Bible society has been organized here among Lutherans, which has as its objective to distribute well done, complete Bibles, of the kind we cannot obtain here in America. As far as the German Bible editions are known to us here, that of Teubner in Leipzig is the best. In the enclosed letter, therefore, the agent for our Bible society addresses himself to that publishing house to order a number of Bibles from it. The need of Bibles is great, but our financial resources are still modest, since our society has just been organized. We would therefore desire that Mr. Teubner for a short time send us perhaps twice as many Bibles on credit as we are able to pay for. But since we are unknown to the publisher, we thought we could establish credit through your good offices and by your guarantee. Therefore in the name of this society, which now consists of about 250 regular, dues-paying members, and of which I have been elected president, I now direct the request to you to forward the enclosed letter and the draft of $110 to Mr. Teubner and to intercede with him that he might grant us credit. The payment will follow assuredly and quickly, since not only do the members continue to make payments into our society treasury, but also since no doubt most of the Bibles ordered will very quickly be sold. Please forgive my openness. But I must confess to you that our visit to Germany has not increased our friends but rather has diminished them. The witness for truth, especially against Romanizing tendencies and hierarchies, which we had to make has almost everywhere aroused considerable opposition. You are almost the only one with whom we recognized and felt ourselves to be totally at one in the truth. You are therefore also the one in Germany whom we feel freest to ask for deeds of love.

The report which I brought along from Germany to the effect that we, that is you and I, after going our separate ways for a long time, have now with inexpressible joy found ourselves again walking together toward one objective, this has been a matter of exceptional joy for your old brethren in the faith and former companions in misfortune. Upon this news the former great love for you, which had only been covered with ashes but was by no means extinguished, now flamed up brightly in everyone. All of your old friends here wish only one thing, that you will come over once more and, since God has so graciously given to all of us a clear evangelical certitude after those horrible days of conscience scruples, that you will now spend better days with us, take part with us in a more blessed struggle against the world, and in our midst die and enter the church triumphant.

It is my firm determination to write to you very soon in much greater detail. Right now this is impossible because official duties which cannot be put off flow in upon me like the tides of the sea. Please, therefore, cordially accept this preliminary letter as only that.

I commend you to the grace of our Lord Jesus Christ at the same time that I express my most heartfelt thanks to you for the great love which you and your dear wife expressed to me, and I ask you to greet your wife from me and to tell her that I remember with profound joy that in her I have found a faithful sister in Christ in Germany. May the Lord also in the future be your salvation and strength.

Your,

C.F.W. Walther

As a postscript I permit myself also to ask you heartily to greet your dear son Victor from me.

To His Nephew Johannes Walther

(Fuerbringer, I, 136—37)

New Orleans,[1] Feb. 24, 1860

My much-beloved Johannes,[2]

I received your welcome letter of the sixth of this month and heartily rejoiced over its content. It is our nature that even when we have no reason to doubt the continuing love of a person for us, we still gladly receive evidence of the same. Therefore it felt very good to me to receive such an indication from you, although I have been always assured of your sincere love for me. Possibly things go with you as with me; therefore I cannot but send at least a few lines to reciprocate your love.

I have really nothing to tell you. A trip within America offers so little that is interesting that it is difficult to write a description of such a trip that would be reasonably interesting. Accidents are as a rule the only notable things on American trips, so that under the word "accidents" we always understand cases of misfortune. But God has graciously protected me against such events.

You know that for my entertainment I took along a few volumes of the dramatic works of Shakespeare. After I had read a little bit, I thought that I had received suitable literature to supplement my edifying reading matter. But I have to admit that on the way I have come to a different conviction. There are a few pieces that one can read, as for example *Coriolanus,* without polluting one's nature and having all kinds of unclean images fill one's mind. I hold therefore that you students and scholars should be very careful in this matter and read only what has been recommended as being harmless. It is true that the newer novels and theater dramas are even more poisonous because they usually put a veil over their immoral imagery and thus inflame one's fantasy all the more and arouse a hellish lust, and because they easily pursue youths in all directions, even during prayer and divine services, where they pop up as

26

heavenly images which invite one to the highest enjoyment whereas they really are messengers from hell which want to drag their victim down into the netherworld with ropes made of flowers. Oh, how many have lost their spiritual treasure through intoxicating literature, have lost their love for Christ and for His grace and communion, and have become slaves of sinful sensuality, often behind the most innocent-looking masks. Be warned! Satan is clever, the world is deceiving, the flesh is weak. After one has fallen, recovery is very difficult and therefore very rare; and repentance is always too late, for the time, energy, and grace that are lost are irretrievable.

Among the so called classicists, it seems to me, Schiller[3] is still the most harmless, and as far as attractive form is concerned, one may learn much from him. But also in Schiller's dramatic works the overarching theme of sexual love plays a main role, for the world just doesn't have anything more intellectual than this refined flesh. But he who loves Jesus will soon see and shun the idolatry that manifests itself in it. Next to Schiller possibly Jean Paul[4] is also one of the less dangerous writers among the German classicists (his name is really Friedrich Richter). The best of those who at the same time were Christians are people like the author of the "Wandsbecker Bote"[5] and Hamann,[6] who is usually called the "Magus of the North," as even Gottfried Herder,[7] who was reared a Christian but became a pagan, called him.

May God lead you, my dear Johannes, that you may not lose the crown which you through His grace still wear, and that your soul may safely pass from the turbulent and foamy period of youth into maturity.

In asking you to continue to think of me and to extend my sincere greetings to all your dear, unforgettable fellow students, I assure you that I will constantly remain,

Your faithful uncle and friend,
C.F.W. Walther

To F.C.D. Wyneken
Ft. Wayne, Ind.

New Orleans, March 8, 1860

My dear Wyneken,[1]

I cannot possibly leave America without writing you a few lines. Tomorrow the *Oder,* the ship on which I will make my journey, will leave for Hamburg. Thus I make haste to bid you adieu. That I only now get to writing you is due to my intention of writing you an enriched epistle. But since I could not get my spirit into the mood, since it was dampened down or not present at all, therefore I now must decide to prepare a few intellectually empty lines for you.

On Feb. 6 I left St. Louis and arrived in New Orleans on the 13th. Metz,[2] who was supposed to make arrangements at a boarding house for me, insisted that I stay in his home. I accepted because otherwise I would have insulted his love for me. I stayed with him two weeks, till the 27th. Thereupon I moved to Hoppe's[3] home, upon his invitation, and stayed with him till today. The doctors whom I consulted here have stated that I would be foolish to undertake this sea journey immediately without first enjoying about one month of the summer climate here, which they call spring. I followed this advice and have discovered that the doctors advised me well. I felt better day by day, except that I could not sleep well at night and thus am not able to do anything intellectual during the day. My throat is almost completely restored. Metzes and Hoppes have done everything imaginable for me to nurse me and to make me a real bum who does nothing but eat and drink, go out on strolls, or lounge around even more, who flops down on the bed and occasionally smokes a good cigar.

I have especially found joy with Hoppe, for he studies Luther very zealously and in his sermons does hardly anything but reproduce Luther with warmth, albeit not always with full clarity or with a strictly observed sequence. Therefore he also has a lovely evangelical relationship with his congregation. Not so Metz. He is somewhat bitter, and he brings up too many personal things. But he is very zealous and diligent, self-sacrificing, and very insistent on uprightness. He is much concerned with a certain emphasis on science, although he is pure in doctrine and sincerely devoted to it in all points. Theory and practice are for him very far apart. But he is basically well gifted, and so God will no doubt enable him to make progress. I believe it would be good if a different place would be found for him. He is by nature not suited for the south as is Hoppe. If he cannot transfer to the north, I am afraid he will soon be worn out.

I now see more and more that it was no doubt the right thing to do, if I am at all to continue living[4] (which is very unnecessary), to get out of St. Louis. I notice that I am more exhausted in spirit than I thought. May God reward you for your faithful love! I have always thanked God that in you we have a faithful watchman of the sound doctrine and of the proper evangelical spirit in our synod. Now I see, what I actually already knew before, that we have a real father in you who like Paul with his Timothy does not forget to encourage care for the stomach also, because truly the stomach plays an important role in the case of servants of the church and can easily spoil everything.

That you refuse to give me a letter of introduction to the Prussian General Synod[5] I see as your playing the role of a grandfather, who often deals with the grandchildren more tenderly than with the children. But basically you are correct. And I will not write it behind my ears, but in front of them, that I am on this trip only for physical recuperation and for that purpose am spending the money of God's children. I do not intend to look for any kind of work except the buying of good books and, if possible, the recruiting of a Lutheran theological professor for Concordia. I am in a mood which could not be worse for Germany. I am full of malediction, yes malediction and bitterness about the shameful trend among the theologians there, among whom I don't even care to visit anyone except possibly Stroebel.[6]

Stephanus[7] [Keyl] is carrying out his duties as my nurse only too well. He has secretly gotten his hand on some money as an above-budget fund, with which he buys all kinds of delicacies such as oranges, good cigars, and the like. And with all this he provides me very generously, in spite of all my protests. Your eyes are going to pop when I return home or when you see the expense accounts. I am fearful that you and Craemer[8] are going to feel a terrible regret at that time. I am also concerned that I'm going to be returning as a complete lazybones, since idleness and an easy life are already now starting to appeal to me, which I would hardly have believed before. Pray for me that God may not only grant me my life but also permit me to work again, because this I have determined, to show in Germany how well off a Missourian is and how noble the Missourian laity are. But in the end I'm going to pull myself out of the sling and put all the blame on you, and I will declare that this is what I learned in a three-day oral examination which you together with an official of presidential rank had with me.[9]

But enough of the jokes, my dear Wyneken. May God be "your shield and your exceeding great reward."[10] May He grant you that to which you have helped me, namely a lightening of your official duties and the burdens of your family. May God make all your journeys into pleasure trips amid full crops, whose gathering you must teach more than their planting. May God's blessings sprout up like a sycamore tree next to your hut and spread its sweet shady branches out over it, under which you may take your ease and rest.

Heartily greet your honored wife from me, little Louise, Henry, and Martin,[11] my little beloved sponsor for whom I promise to bring something nice from Germany as well as all your olive branches.[12] Greetings in the Lord also to your parents-in-law as well as brother Jaebker.[13]

When you pray the fourth to the seventh petition, please think of me occasionally, not to exclude the first three petitions.

Now, I commend you to God.

Your eternal debtor in Christ,

Carl Ferd. Wilh. Walther

To His Wife

St. Louis, Mo.

(Fuerbringer I, 138—43)

On board the ship *Oder* off Helgoland, May 2, 1860

My precious, heartily beloved Emilie,

Just now we have come to the last port before reaching Germany. Therefore I make haste to record our anticipated safe arrival, so I can mail it off to you immediately upon landing.

As you can see from the above date, we have had a fairly long journey. Today is the 52nd day on board ship. But we have nothing to complain about. Indeed we have reason only to be filled with thanks and praise to our Lord God. He has not only graciously protected us against all danger, but has blessed our trip more than we asked and can comprehend. My throat ailment has completely disappeared, and my whole constitution is strengthened. I have always had the best appetite and was able to endure even the heavy shipboard cuisine, since I never had even a hint of seasickness. Even the crew and passengers congratulated me for looking so much better—people who know me only from the time we boarded. I have even been able to do a little intellectual work now and then. To be able to do this on board *ship* is by itself significant. Even the bitter cold during the storms we often encountered did not hurt me, even though I was daily exposed to it when I would take my walks on the upper deck above the cabin and the stove in the cabin was not lit because of lack of firewood.

For disobeying the doctor's orders not to go over the North Sea but to go to Havre, we have been severely punished, and as you will have seen in my travel account sent to Ferdinand[1] we were whipped by icy winds precisely in the North Sea and at the entrance to the English Channel. But as I stated, all this seems only to have strengthened my nerves and tuned my whole system. Without doubt God turned our foolishness into good, for cold weather on land would not have been as kind to me as on the sea,

30

where the coldest wind not only lays hold of one but also hardens a person. After I have this year experienced two winters, between which the New Orleans spring intervened, so I am now also approaching my second spring, which I can now (on 2 May) already feel wafting out on the breezes from Germany.

But the ocean trip has not only had a beneficial effect on me, but also on Constantin.[2] In New Orleans the boy gave me great concern, since he simply did not improve any at all. In fact in the first weeks on shipboard he seemed visibly to be going downhill. He coughed and wheezed much, and became constantly thinner and paler. His brief seasickness really affected him. He thus gave me great concern and drove me to prayer. But behold! After about the first four weeks things turned for the better also for Constantin. In spite of the inhospitable weather, his coughing and congestion abated, and with that, his whole appearance soon improved, so that I think he hasn't been as robust for years as he is now. I am thinking of having him stay with your sister in the country if it is at all possible to arrange this, so that he can there go on a goat's milk diet and by God's blessing be strengthened by the fresh country air.

Oh my precious Emilie, let us thank the Lord fervently because He has done great things for us, and let us rejoice in Him. I am unworthy of all the mercy and steadfast love which He has shown me, this most miserable sinner. May He grant me His Holy Spirit to make me grateful. I so much want to be just that.

When I write this, you should not think that we had a trip that was physically *comfortable*. Not only was it uncomfortable to endure a number of storms as we did and to be beset day and night by bitter cold, but a journey on a sailing ship is for the most part uncomfortable. I had difficulty getting used to the relatively good but very heavy ship's fare; it was also the cause of a rather painful swelling of the finger joints, which I have not gotten rid of yet. In all that, we often wished we could eat your cooking at least once a week and be able to enjoy your tasty and wholesome dishes.

Our ship's crew and fellow passengers were certainly not the worst of people, yet to be cooped up with non-Christians for almost two months in such a tight space as the ship's cabin was certainly nothing to enjoy. How often didn't we (Stephanus, Constantin, and I) speak of you and imagine ourselves back in your midst, in order to forget about our prison. How often did we say to each other, "Now they are getting up, now they are at table, now they will still be sleeping, now they will be going to church." The most painful was our realization that we could not go to church on Sundays, and everything about us was so unlike Sunday. How much we

31

would have given to hear a live sermon again, instead of the idle words we were compelled to hear. But, thanks be to God, we did not hear any real godless talk on the ship except at the beginning from one passenger, who later was very circumspect though and took care not to utter one godless or offensive word.

On board the *Oder* off the city of Stade, May 3, 1860

Today we finally are on the Elbe, and since it has quieted down a bit here now with the ship lying at anchor, I will continue the letter I began yesterday, so that I might, God willing, mail it in Hamburg tomorrow, lest you be burdened with all kinds of worries about our trip, since it has become unusually long, if the news of the successful conclusion of our sea journey were to reach you even later.

Our plan is to stay over in Hamburg tomorrow (Friday before Cantate Sunday) to visit the sainted Professor Biewend's[3] brother and to visit the used bookstores. The day after tomorrow we want to leave for Leipzig and spend the following Sunday there in order again to hear the Word of God publicly proclaimed. On Monday then we hope to leave for Zwickau, in order to visit Aunt Zschenderlein[4] there. From there we will proceed to Lugau, where Robert Engel is pastor.[5] After that we go to Chursdorf to my sister Constantine and to Chemnitz to my sister Julie. When we are satiated in the Muldental, then with Constantin we will go on to your dear sister Emma, and as I have already remarked above, Constantin will remain there till I return from the spa.

But that is my *thinking;* God will do the *guiding.* Whether God has given His consent to my plan you will learn in the next letter. In that letter I will also enclose one for the congregation and one for one of our periodicals. For the time being, I only ask our dear Brohm[6] to announce to my friends my safe arrival in Germany on the pages of the *Lutheraner.*

It probably goes without saying that day and night I think not only of you but also of all my American friends, especially all the brothers, sisters, friends, and benefactors in St. Louis. I am sometimes so overcome with homesickness for these precious souls that I hardly know how I can bear the long separation and how I can recuperate here in my German loneliness. If I were not convinced that it would have been better not to do anything for my health rather than to make a *halfhearted* application of the chosen remedy which is costing so much sacrifice, I would right now turn around and go home. But after so much effort has been expended for me, I consider it my *duty* to do everything possible in order to return home in as robust a state as possible. No day passes but that I pray to God from my heart that He would bless my benefactors physically and spiritually for the mercies they have shown me, and to permit them to see the fruits of their love, and to sustain their love to me. The latter two points challenge my faith every day, whereas I do not have any doubt in my heart as to the first point. I sing in my heart already at the thought that in the person of Mr. Heinicke[7] I will, as I hope, have an American visitor. That will be one of my more memorable days.

If God sustains my health and further strengthens me, then Aug. 1 will be the latest I will start the return journey, for that is the day on which at the latest I am thinking of leaving for New York on the Hamburg steamship, which as a rule takes two weeks to New York.

At the same place, Friday, May 4, 1860

We are still at anchor. Called away by the family of the captain to make an excursion via lighter to the land, I was unable to finish my letter yesterday. Now while we are packing, and everything on the ship is thrown about helter skelter, I can barely find time and place quickly to add the last lines. In a few hours we will be in Hamburg, since the tugboat to tow us in has now arrived.

Please greet all the dear friends, brothers, and sisters in St. Louis from me individually, especially my dear colleagues with their families, the Tschirpes, Brohms, Heinickes, and Estels, Ercks, Weises, Ameises, Kampmeiers, Tirmensteins, Kalbfleisches, Augustins, Scheels, the new houseparents, Schroeters, Niedners, Schallers, both Buengers, Burkhardts, Roemers, Ahners, Uhliches, Bischof, all the teachers in the city—but when would I finish if I would name all those whose names are indelibly written in my heart? Greet all of whom you think that they remember me in a kindly way. As far as I remember, today the annual pastoral conference meets in Altenburg. Would God that I could be among the brethren and there again have my drought-afflicted heart brought to a new greening!

One more thing I have to call to your attention, since I do not know whether I have already mentioned this to you. You are never in my absence to allow Lenchen[8] to take part in the students' games. She is now of an age where that is no longer proper and where it could become harmful for her character as well as her reputation.

Please content yourself this time with these few lines. You may be surprised that the letters to the children are longer than yours. But do not thereby measure my love for you nor think that I prefer the children to you, my dear and faithful wife. What I have crammed into the letters to the children may be of greater significance and interest to you than to the children themselves. Stephanus sends hearty greetings. How he has fared here, you will see from my travel journal, addressed to Ferdinand.

May God bestow upon you good health as upon Sarah, good fortune as upon Esther, and grace as upon the God-fearing Elizabeth. May He give you strength to carry out, besides your motherly duties, also my duties to the dear children He has given us. May He incline their hearts to obey you in a pious attitude like dutiful children. May He constantly fill your heart with comfort and joy in your loneliness. May He help that we may see each other here again and in Him together joyfully walk the path towards our heavenly Zion. May He be a protecting wall of fire around all of you and preserve all of you like the apple of His eye.

You will see from the postmark that we have today safely arrived in Hamburg.

I am and remain till death
Your faithful spouse and intercessor before the Lord,
Carl Ferd. Wilh. Walther

To Ottomar Fuerbringer
Frankenmuth, Mich.

St. Louis, Mo., May 17, 1864

My dear brother-in-law,

I must say that I respond to your request to express myself over M.,[1] who has requested the hand of your daughter R., not without some hesitation. But love not only requires but even urges me at least to tell you briefly what I know, which might serve as a support for your following decision. I am assuming that whatever I divulge to you you will not use directly but rather consider as confidential, for you and for your dear Agnes[2] alone.

M., to say it forthrightly, belongs to those students who have from the beginning filled me with many a care. But I cannot complain about lack of diligence, nor about his deportment, nor about any lack of gifts, and certainly not about lack of results in his studies, nor has M. failed to carry out his duty in view of his assignments. In fact he has distinguished himself in his conduct toward me and the other professors, so that one can see in his case good home discipline. His strong points are a good understanding, a masculine attitude, skill in interpersonal relationships, a good memory, etc.

What gives me concern is that I have not been able to discover in him a

34

humble spirit of faith before God. It always seems as if he were physically in this preparatory institute for the office of the ministry, but with his soul in the world. At one time he made the confession to me that he was not able to believe God's Word and therefore would rather give up his studies. But to my joy I noticed immediately that in the very depths of his heart there was a certain sorrow over this situation. He gladly took it back, and it seemed that the ice in his heart would melt. Although he was always very polite towards me and deferential, I always thought to have good reason up to half a year ago for assuming that his heart was not inclined toward me. It seemed that his heart was inclined more to Rector Goenner, my constant antagonist, from whom without doubt he was constantly being filled with a certain measure of antagonism toward me. Goenner also infected him with abolitionist principles, which made our mutual relationship even more difficult, the harder it became for me to intervene in this matter decisively, since this was considered an unjustified intervention in an area in which I was not to arrogate any control over my students, namely the political area.

When I announced to the students about half a year ago that I intended to make a thorough presentation to them on the basis of God's Word concerning the difference between the political and the ecclesiastical estates and pertaining to the difference between the kingdom of God and the kingdom of this world, then M. reported in sick, and this under suspicious circumstances. I do not think I did him an injustice when I said I thought the illness was a fiction. I let him know this. So then he came to the next presentation and gave the appearance as if he wanted to have people notice that he had finally overcome and was now willing to yield to God's Word.

But our relationship continued such that I did not dare to ask him directly, because I feared that if I would want to extract a decision too early, the good work begun in him might be disturbed and I might achieve the opposite of what I desire. Mostly, though, I have had concern that M. has never had a good relationship with those of his colleagues who combine with a Christian earnestness outstanding gifts and knowledge motivated by curiosity. With those colleagues he constantly had some argumentations. He always sought to deflect them. As polite as he always was to me and other teachers, so inconsiderate even to the point of hardness and rawness was he to those colleagues.

But I must remark at this point that I have the suspicion that M. was in a legalistic attitude and thus was not able to take any different course in view of his natural energies and lack of a greater power of faith, except that he strove to get intellectual room. Perhaps it was precisely that period in which a human being in whom God is working first has a falling out with God and with the whole world, in order finally to surrender himself to God. At least in the last months there was a very clearly recognizable change in him. It seems that a certain joy entered into him, that he now saw his objective, that he now saw what God wanted of him, namely to have him for His servant. He became more sincere. Also Brauer said that M. had opened up on the occasion of the Saxon Jubilee in February and had said that in the past he had not given up the study of theology only out of love for his mother, but now the situation was different.

I must also admit precisely this, that the fact that M. is seeking the hand of your daughter R. seems to me a remarkable proof that he is undergoing a substantial change. If he were the same old person, he would not want to marry into a Christian pastor's family, and certainly not yours. I cannot help but believe that he must be serious about wanting to start a Christian family life. To this is added the fact that there was always, I would like to say, something noble in his nature. He was always upright and never threw himself away, as some other students do. I believe that he has enough strength of character that he would take great pains not to lose the respect of his wife.

In short, you can see that I am fluctuating between two views. I do not dare to express a joyful positive response to this marriage, and even less do I dare to give a decisive no. You are a more profound student of human nature and of psychology than I am. I hope that this forthright description of this young man, which is throughout objective, will suffice to help you arrive at a clear understanding about him and that you will come to a certainty through this portrayal, with the gracious help of God, as to whether with your dear Agnes you may give your parental blessing to this proposed marriage. M.'s brother has a certain tendency towards melancholy, which has already led him to many an eccentricity, and this in spite of all his good-naturedness, but of this kind of tendency I have never noticed any inclination in M. My inner wish is that this matter may be resolved to R.'s welfare, for I have a deep affection for her and for the joy of your whole beloved family. I will join in prayers to God for this.

You will probably have been wondering, in fact it has probably somewhat alienated you, that immediately upon your essay I published my basic theses dealing with church order and church government in *Lehre und Wehre*. The reason is the following. Brunn[3] sent in similar studies, which he was going to present to his conference, and sought my opinion. But there were so many things so badly dislocated therein, that I feared confusion. I therefore prepared my own presentation, but also in order to really make clear my own sense to him I presented the antithesis to serve as the foundation for an understanding. But since my time and my strength is so limited at this time, so that I can do so pitifully little for our periodicals, I utilized the opportunity and put those propositions into *Lehre und Wehre* at the same time.

Kindly greet your dear wife and daughter from me. May God be with you, and please let me hear soon that you have joyfully found a decision in the Lord. In this case either turn of events will be joyful news to me.

Yours,
Walther

To His Daughter Julie
Philadelphia, Pa.

St. Louis, Jan. 8, 1866

My dearly beloved Julie,[1]

First of all I want to express my heartfelt thanks to you for your lovely New Year's wish. I also thought of you at the turn of the year and prayed to our dear Lord that in this new year of your life on earth it may go well with you in body and soul.

Above all I wish that this year you may be joyful in God and in your Savior. Earthly things cannot put our heart at ease or make us satisfied and blessed. There is always something that gives one concern and fills one with care. And if a person were to receive whatever he wishes in temporal things, he would still not have peace, but his wishes would only grow that much larger. The joy of the world is like drinking salt water—the more you drink, the thirstier you get. But it is something totally different when one says: "World, adieu! I am tired of you, I have something better than what you are with all your glory. I have a gracious God; He is rich, and therefore I am a rich child. He is the greatest, and therefore I am of high estate. He is joy and salvation Himself, and therefore I am a joyful and blessed person." Even if one then experiences need and tribulation, one can think: "All suffering endures for only a short time. How long will it take and I will be completely joyful from eternity to eternity." O my beloved daughter, if only this joy would enter your heart, then you would soon say: "How blessed am I!" and you would always give praise and thanks, sing and leap for joy.

We had very joyous holidays in the spiritual sense, but in the physical sense the days have been really quiet. It was the first time in my life that at Christmastime I was at home alone with Mother. You can well imagine

37

how much we have missed you. So much more vividly we have thought of you. In spirit we saw you laughing, and saw the little Emilie jumping around for joy and clapping her hands, and we saw the little Teddy[2] with his popping eyes in front of the sparkling illuminated Christmas tree.

Since the very hard winter has set in, our beautiful choir has suddenly wilted. There were many who were going to participate in it, but there were not enough men who wanted to help in getting together the young ladies living so scattered about and then to take them home again. Therefore it was decided that the choir take its summer vacation in winter—then in spring, when the flowers bloom again, to emerge in its full beauty once more.

I have now also begun to invite a few students from my department[3] for Sunday dinner. I would not have thought they would accept so gladly. From now on I always want to invite some every Sunday that I am here. These days I have also received the news that Mr. Crull,[4] for health reasons, cannot stay in Milwaukee but must resign his office and go to New Orleans to his parents to be cured. Also last Sunday our dear Pastor Birkmann,[5] near Waterloo in Illinois, was buried. I hear that also Pastor Wyneken is very ill. So one after another is stricken and falls.

Today I am not able to write any more. Please give my excuses to our dear Lenchen[6] and her dear husband. Tell them that in this new year I wish them with all my heart nothing but the sunshine of God's goodness, especially that their tender shoots may grow in a lovely way and come to bloom for the honor of God and for their joy and happiness.

Now, my sweet little daughter, may the Lord be with you and with

Your faithful father,
C.F.W. Walther

To His Nephew Johannes Walther
Wyandotte, Mich.

St. Louis, Sept. 27, 1866

My dearly beloved Johannes,[1]

First I congratulate you sincerely that the Lord has done such great things for you and has permitted a tender shoot to spring forth in your vineyard. May the Lord's blessing rest on your dear little son in time and eternity. May He preserve him for you and may He grant that your son will sing His praise before your ears in the congregation. It is proper that you call this new Walther Hermann. Your sainted father wrote that he had not called you Hermann, but Johannes Gottlob, so that you would praise God's grace after he himself had dishonored God through his emigration.[2] This he said in his singular humility. He is worthy that now your son honors the sainted grandfather by bearing his name.

As for the conditions in your congregation, they are truly deplorable. In the past I had never replied on this point, since in your last letter you had not given any indication that you wanted my opinion and my advice. My conviction in brief is this, that you endure there as long as you are not forced to take part in the sins of the opponents of the truth and of discipline, and as long as you are not prohibited from protesting. If they would be successful in appointing an unbelieving or a heretical schoolteacher, then you would have to disassociate yourself from everything and everyone who stubbornly wants to hold to this shameful injustice. Apparently at that point a division would follow, in which case you would have to be wisely concerned that the church property would go to the upright members, whom you then would not dare leave till they could be provided for properly in some way. There is no question that it is drawing to a separation. Do not encourage this, but do not try to prevent it by taking part in error and sin. In any case, you certainly will not take any decisive step without your father.[3]

I am not in a position to recommend a schoolteacher. The need for teachers is as great as for preachers.

Everyone here greets you and your dear wife, whom we especially wish healthy recovery and churching, with joy from the heart.

Tomorrow it is to be decided whether this year we can still invite the synodical convention to meet in St. Louis. The prospects for this are good. The cholera plague has declined visibly; yes, it seems to be disappearing.

Your uncle who rejoices with you and prays with you,
C.F.W. Walther

To His Daughter Magdalene
Philadelphia, Pa.
(Fuerbringer, II, 93—94)

St. Louis, April 18, 1867

My most dearly beloved Lenchen,[1]

With the approach of the beloved Easter festival I am burdened with a double load of work, but in the midst of it my heart urges me to again share a few words with you after a rather long silence.

I noted with joy in your last letter that the Lord has again blessed you with maternal hopes. That of course again poses a heavy burden for you and brings with it many a care and also some danger. . . . Ever since I have known of it, therefore, I have daily implored our dear God to continue to be with you, to protect and keep you in all your ways, to lighten your burden, and in His time safely to deliver you and make you a happy and blessed mother of children.

But at the same time I must also remind you not to forget in your cares and burdens what a great gift of God it is to be blessed with offspring that way. Think of it, is it not something great that God deems you worthy to bestow life and existence on an immortal human called to eternal life and dearly redeemed through Christ? If that little babe is successfully born into the world, this is a greater achievement than one thinks. For the little child is then there in order to know God in all eternity and to praise Him and receive salvation. If God would give you a million dollars, this would be a lesser gift than a little child. Gold and silver will not only pass out of existence on the day of judgment, as will also the whole world, but in dying you must leave everything behind here; but not so with a little child. Whether it dies before you or after you, it still remains your little child; and when through God's grace that little one learns to know the Savior and to believe in Him, you will rejoice with it in all eternity.

Therefore do not be sad about the present inconvenience which the blessing of children brings with it, but thank God for it and spare your life and your strength, because a second life now is dependent upon yours—a precious, costly treasure, more splendid than precious stones and pearls. This you certainly are experiencing daily in your little ones, namely in your Emilie and your Theodore. Isn't it true, you would not be willing to trade them for a whole kingdom? See from this how God has enriched you.

You cannot believe how we rejoice every time you write us that your children are well and healthy. We hold them as dear as our own lives. Would God that we could divide ourselves so that we could have them and you could still keep them. But only Jesus and His gifts can be completely possessed by several people at the same time; other possessions do not have this perfection. Well then, we shall share the Lord Jesus and His grace. I look on the little offshoots of your marriage as my own children and rejoice in them as a sweet gift for my wilted old age, a gift through which my old age is again greening and blooming.

. . . Mother[2] is now loaded with work in her garden since after a long winter and a raw beginning of spring the sun has suddenly asserted its full rule and the sleeping life in the garden is awakened as by storm.

. . . Greet your husband from me. May God stand by his side in these busy festival days, and may the faithful Savior grant you a rich strengthening of your faith through the preaching of Christ's victory over sin, world, death, grave, and hell, and help you that you follow after Him, the Breaker of all bonds, on the wings of faith, and rejoice in His victory.

Greet and kiss your sweet little ones from me,
Your faithful father,
C.F.W. Walther

To His Nephew Johannes Walther

Concordia Seminary, St. Louis, Mo., May 24, 1870

My dear Johannes,[1]

I was astounded to read in your letter that Sprengeler[2] has rejected the call to Venedy,[3] but was happy to hear that he soon again was willing to reconsider. I myself am convinced that Venedy must get the most careful consideration. After this congregation has experienced those great difficulties, it absolutely needs a pastor whom the people can trust, and I hope that Sprengeler is such a man. Besides that, we have the additional consideration that the pastor to be called should not have too large a family so as not to be a heavy burden on the congregation. I shall do what I can that Venedy will call a pastor.

Your dear father[4] and father-in-law, who both send hearty greetings to you, have great concern and worry about you, as you can imagine. Your father is of the opinion that an overseas trip with your family is not practical. He believes that it would be best if you would seclude yourself somewhere in the bush. This is also my opinion. But in any case it is an unfortunate thought that you now want to work as a correspondent. During this time of unemployment which God has laid on you, you should do nothing but easy manual activity, and besides this nourish your soul with the milk of God's Word. You have flown too high; you must now come down to earth and become like a child, quietly in the lap of God awaiting His help. You must learn to say to God, "I am Your clay; You be my Potter, and make a vessel of me pleasing to You." "I am nothing," that must become your motto, and you must rely on the grace and mercy of God. Wait on the Lord. Be of good comfort and do not despair; wait on the Lord. When you look to Him, naked and bare in faith, He will help you and you will yet thank Him that He has led you in this inscrutable and marvelous way.

Greet your wife from us all most sincerely. We think of you daily and remember you before the Lord.

Pastor Hattstaedt[5] very much wishes that his son return to St. Louis. Greet him from me. We commend you and your dear congregation to the open arms of the Divine Mercy.

Deeply bowed with you but firmly trusting in the Lord, I am

Your uncle,
C.F.W. Walther

P.S. Please let us hear from you from time to time. In your condition I fear to write something to you, since I do not know what might dangerously excite you. As soon as you have come to a resolution on your father's letter, let me know. In whatever I can serve you, I shall do so gladly from the heart.

To His Wife
St. Louis, Mo.

New York, Aug. 21, 1871

My dear wife,

The love of God, the grace of Christ, and the communion of the Spirit be a salutation to you.

I want to let you know that I arrived in New York safely last Friday noon after 11:00. Stephanus[1] [Keyl] to my great joy met me at the train station; otherwise I would have been completely lost in this large city, like Peter in a strange land. We took the streetcar to Strovel's, where I met Mr. Birkner, Mr. Saxer, and Pastor Traugott Koerner[2], with whom we then had lunch. Shortly the students sent by Brunn[3] arrived, appearing in person one hour later. At 4:00 p.m. we went to Port Richmond, where I met Lena[4] hale and hearty with all her children. Yesterday, a Sunday, we had the baptism. I baptized the little Emma Mathilde.[5] We had a high time. The whole circle of friends was there. We were overjoyed, and we thought of you with the heartfelt wish that you could be in our midst too.

This evening I will leave for the pastoral conference in Buffalo. Next Tuesday, eight days from now, I plan to leave Buffalo to go to Keyls in Willshire.[6] My plan is then to arrange it so that either on Saturday, Sept. 2, or Sunday, Sept. 3, I will arrive in St. Louis, if the Lord would graciously lead me. If possible, I will write you again on this.

Since Ferdinand[7] has not written, he probably has not yet left for

Brunswick. Greet him and the bride Julie[8] from me heartily. Everyone here sends a thousand greetings.

Greet Brohms, Langes, Craemers, Brauers, and Preusses from me if you see them.[9] May God keep you all in His protection and grant me that I will see you again.

Your faithful husband,
C.F.W. Walther

To His Son Ferdinand
Brunswick, Mo.

St. Louis, Dec. 13, 1871

My dearly beloved son,

Only today did I receive your letter written Dec. 8 but stamped Dec. 11. I opened the letter with the great hope of getting good news. This your last letter still contains the complaint that despair often overcomes you, so that your heart would nearly break. But I hope that our faithful God will not permit you to go under completely in this your need. For He has created you, redeemed you through the blood of His Son, and in Baptism has received you as His child and heir. And He has called to all sinners through the prophet Isaiah: "Though your sins are like scarlet, they shall be as white as snow; though they are red like crimson, they shall become like wool."[1] God has worked in you the will not to serve sin, and thus He will not permit the spark of your faith to be extinguished, but will blow it up into a bright flame by the breath of His mouth through the Word.

And if I go through into night
And see again the morrow,
Not even then in God's strong might
Will I doubt or ever sorrow.

"They who wait for the Lord shall renew their strength; they shall mount up with wings like eagles, they shall run and not be weary, they shall walk and not faint" (Isaiah 40:31).

You wrote that when you preach you show others the way to salvation but feel that you yourself are going lost and that your preaching is only lip service. But this is only the voice of the flesh and of the wicked foe, who wants to throw you into despair. In all confidence continue to preach Christ and praise His grace, for that is the doctrine which the Lord has commanded His disciples to preach. This preaching is therefore the best

43

work you can possibly do in your present calling. And believe what you are preaching, and thus your preaching will not only benefit your listeners but also yourself. That is the way it should be. For the apostle Paul writes: "Take heed to yourself and to your teaching; hold to that, for by so doing you will save both yourself and your hearers" (1 Timothy 4:16). You should not think, even if you feel you are dead and unbelieving when you preach, that your preaching is therefore dead lip service. Oh, no! God's Word is and remains living and powerful (Hebrews 4:12) and as far as you yourself are concerned, you need to think of it that faith is not just a feeling, but it is a trusting in the Word and the promise. We hope without doubting, for that which we do not see (Hebrews 11:1), and thus we do not perceive it.

When that father brought his possessed son to Jesus and asked for help, Christ said to him, "If you can believe." Then the father felt how difficult it would be for him to believe, and thus he cried with tears, "I believe, dear Lord, help my unbelief!" And what did Jesus do? Did he say to the father, "Your faith must first be cleansed from all unbelief?" No, but he helped him (Mark 9:17-27). See yourself in this fine example. I think you are also such a patient as that father was, and therefore when you say "I believe, Lord," you must immediately add, so as not to lie, "Help my unbelief." This is a sign of a weak faith, but not of unbelief. For he who very much wants to believe, already believes. Christ does not reject the weakest faith, for it is written of Him: "He will not break a bruised reed or quench a smoldering wick" (Matthew 12:20).

O my dear Ferdinand, learn just to trust in your Savior. He is friendly and gracious; he who comes to Him will not be rejected. Let me tell you what it says in the epistle for the Fourth Sunday in Advent: "Rejoice in the Lord always; again I will say, Rejoice" (Philippians 4:4). Open your heart to the joy of Christmas, for there a joy is announced which shall be to all people, among whom you are also included. You can say it in the words of the hymn:

> Hence, all fear and sadness!
> For the Lord of gladness,
> Jesus, enters in.[2]

Recently I wrote to our dear Wyneken that you were experiencing great difficulty and I asked him to include you in his intercessory prayers. Yesterday I received a letter from him in which he wrote: "I have put your dear Ferdinand on the list of names of those for whom I pray daily, right next to the name of his father. When he is again out of the fire, I would very much like to know it, and then I shall place him in my general prayer list and there will certainly be another name to put in his place on my special list. May the Lord, who looks upon those who are wretched, also look upon him in mercy and make something of him to the glory of His name, which cannot happen without serious temptations." See, so you have another good intercessor besides me. We shall not cease to cry out to God for you and say "we will not leave Thee, except thou bless us." Therefore wait on the Lord. Be assured and do not despair; wait on the Lord.

We here also have lots of problems, as you can imagine. For I know that just because of this the devil is raving and raging against us, because we get in his way. Even though he can always get a Judas among the disciples of Christ, this will not only not help him but will rather hurt him and help us. Let the world and the false church deride us. He who laughs last laughs best.

The *Lutheraner* of the 15th of December contains many good items. Read, and refresh yourself therein. How beautiful is "The Life of Gerhard" by Pastor Guenther.[3] Gerhard as a student endured great conscience troubles.

You can well imagine how happy Julie is that she once said no.[4] Dear Mother was seriously in error when she at times threw it up to me that I had not encouraged Julie. Now also Mother thanks God for it. Julie sent off by express a beautiful watch chain made of her own hair, for her future husband.[5] Mr. Kramer, Niemann's landlord, is to present this gift to him on Christmas Eve.

In the place of Preuss, Professor Schmidt[6] of Decorah was called. This was done only provisionally through the Board of Control, to which I also belong. I am anxious whether he will accept.

I must now work diligently since I am almost alone in looking after the editing of our periodicals. On Christmas Day I must again preach. God willing, I shall arrange the sermon so that I can deliver it also in Brunswick,[7] so that I need not write a new sermon but at most a new little introduction.

We are all well. Everyone greets you a thousandfold. May God preserve you in your arduous tasks and keep you in good health in your winter toils and give you a joyful heart, for as Solomon says "A cheerful heart has a continual feast" (Proverbs 15:15).

God strengthen you in your work at Christmastime and bless it richly.

Your faithful Father,
C.F.W. Walther

P.S. When you write us, don't write deep into the night. You need rest from the day's labors in the cold weather, and you have to spare your eyes as much as possible.

To His Son-in-Law Stephanus Keyl

Port Richmond, Staten Island, N.Y.

St. Louis, May 22, 1872

My most heartily beloved Stephanus,

Man proposes, but God disposes. How beautiful and beneficial we thought those days would be when you and your family would again stay at our house.[1] This would have been a time for refreshment and recuperation after a time of daily care, concern, and labor.

But it turned out totally different. Soon after the greetings at the arrival were spoken, we noticed that our dear God had given you a cross to bear. I really hoped that God would hear my daily sighs and prayers so that you would not be deprived of any of your dear children. But see, our thoughts were not God's thoughts, nor were our ways God's ways. As far as the heavens are higher than the earth, so His ways were higher than ours.[2] Two children were left to us, but one, our dear, sweet Emmie, He took from our lips, from our lap, and from our arms. Besides the measles, Emmie had pneumonia, and just at the time when she was teething. For God these three enemies of that young life would not have been overwhelming, but for the tender little child it was too much, and since the Lord of life had resolved from eternity that this innocent child should never know the evil of the world, there was no delay; God hurried it out of this miserable life and refreshes it now even with joy before His own countenance.

She never cried, never expressed the least impatience. As a lamb she lay there, and only the quick, short breathing sounded like a constant sighing and moaning. The doctor did everything he could. He was very tireless, and his visits were never hurried. It seemed as if the course of the illness would turn for the better, but we soon saw that this was only outward appearance. As human beings are always encouraged at every flicker of small hope, so also we were here. Yet the Lord's will had to be done.

Well, then, my dear Stephanus, let us subject ourselves to His will in humility, for we do not belong to those who have no hope. We know that the blessed child only preceded us to receive us there above with joy whenever our own hour has come, and then to be with us there eternally. We also know that when God lays a cross on us, this is not His anger but rather a sign of His love. With this He clothes us with the livery of His children, who must enter the kingdom of God through many tribulations.[3] We are thereby to become like the father of all believers, who was required to prove his faithfulness thereby, that when God required him, he had to lay his own son, whom he loved, as a sacrifice on God's altar.[4] But above all we are thereby to become like the picture of the Son of God Himself, who never laughed, but wept much in this vale of tears. Well, then, my dear son, if it is God's will that the good will be preserved for us only for eternity, then let us say to Him: "Lord, as Thou wilt, deal Thou with me."[5] It is better to weep here and to be eternally joyful there, rather than vice versa. Join us in drying your tears and speaking with Job, "The Lord gave, and the Lord has taken away; blessed be the name of the Lord."[6]

We are exceedingly sorrowful that you now in your loneliness receive this tragic letter, and would God we could fly to you and weep with you and comfort you; but even this also is God's gracious leading. He will certainly strengthen you, also to bear this cross. God already has led both of you through the school of affliction, and has exercised you herein so that with His help you will also this time not murmur against the Lord but bring Him also this offering, even though with tears.

Now, we commend you to God. May He comfort you with His everlasting comfort, and may you experience in yourself the word of the Savior: "Peace I leave with you; My peace I give to you; not as the world gives do I give to you. Let not your heart be troubled, neither let it be afraid."[7]

Your uncle, father-in-law, and colleague,
who sorrows with you but also shares tribulation
as well as membership in the Kingdom,
C.F.W. Walther

To His Daughter Magdalene
Port Richmond, Staten Island, N. Y.

St. Louis, Jan. 15, 1873

My precious daughter,

According to the last letter I received from your dear husband, he is presently bobbing between water and sky on the ocean and drawing further and further away on his ship, many miles removed from you and your children. That is certainly something difficult for you. But it is also something beautiful. For it is certainly preferable to you to have a husband who has to accomplish something significant and difficult in the world, compared to one who could not be used for anything. Also you know that many prayers go with your spouse as with a man who is beloved by everyone who knows him and who has to accomplish an important task in the kingdom of God.

That you have to live so long in loneliness, like a widow, will not be easy for you, but you are already prepared for being dependent on yourself most of the time. You will be able to say with the pious poet Schmolk:

Alone and yet not all alone
I am in this loneliness;
For when I feel completely abandoned,
Jesus Himself helps me pass the time.
I am with Him and He with me;
Thus nothing is really lonesomeness.

Furthermore Milcha and Clara will see to it that you will not become too bored. Greet them from their grandpa and say to them that they should be obedient to their lonesome mother. Tell them Grandpa asks you to write him each week or two whether your little children are nicely obedient, whether they give you nothing but joy, and whether they pray diligently and reverently for their papa.

You can also be comforted with us. We too are now totally alone. Everyone has flown the coop, and we alone are perched in our little nest. But we rejoice that our young nestlings became capable of flight and now can fly out to search for their own food.

It is a great joy to us that Ferdinand[1] has now decided to end his own loneliness. Till recently he always said that he would have nothing to do with getting married. He always said he was an unfortunate being and did not want to make anyone else unhappy. [This last sentence was written but crossed out by Walther.] How gladly he would have become your husband's assistant! [A part of the letter seems to have been destroyed at this point.] But his congregation . . . would have to say, "I will have to be like one who has been robbed of his children." Constantin[2] is now again in Perry County active in his mill in Wittenberg. I am very happy that he again is working at his calling, since inactivity is the beginning of all vice.

On my birthday we had a right good time. Besides my colleagues and their wives, there were also Schaller, Brohms, Dr. L. L. N., Mrs. L. and her daughter, Mrs. G., Er. Mueller, L., and the apothecary M.s.[3] In the evening we put on a little concert in which I played piano, student Maas played the cello, E. Erk played the violin, and the girls sang. My students presented me with a beautiful sofa. Your dear present, the picture, has not yet arrived. I only regret that you poor people have endured such expenses on my account.

For the Reformation Festival I preached in Immanuel Church, where all the "districts" were assembled, and therefore the church was full to choking. The children from all the districts, an enormous crowd, sang the hymn "Lord, Keep Us Steadfast in Thy Word,"[4] after the sermon. All the singing was accompanied by brass instruments, and the choir rendered a motet. It was a beautiful festival celebration. I chose the theme "The Promised Fall of the Antichrist Is One of the Great Blessings of the Lutheran Reformation."

If you, God willing, soon come here again, you will not recognize this area.[5] Now the main highway with its street lights leads from Carondelet Street past the college. In the college area, there are now the beautiful new teachers' residences fronting on the so-called Bishof's land. There are now already a number of residences there. In our yard we have our beautiful house, and adjoining on the exercise grounds is the new printing establishment of Synod, and on the cemetery is our beautiful Cross Church. This area is becoming more and more like a city.

Please content yourself with these few lines then, which I have written with many interruptions. Greet your dear husband a thousand times from us all, and give your Milcha and Clara a hug from me. Mother and your sister and brothers will send greetings. As you have opportunity, greet G.S. and your neighbor. The Lord be with you, my precious daughter, and may He grant you a heart joyful in Him, sustain you and your dear husband and your offspring hale and hearty, and grant us soon the joy of seeing each other again.

In abiding love, your father,
C.F.W. Walther

To Pastor E. A. Brauer
Crete, Ill.

St. Louis, Mo., Feb. 26, 1881

Heartily beloved friend and brother in the Lord Jesus,[1]

What might you be thinking of me? It is so long a time ago that you and your dear wife again[2] bestowed such an undeserved gift on me without any merit and worthiness on my part, and I have not yet expressed a word of thanks for it. "O world, ungratefulness is your reward!" You may often have said this in your heart when you thought of me. If this is the case, then I cannot complain. I have richly deserved it.

But permit me to share with you some mitigating circumstances so that your righteous anger may not wipe me completely off the list of your friends and brethren. When the precious liquid arrived, I was preoccupied with so many evil matters, and was loaded down with so many articles approaching deadline, that at the time I could only rejoice, although deeply ashamed, first because there were still hearts that beat for me, this miserable person sitting in shame, and secondly because enjoyments were again waiting for me which could sweeten my bitter life.[3]

To avoid being too much taken in with this earthly good, and thus being distracted from that which is most necessary, I immediately commanded that the tempting bottles be immediately deposited in the nethermost part of the house. As soon as it was said, so it was done,[4] as the ancient Greeks said.

But the result of this regulation was that in my ascetic zeal, in combination with all kinds of things that weighed on my spirit, the glorious gift almost completely escaped my consciousness, and in moments when I did remember it, I couldn't do anything about it but make good resolves. But recently, when I had emptied a glass of Schuricht wine for my breakfast, I again recalled the hidden treasure and immediately issued the order that one of those captives be freed from his dark prison and be presented to me, the judge. And then the judgment followed that the culprit is to be taken apart piece by piece and, to make his sufferings last longer, to be emptied of his innards by only one wineglassful a day.

But in doing this, my sins against you weighed heavily on my heart, as you can well imagine, and especially so when I partook of the first serving. Well then, be kind enough to receive my confession. But be satisfied with my attrition, because I could not come up with contrition. And excuse me from the satisfaction,[5] according to the glorious old saying, "Where man has a choice between two things, God will not require either of him."[6]

But, all joking aside, accept my belated but sincere and deeply felt thanks. God bless you for your kindness shown to an old friend. May God grant me an opportunity to return this kindness.

With exceptional joy I received the postcard which announced the engagement of your daughter Helene to Pastor P[fotenhauer].[7] They will make a beautiful couple. He has always been a favorite of mine, and thus I do not begrudge him such a pearl as your Helene is, and to her I express my congratulations for getting such a deserving, outstanding husband as our dear P[fotenhauer]. May God grant both of them a happy and a blessed marriage in every respect, and may God also thereby sweeten for you, the parents, this bitter life. And all this on account of our dear Lord Jesus.

These days I received an epistle from Pastor Huebner in Dresden.[8] This nephew of yours is a beautiful person, a jewel of the poor Saxon Free Church. Among other things he informs me that H[ein][9] in W[iesbaden] has become a raging Schmidt follower,[10] that he has declared his separation from our "Calvinistic sect," and that he is becoming ever more unapproachable. Thank God that all other members [in the Saxon Free

Church] stand firm and are clear. Huebner states that already through the article on "Selbstentscheidung" ["One's Own Decision"] in *Lehre und Wehre,* Volume XVIII, he was able to grasp the proper doctrine of predestination.[11]

Now, finally, many thankful greetings to your honored spouse and to all your dear ones from me and my better half. The Lord be with you personally, with your family, and with you as pastor.

Yours till death,
C.F.W. Walther

To His Son Ferdinand
Brunswick, Mo.

St. Louis, Mo., April 9, 1884

My cordially beloved Ferdinand,

Unfortunately I have to inform you that Mother has been ill with a most painful rheumatic fever for already 10 days. Right now she seems just a bit better, but even at best the recovery will be very slow since our precious patient suffers from great weakness. Please help pray God that He will grant her recovery and sustain her for us once again. It would be shocking to me if I were in my old age to lose my very indispensable helpmeet. I am not giving up hope that when you come to us for the synodical convention again, she will be our busy Martha once more.

May God grant you a joyous voice to proclaim the great deeds for the salvation of the world of sinners to your congregation under the direction of the Holy Spirit on the Easter festival. Anyway, the circumstance of Easter is so glorious that it penetrates the hard rock of hard hearts even if we can only very inadequately speak thereof.

I have, besides your father-in-law,[1] also invited your dear mother-in-law to stay with us during the time of our synod, but the latter has declined our offer. Julie also, who is ill now, will hardly be able to come, nor Lenchen,[2] since she is even this month expecting her confinement. All the more necessary, therefore, that you bring your wife Bertha along so that we can have the pleasure of at least one daughter in our midst here. Naturally then you will have to bring your children. Please feel free to do so. We have plenty of room. And half of the travel expenses I will bear with great joy.

Humbly in love,
Your father,
C.F.W. Walther

To His Son-in-Law Stephanus Keyl

Port Richmond, Staten Island, N. Y.

Concordia Seminary, St. Louis, Mo. Aug. 30, 1885

My heartily beloved Stephanus,[1]

Ferdinand just left to return to Brunswick.[2] It is now high time that I sit down to write something to you dear people in Port Richmond about the illness and the blessed death and funeral of our dear mother.

Her last illness began apparently as a result of a cold which she contracted after a bath on a cool evening. She got serious heart cramps, which caused her to have the most terrifying breathing difficulties for weeks on end, day and night with only short interruptions, which made virtually all sleep impossible. These difficulties always were a real wrestling of life with death, because it always seemed to her that the very next instant she would be completely unable to breathe and would choke to death. Her anguish was therefore great. Day and night she sighed, groaned, and whimpered. She would say, "O, Lord Jesus, help me! O, my most dearly beloved Savior, have mercy on me!" In this and similar manner she prayed without ceasing. She often complained, "Oh, I can no longer endure this!" But she never expressed one word nor even gave one facial expression of impatience. As patient as a lamb for the slaughter she lay on her bed of pain.

Dr. Bosse, an excellent, experienced, conscientious, and involved physician, at first did not dare to give her any opiates to permit her to rest, since he feared that precisely this way she could lapse into the sleep of death. But since her pains and her anxiety increased constantly, Bosse finally did resort to opium as also some other means. This finally resulted in our good mother being freed suddenly from her breathing difficulties and pain, so that after the first sleep of several hours she said, "I am as if in heaven."

Only now a frightful almost burning, glowing fever set in with her, which did not want to yield to any medication. It became more and more difficult for her to speak, till in her last days she lost the power of speech completely. But it seems as if all pain had left her and that she might not even feel the burning fever because of her weakness. As often as I leaned over her face she regularly commenced to smile in a sublime way, and did this till her death. The physician had soon noticed that the illness had also affected the kidneys, since there was evidence of albumen in the urine, which he examined chemically each day. So she became weaker and weaker till eight days ago today about noon also her consciousness faded.

Up to then she audibly repeated all the prayers said for her. It was highly comforting to see and to hear how she busied herself with the Word of God and how she was refreshed thereby. She had soon realized that she would die, and she was prepared to depart with joy in the name of her Lord Jesus, then to be with Him eternally. She had no spiritual afflictions in all of this. She believed firmly that because of Christ all sins had been forgiven her and that she would be saved. When she had further serious attacks in the night from Friday to Saturday, I heard her confession and gave her absolution and the Lord's Supper.

Saturday evening the physician no longer gave her any medication. Then he said, early on Sunday, that the time of her departure was at hand but that the struggle for life might extend until Monday morning. But God heard our cries. Sunday afternoon her breathing became ever weaker and in the last hour even more soft, till finally five minutes of five in the afternoon her precious soul left her softly and quietly so that even for a little while we did not even know whether she had gone to sleep or whether she was still awake.

Mrs. Lange,[3] Mrs. Tschirpe,[4] and the widow of Pastor Buenger[5] stood faithfully by her side till her last breath, for which the patient always looked on them with an expressive smile, also at Katharina[6] and at her nurse, a very likable woman.

Please do not let this description of her last suffering send you into too great a sadness. God has purified her in this crucible of suffering like gold and silver. She struggled like a genuine heroine and conquered gloriously. Her faith, her love, her patience were tried by God and found adequate. Her suffering, as great as it was, is not worthy of the glory which without any doubt she now enjoys. Her mouth is now full of rejoicing and her tongue filled with praise. We yearn to be with her, but she does not yearn to be back with us. She is in a state of certainty, we still in a state of danger. We still struggle and strive, she rests triumphantly. Her memory will be a blessing as long as there are people who knew her. She had no enemies, because she never did any evil and was polite and well-meaning to everyone.

My tears naturally flowed freely, because it is inexpressible how much I have lost in this my faithful helpmeet. But the more I think of it that next to God she lived and labored for me night and day, the less I have to begrudge her that she now has found her rest and her works indeed follow her. Oh, if I had only honored her more than I did in all the pressures of my official duties! This humbles me greatly, but her gracious glances to me have been a comforting absolution for me. Oh, how I rejoice that I shall soon see her again!

Her tired body, as you know, we brought to its place of rest last Wednesday. Stoeckhardt[7] conducted a fine funeral sermon on the text Acts 16:13-15. He presented her as a believing and God-pleasing Lydia. The attendance was great. The church could not contain the congregation. More than 70 coaches and carriages followed the flower-covered casket, with the professors and St. Louis pastors as pallbearers.

How much we regretted that no one of you dear ones were able to come to accord the departed one your last respects, you may well imagine. If after the receipt of your telegram there had still been time to summon you to the funeral on Thursday, we would have delayed till then. But enough of this! I do not want to further burden your hearts through my words. Unfortunately Julie[8] also was unable to come, but only her dear husband. Also Ferdinand and Constantin[9] did not receive the last telegram in time, so that when they did come, they had not yet received any news of Mother's blessed death.

Probably by late fall Julie may be well enough again so that with Lenchen[10] she may come and comfort me, this poor forsaken widower.

It is a great blessing to me to know that I have Katharina, who has already served here faithfully for 14 years and will be able to carry on the household even as my blessed God-given helpmeet always carried it on.

Greet all your precious children. I am not yet going to send any mementos. When the daughters come, then you can take and distribute whatever you wish.

Heavily afflicted, yet yielding humbly to God's guidance, I am yours,

C.F.W. Walther

P.S. . . . Please forgive me that also this hastily written letter reaches you so late.

Walther as *Seelsorger,*
Pastor of Congregations

To Mr. F. Sproede
Perry County, Mo.

[May 1841]

Honored Mr. Sproede,[1]

Since I again have a chance to send along a letter to Perry County, I cannot but take this opportunity to express myself in writing to you on several points of difference between us. Already more than a year ago, as you will remember, I sent a request to you through Pastor Fuerbringer,[2] at that time a candidate, that you would set forth in writing those things you hold against me, so that I would either defend myself or apologize to you in those things in which I would be shown to have sinned against you. This way for reaching an agreement was rejected by you at that time, and I could not agree to accepting your proposal that you would charge me verbally, since at that time I was too afraid of your irritable temperament; I had no hope that in these circumstances the latter way would lead to the desired results. Thereupon I became ill, and with that there was a new obstacle in the way of a thorough discussion of all things that happened between us. Such a discussion was absolutely necessary if we were to arrive at a cordial consensus. At that time, when God's hand rested heavily upon me, I would gladly have humbled myself on many points in which I recognize my indebtedness to you, but I knew that for a reconciliation you demanded an admission on my part which I could not make with a good conscience and without hypocrisy. I was always afraid of your heatedness in oral debate.

I was very happy, therefore, to hear before Christmas last year from candidate Kluegel[3] that you yourself were ready for a quiet discussion of our situation. Besides, you yourself in those holidays told me of your readiness. We agreed then that, as soon as the debilitated condition of my physical and intellectual powers would permit it, we would arrange for a conference to achieve reconciliation. As sincerely as I yearn for that, I was always deterred by new attacks of fever which kept me confined to my bed but which also made me unfit for a dialog which would have agitated the emotions and for which full alertness and intellectual powers, especially of the emotions, are necessary.

Shortly before Easter of this year the fever attacks declined more and more, so it might have been possible to carry through this projected discussion with you. But I was hindered from this by the task of working out an essay, partly familiar to you, which demanded all my time and energy but which I had no hope of ever really completing. . . . [text missing] . . . to touch on many things and illumine them, to which we would also come in our discussions. I believe that if I could lay this finished essay before you, an agreement and understanding between us would take place all the more easily. But I was not able to carry out my intention in Perry County, and I felt conscience-bound not to delay the acceptance of a call extended to me.[4]

I was going to utilize the last hour I had in Perry County to discuss reconciliation with you, at least to make a beginning of trying to reach an agreement with you which could have been followed from time to time with other written and oral exchanges. Therefore, with Pastor Buenger,[5] I stopped at your house but did not find you at home. Although you were probably reachable if there had been enough time, I did not hope for anything beneficial from a momentary discussion, and thus I only notified you that I was ready to talk to you.

I am here already a few weeks and did not yet write you, but certainly you will believe me that now it is not so much a matter of willingness but a lack of time and energy. I have barely been able in my debilitated condition and with occasionally recurring attacks of fever to perform the most necessary works of my office. Since now, however, I can find a free hour, I am using it to reach out to you.

I confess to you, dear Mr. Sproede, that my functioning as a pastor in the time I was associated with you was exceedingly feeble. At that time I was crushed by many wounds sustained in my emotions through the Stephanite association. I was also led by many Stephanite tendencies and errors. I confess to you that, in my dealings with you in respect to your relationship to other members of the congregations, I out of inexperience and unknowingly, did not always follow proper church order without knowing it or wanting to know it. I also did not make the proper distinction between the spiritual and the secular. I confess to you that I did not always deal with you with the patience, humility, and love befitting a servant of the Gospel. I confess to you that I did not always proceed in a truly evangelical manner in dealing with you and advising you spiritually. I confess to you that I did wrong when at one time I gave you only a conditional absolution. For all this I am sincerely sorry and I beg you humbly to forgive me.

It would be very heartening for me if you could right soon favor me with a word of reconciliation. I am also prepared to give you a further explanation on whatever you may consider insufficient or if you have any reservations on the above points.

Be so good as to remember me to your dear wife and your mother-in-law.

Your most humble servant,
Carl F. W. Walther

To Rev. E. J. M. Wege

St. Louis, Aug. 20, 1842

To M. Wege[1]
Dear and honored friend,

In all haste, I have time for only the following.

First of all, I am sending you herewith an answer to the first letter from Benton County. From this you can see what I have done and how I have prepared the way for you there. At the same time as the first letter from there reached me, the second arrived also. I consider that the main content of the second letter is the result of a number of misunderstandings. I am of the conviction that they have conceded in essence what I required of them. That they do not want anything to do with subscription to particular books is understandable, in view of their misunderstandings, and is no cause for suspicion. (A marginal note: I have made no use of the documents you sent me.) Suffice it that they wanted just that kind of a pastor as I had expressed it. I would think that one should not make further demands of them. My letter and the response to it will be very important documents for you in the future. I cannot but believe that God has His hand in this, since I addressed them so forthrightly and yet they were not alienated. Neither Schieferdecker nor Buenger would be inclined to accept a call like that in America, and I would have to agree. My advice to you does not demand conformity to it, but I would say you should start out for that post without delay. Now I suggest you read in Luther's works Vol. III, pages 1076—77, and Vol. X, page 2788.[2]

Don't permit anyone to raise too many scruples for you, neither from your own family nor from others. You will not be going into a true Lutheran congregation, but are going among people who are mostly heathen, whom you are to convert and whose community you are to transform into a Christian congregation. See Luther, Vol. X, pages 271—72.[3] You will be among murderers, and in such a situation it would be wrong to come on too strong. In such a situation one has to suffer certain things for a while, as the apostles did with circumcision, in order to win many eventually. Just let me, the least knowledgeable, tell you a number of things from experience.

It is completely impossible for me to write also to my brother-in-law,[4] but I just send him greetings and enclose herewith for him the letters from Einsiedel[5] and Schieferdecker.[6] I urge you to send back Rudelbach's[7] communication. Till I have that, no new installment will be forthcoming.

May God watch over you for His praise, your peace, and the salvation of many. May He enlighten you, refresh you with grace, and strengthen you through His might.

Yours,

Walther, pastor

P.S. I have not yet made any use of your documents. Greetings from Buenger. The letter of Schieferdecker to Veym I cannot locate. Did I already . . .[8] it?

To Church Members
Benton County, Mo.

Aug. 30, 1842

Dear brothers in the Lord,[1]

Your precious letter of last month is at hand, and I perceive that you did not resent the forthrightness with which I expressed myself to you but that you rather agree with me that from your pulpit there should be proclaimed not human wit and wisdom but rather the Word of Him of whom God Himself has witnessed from heaven in the words, "Him shall you hear" (Matthew 17:5).

On the second point I am in complete accord with you. I had not meant that you should make a lifetime contract with your pastor, for the time and conditions change so quickly, and what you would promise today, you might not be able to fulfill after a few months. My intended meaning was only that you should not, as is often the case here, hire a pastor as an ordinary servant but rather call him as a servant of Christ and of His holy church, and that you would at least give him the verbal assurance that you consider him a servant of Christ and have him carry out his office in your midst till our dear Lord Himself would dissolve the bond between pastor and congregation through some other compelling circumstances. That you renew the contract and change it according to circumstances because of the salary each year, that is quite proper. The pastor is not to get his hands on anything that he could use against you later.

The main thing, as I see it, is only that you recognize that the establishment of the office of the ministry is not a human arrangement but is of divine institution and may not be suspended by human whim. Far be it from me to try here in this free land again to lay a human yoke upon our congregations; but as much as they love their freedom, yet they certainly would not want to be free of God's order. For whoever is free of God becomes a slave of his own impulses, but whoever is a servant of God is a free man even if he were the slave child of a Negro.

It is one of my most important duties to take part in the defense of the freedom of the congregations. No pastor dare lord it over his congregation (1 Peter 5:2-3); no pastor may force anything on his congregation, but in all church matters all franchised members should have the voice and vote, for in matters that are the concern of all, all must be satisfied, not just the pastor. This you must hold fast, and your new pastor will also diligently encourage you to do so. Only this one thing must be established among you: No human being should lord it over others in church matters, for One is your Lord, namely Christ. The Word of Christ must be the Book to which the whole congregation, young and old, the great as well as the lowly, humbly bow in childlike spirit (Matthew 23:8; Luke 22:24-26). This must be the highest principle in a truly Lutheran congregation, that they harken to Him who can establish any matter in a clear word of Scripture.

Your letter I have forwarded to Mr. M. Wege[2] and given him encouragement to accept your call. He responded that within these next days he would personally come to St. Louis. I am awaiting him just anytime. According to your wish, I will then urge him to hurry to you, and I shall give him a letter of introduction.

Because of lack of time, I am not able to write more today. Excuse my haste.

God be with you.

Your humble servant,
Carl Ferd. Wilh. W.

Probably to Pastor L. F. E. Krause
and His Congregation
Wisconsin

St. Louis, Jan. 19, 1846

Grace, mercy, and peace from God the Father and from the Lord Jesus

Christ, the Son of the Father in truth and in love, be with you all. Amen.

Dear friends and brothers,[1]

It certainly will have alienated you that I have so long been silent in view of your letter of Oct. 30 last year. The reason for this was that I wanted to write a real detailed response to you, but because of the great amount of official duties which constantly weigh upon me, I could not get to it. But since I now see that I will look in vain for the kind of lightening of my official duties that would be desirable for an explanation of the things you touch upon in your letter, I now will no longer delay my answer but will serve you with as much as I can.

First of all, you were offended by the fact that in a written explanation I was not able to declare the so-called pietists[2] as being pure teachers, and had to take exception to their teaching especially in the matter of justification. At the same time you could not harmonize how I would then recommend Arndt,[3] Mueller,[4] and Scriver[5] in the *Lutheraner.*

I would first say the following in response. Pietists admit the thesis that faith alone justifies without works, and they do not deny this expressly anywhere. But to admit this is not the same as teaching justification in a pure way. To this belongs such a distinction between Law and Gospel that a human being is turned completely away from his own works to Christ alone. But this is the point that is missing in our dear pietists. Among them are to be understood Spener and Franke and those who have come out of their school, such as Bogatzki,[6] Freylinghausen,[7] Porst,[8] C. Schade,[9] Joach. Lange, [10] Gerber,[11] Fresenius,[12] and others. These all indeed adhere to the basic principle that man is justified alone through faith, but with that they to such a degree emphasize repentance and crushing of the heart, and the particular circumstances in which a person first has to find himself before he would dare to believe, and they identify so many signs of a truly penitent heart, which then first can dare to approach Christ—they emphasize all this to such a degree that Christ with His grace and mercy is pushed very much into the background. The result is that Christianity appears more as a serious burden, that Christ is made out to be a hard, demanding Savior rather than a gracious one who brings everything.

The whole character of pietistic writings is not that they seek to lead poor, impotent, true sinners to Christ, but rather that they prevent anyone from coming to Christ who does not truly belong to Christ, that they build a fence around Golgotha as there was around Sinai. They incessantly work on their readers, if the latter feel any kind of inadequacy, to doubt their state of grace, to throw away everything as useless that they have experienced heretofore, and to subject themselves to another great process

60

of repentance to enable them to appear properly before Christ. Instead, they should think of how to give certainty to doubting sinners and move them to hold firmly to the word of the Gospel from which alone light, life, and strength come into the human heart, by nature dead. The fact is that such doubting sinners precisely *because of their doubts* lack power in sanctification and *for this very reason* constantly defile themselves again with new sins.

I would be able to cite a large number of passages from the writings of the pietists where they express themselves completely contrary to the pattern of pure doctrine, but I do not want to stop at individual passages and I would like to overlook and put the best construction on incautious expressions on their part, in which they speak of the presupposition of good works for the bestowal of grace. But I beseech you to pay attention to the whole matter of dealing with souls which is expressed in pietistic writings. If you do, you will readily see that they put a thousand times more emphasis on what man must do than on the reception of what God has done for man. The result is that anyone who entrusts himself to the cure of souls embodied in these writings will not easily remain certain of his state of grace, but will constantly be assailed by doubt, will be tempted to engage in running hither and yon and will perhaps even be plunged into despair. I speak from experience![13] To this must be added that the pietists have a dreadful hesitancy when it comes to the rejection of false, enthusiastic teachers, if these have a pious, holy, spiritual appearance, and that all of them dream of a thousand-year reign or at least of better times that can be expected in the church.

As for my urgently commending Arndt, Mueller, and Scriver in spite of this, you have to consider that these were not pietists, for they did not come out of either Spener's[14] or Francke's[15] school, and they lived either before or contemporarily with Spener. In a letter to Watertown[16] I made reference to these men but not because I held them for pietists, but because Kluegel had simply included them under the pietists without making any necessary distinctions. Between these people and the pietists I still make a major distinction, although I find Luther's doctrine of the Holy Scriptures more Biblical, evangelical, and purer than the teachings of these men. If you, for example, would make a careful comparison of Scriver's seventh sermon in the second part of his *Seelenschatz,* which deals with justification, then you would observe that as gloriously as Scriver speaks of justification and of his own experience of it, that nevertheless he constantly inclines to the view that faith justifies because through it Christ is united with us and because in that way we become partakers of the divine nature. The citations he has from Luther are not given in their real sense. I am sorry that I am not in a position to prove all this in more detail, which of course could be done verbally very quickly.

Furthermore, you should not forget that a judgment of a book will turn out differently when it is made to those who do not know anything about pure doctrine, or who do not want to know anything of it, compared to making such an evaluation to those who are capable of distinguishing the better from that which is only good, or finally when such an evaluation is made to those who probably are greatly intrigued by such writings, who may have some motes in their eyes but nevertheless are rich in their Christian experience. It is in this last category in which I classified the Watertown people, and I wrote to them as such. I consider them, then, to be people who have been misled, to whom one should yield as much as one can with a good conscience. I have reference here to my criticism of such men as Arndt, Mueller, and Scriver.

Finally, consider that the most competent theologians have spent lifetimes researching the real standpoint on which the pietists stood, yet without really understanding it totally. Therefore do not be surprised if you yourself make only slow progress in this before you see these circumstances real clearly. First of all, Law and Gospel has to be distinguished in our own hearts through longer experience, and then we will attain to greater powers of discrimination which will enable us to detect the aberrations of those who still try to build on solid ground. If you should desire further elucidation, certainly Pastor Keyl, who has been preoccupied with research into the pietists and their relationships to Luther for a long time, will gladly serve you more than I could in the very limited time I have now. I commend you to the grace of God,

Your

Carl Ferd. Walther, pastor

To An Unidentified German Churchman

March 19, 1849

Honored sir, dearly beloved brother in the Lord,[1]

The day before yesterday was an unusual day of joy for me. It was the day on which your worthy letter of Jan. 11 of this year reached me with its enclosure. Already when I read your letter I thanked God in my heart for the precious gift which I received from you, and now I make haste to express to you also my thanks.

When five years ago I decided to publish the *Lutheraner*,[2] I did this in no way because I considered myself equipped for this kind of an enterprise, but I did it because I could no longer bear to see the enemies of the church carry on as they did without let or hindrance, that every error should be permitted to be voiced without any kind of challenge and to be spread all over; and I did it so that the truth once more should have a public defense and a confessor, so that the German Lutheran immigrants would not in whole groups be enticed into the sects when there was no one who took care of the innocent and neglected people who for the most part were already so helpless in the fatherland. I was pained over the insults to the honor of God and over the seduction of so many unsuspecting souls into all kinds of false beliefs, and this finally overcame the feeling of inadequacy for editing a church paper.

Without confidence in myself, but with total trust in Him for whose truth I wanted to witness, I began sending out this little leaflet to the world. And behold, the Lord blessed this modest effort beyond all prayer and understanding. This paper is not only the chief means of a blessed union of the friends of the church, but has also won for itself a large number of new friends among pastors and laity, has strengthened many a person who was uncertain, and has led many a person back to the truth who had been misled before. I have a whole box full of letters which are documentation for this.

This experience has mightily strengthened me in this faith, yet I have by no means become blinded as to the shortcomings under which the *Lutheraner* is suffering under my editorship. I not only agree in my heart with the complaint of our honored Loehe about the inept, old Frankish and yet un-German language in which the *Lutheraner* is written for the most part, no less do I see too well on what a low rung this paper stands in respect to the selection and treatment of the material in it, and God alone is aware how I pray to Him inwardly without ceasing that He would help us so that the editorship of this paper would be transferred to other more capable hands.

I have been especially sorry that thus far I have not been in a position to gain a correspondent in the old fatherland who could make regular reports for the *Lutheraner* about the ecclesiastical and political affairs of our homeland. Reverend Brohm in New York was appointed in the synodical convention during its last session to give short reviews on world affairs for the *Lutheraner*, and although Brohm has done everything possible to fulfill this assignment, yet the comprehensiveness as well as the precision of his reports naturally suffered from the fact that almost always the news to which he had access was made available to him only in the biased and radical political press.

63

Therefore I cannot say what joy it has brought me to hear that you, honored sir, have kindly agreed to take over the business of a German correspondent for our poor meager *Lutheraner,* and that your first attempt is now in my hand. What I have received is completely as I would wish it. May the Lord grant you time and health so that you may continue in the way you have begun. You will thereby not only win the gratitude of all true Lutherans, but you will also receive much blessing. I hope not only that the *Lutheraner* will through publication of such interesting correspondence become more appreciated and more valuable to all its readers but that through them this paper may gain entree with many people who feel repulsed by the dryness of most of the articles in the paper and by the exclusive character that it reflects. I am very much looking forward to some substantial help, viewing the content of your correspondence, to aid me in revealing the truth and in fighting for the same.

Of special interest to me right now is the witness of a German correspondent against the revolution. The teaching of the Scriptures on government, as you may well imagine, has now everywhere become a sign that is spoken against and on which the thoughts of many hearts are revealed. [A footnote adds:] How things are done in this connection here defies all expression. In Philadelphia there is an association organized among the Germans there which has set aside large sums of money as bounty for the murder of every sovereign of the German states. It has now through its secretary, the newspaperman Wollenweber, challenged people openly to take part in assassinations. [End of footnote.]

Here it is not only the open rationalists who speak in favor of the revolution, but all the German religious periodicals blow the same horn as the radical papers do. One can hardly believe how far the blinding of even the so-called "believers" has gone on this point. I have read these days that the so-called North German Lutheran preacher Suhr[3] in Cincinnati had written that the revolutionaries only want to establish through deeds what the Christian preachers are pledged to achieve through the preaching of the Word of Christ. "If anyone among you would be lord over you, let him be your servant," etc. Christ was the first one, it is said, who wanted to put into effect the principle of republicanism in its total implication. As far as the Romanists are concerned, they speak a different language since the pope has gotten into a bind because of the revolution. The *Lutheraner* is the only periodical which publicly confesses the Scriptural doctrine of the divine institution of government. Praise to God that the *Lutheraner* in its witness is not without visible and wholesome influence both in the people and on the editors of other religious papers. I hope for much good to come from the clarifying and reporting of the first segment of current history which you share in your correspondence.

Assuming your kind permission, I have deleted the words in your correspondence which deal with Hecker,[4] "in the procession of a Rinaldo Rinaldini." Hecker is staying in our neighborhood and is fully deified here. Thus I thought it was a matter of Christian prudence not to arouse the wrath of the mob with such an epithet. The liberals of our city are already much aroused against me. On New Year's Eve somebody fired a shot through the glass window just over my bed, which stands very close to the large window and in which I was fast asleep with wife and child. It appears that the shot was only intended as a scare, but it might also be a prelude to real intentions. You can well imagine that I, though not afraid of a martyr's death, do not consider myself worthy of the death of a martyr, yet would not really care very much to seek martyrdom.

It has been a great joy for me that you promise to include something of church affairs when you send in your next material for the *Lutheraner*. May the Lord grant that you will be able to forward more encouraging news than you had hoped when you did your first report. For our Lutheran church in America it will be of incalculable effect how you describe our mother church in Germany.

For a long time already I was supposed to write to our most revered fatherly friend Pastor Loehe in behalf of Synod, but I was at the same time supposed to present to him a justification of our synodical constitution. But with all the mass of official duties, editorial duties, and presidential affairs[5] which sometimes almost crush me, I have not had the leisure to do so, and thus to date the response and expression of gratitude to the dear pastor [Loehe] and to you have not been forthcoming. Immediately after Easter I will carry this out, however. In case you would be speaking with Loehe soon, kindly convey to him my most respectful greetings and as much as possible excuse my negligence.

With heartfelt respect, your fellow believer,
C.F.W. Walther, pastor

To Wm. Sihler
Ft. Wayne, Ind.
(Fuerbringer, I, 55—57)

St. Louis, April 19, 1849

Beloved brother in the Lord Jesus Christ,[1]

After returning from my official visit in Altenburg, I hasten to briefly

65

answer your letter of March 26, which has only recently arrived. According to your wish, I have decided to make the trip to Buffalo myself. Although I am fully convinced that only your humility causes you doubts as to whether you are the right man to step in between the opposing parties in Buffalo to restore peace, yet I gladly admit I have an advantage in this over you since I saw that situation develop before my very eyes for years.

My letter in which I share my opinion about that engagement case you will, I hope, have received after you sent off your letter of March 26. In that letter I expressed myself to the effect that I consider that engagement null and void.

One question I have. Don't you have a man whom we could post to the so-called Dutchman's Hill[2] in St. Clair County, Ill., where they are pressing us for a pastor? That is an important post. It is a large congregation with a considerable number of rather well-educated members, who are however quite friendly to us. Besides that, there is the fact that St. Clair County is almost totally German and is pretty well dominated by the *Lichtfreunden.*[3] In it lies the city of Belleville, which probably is one of the largest cities of the west with a German majority. It pains me to think of the great shortage of pastors, since I am almost assailed by many congregations to find them pastors, without having suitable persons. If you have any, don't forget the promising far west [today's Middle West]. I see more and more how necessary it is that we concentrate our resources on the improvement of our seminaries.

Two weeks before the festival [Easter], Poeschke[4] wrote me a real impertinent letter from Kindermann's[5] place, signing himself as "Lutheran priest." In his letter he challenges me with threats to draw up a testimony for him saying that *he* had dissolved his relationship with our synod—only this and not one word more. He writes among other things that I am a Jesuit but am also too dumb to be one, that I am a pope, that Synod is a fallen and hypocritical body, and that he was unjustly evicted, against our constitution. I did not answer that miserable man, and all his future letters I will return unopened. I will bring that document along to the synodical convention and there publicly justify myself and explain why the expulsion of that rascal could not wait till the next synodical convention.

With real sadness I have heard that, as a result of your article against revolution,[6] a revolution erupted in your congregation. May the Lord strengthen you and grant you great joy. May he protect the weak ones among the good people, that not one of them may fall and perish in such a fight.

Greet Professor Wolter[7] and thank him from me for the fine article he recently submitted against the *Katholische Kirchenzeitung.*

66

With great joy do I look forward to my departure for my trip to you. May our gracious God bless our meeting. Many who would like to come probably won't. We will have to deliberate how a dividing of Synod can be put into effect without splintering it.

May the Lord be with you and your dear ones and

Your

Walther

P.S. If you received my last letter, then you will, I hope, have according to my wish assigned preachers for the First Sunday after Trinity in the morning (Wyneken?), for the Wednesday and Friday evenings before (Sievers and Schaller?), and for the afternoon service on the Second Sunday after Trinity (Hoyer or Baumgart?). For the other services I have appointed Biltz, Brohm, Fick, and Lange.

To an Unidentified Pastor
Probably in Canada

Concordia College, St. Louis, Mo., Feb. 11, 1856

Dear brother in the faith,

Grace, mercy, and peace from God the Father and from the Lord Jesus Christ, the Son of the Father, in truth and in love. Amen.

Your worthy letter of the 21st of January I have received properly. I was very happy to see therefrom that also in the far north[1] in your area the Lord is beginning to arouse souls and that the pure Gospel, as God permitted it to be preached again through His precious servant Luther, is finding a place there. May God bless and further these God-pleasing undertakings. For it is certain that anyone who thinks only about having a church, without also asking and inquiring whether the unfalsified Gospel will be preached therein, will only help in the building up of the tower of Babel which here in America is being constructed so eagerly by a hundred different sects. All sects come and go like comets, but the star of our true orthodox church of the Unaltered Augsburg Confession will continue to shine forth, even if the star here and there is clouded over somewhat. For "God's Word and Luther's doctrine pure shall now and evermore endure." "The Word they still shall let remain, nor any thanks have for it; He's by our side upon the plain with His good gifts and Spirit." As much as our small Lutheran Catechism is despised, yet it is a fortress that cannot be conquered no matter how much the world assails the Bible fortification. For in all other catechisms of the sects there are all kinds of rationalistic

67

propositions, yet in the treasury of our precious catechism there is nothing but pure gold, nothing but the pure, genuine gold purified and seven times refined, the precious ore of the divine truth. May God strengthen you to raise up high the pennant of our church there so that all the misled children of our church may again be gathered under this banner and many others also be attracted into the one faith confessed in one love and one hope.

As you report, the situation in your area now is such that a married pastor would hardly dare to cast his net out into the deep there. It might be more suitable if a young, single, energetic man could be posted there, suitable for shepherding and defense, without immediately having the care of his family to burden him. Since I well see how important Rock Island and Davenport are, I will gladly offer my good offices that you secure a man who will not be out to fleece the sheep but to shepherd them, who is well equipped to establish a proper church enterprise there. Unfortunately before the beginning of May I could hardly find that kind of man for you. In April there will be five students of theology here who will finish their studies and who will then enter service in the vineyard of the Lord. Of these you could call one. I am convinced that you would be well supplied. I would be willing to recommend the best of them to you, a young man of about 25 years of age named Hugo Hanser,[2] a Bavarian by birth.

But I have to tell you in advance that you can secure such a candidate only if you are willing to call him on the basis of the Word of God and the confessions of the church. We will not permit any of our preachers to be made into servants of men, and therefore we do not permit them to be hired for a year, or for several years, but only on an indefinite basis, for as long as the Lord wills it and as long as the respective pastor remains true to his office, or till he will be called to another ministry, or till the Lord calls him through death. With this we do not intend to say that a congregation cannot at all get rid of its pastor. If a pastor becomes guilty of false doctrine, if he departs from the pure Gospel, or if he is not faithful in the carrying out of his office, or if he lives a sinful or offensive life, then the congregation can remove him from office.

Another condition is this: Our pastors accept only such people into the congregation, for attendance at Holy Communion, who believe in the Word of God and want to be Lutherans and live a Christian life. We do not have anything to do with religious syncretism and with false church union. Our pastors also will not admit anyone to Communion attendance who has not first come to them for announcement, for we will not cast holy things before dogs nor pearls before swine, which is something the Lord so earnestly forbade us.

The people should not think that thereby we want to exercise lordship over them, for we detest from the heart every type of clerical authoritarianism and all popery, and on this account we have already had many a battle and suffered much. But we want to build up proper Lutheran congregations which stand on solid ground, and not merely loose aggregates of human beings which may hold together today and dissolve tomorrow. According to the constitution of our synod a pastor cannot command the congregation in anything. He is only to preach God's Word and exhort to obedience to it. In other matters the pastor only gives his good advice, and the majority of the voting members of the congregation (that is, those registered members of the congregation who are over 21 years of age) formulate the respective resolutions.

This, my dear brother, would be about what I would like to write to you for the time being. Please consider this matter and discuss it with your brothers in the faith there and do write me soon again. Do not tire of planting the church of our pious fathers in your midst and do not fail to do what you can towards this purpose. For since this matter is most important and obviously displeasing to Satan, but pleasing only to God, therefore the flesh, the world, and the devil will thoroughly oppose it and will seek to weaken you in your undertaking and make you discouraged.

The enthusiasts and the religious syncretists have an easy go of it, for they yield here and there to the devil, the world, and the flesh. For such people to make a beginning in church work is therefore usually not very difficult. But they build on sand, and when the rainstorms come, the whole structure will collapse. The orthodox however have a difficult beginning, for they usually have only a few people, and sparse resources, and are despised by the proud children of the world and by the false saints. But pursue the right course, and your structure will stand firm, which no storm can blow down, because it is built on the rock, namely the rock of Jesus Christ and His eternal, pure, divine Word.

The Lord be with you and yours and all those in your church. Please greet everyone for me in a fraternal manner, those who love the Lord and love His undiluted Word.

Your friend and brother in the Lord,
C.F.W. Walther

To Pastor J. M. Buehler
San Francisco, Calif.

St. Louis, Sept. 30, 1860

My dear beloved brother in the Lord,[1]

With great joy I received your letter of Aug. 26 the day before

69

yesterday, and I see there that the Lord has heard our sighs and has safely brought you to your destination hale and hearty. May His faithfulness be praised always and forever! That on this trip you lost a sum of money to a thief is such a small misfortune that it is hardly worth mentioning, and certainly not worth any grieving. Don't by any means do the devil the favor of grieving over it. This evil spirit, who guided the hand of the thief, has no other objective but to make you lose heart thereby, since he notices that you are coming in faith, with the weapon of the Word of God to capture his palace. Therefore just laugh at him and show him that you have not placed your confidence on the god mammon but in the God whom Satan nailed to the cross but who on the third day arose victorious from the dead. Joyfully sing the beautiful hymns of cross and comfort which you find in our hymnal, also that beautiful verse of hymn number 355:[2]

> Though all the powers of evil
> The will of God oppose,
> His purpose will not falter,
> His pleasure onward goes.
>
> Whate'er God's will resolveth,
> Whatever He intends,
> Will always be accomplished
> True to His aims and ends.

Consider this, that you need faith, a strong faith, to achieve anything in California. It is therefore no wonder that our dear God does everything to *exercise* you in the faith even upon your arrival. He tears away all your supports under your arms, so that you will trust only in Him, who will do His work through you. For you certainly did not go there on your own impulse. You were urgently summoned to go, after a call for help was sounded. You could have remained here in comfort, but the challenge had penetrated your conscience, so that you could not pay attention to the voice of your own flesh or anyone else's, if it had wanted to hold you back. The honor of Christ and the need of those souls gave you the first impulse. Even if the weakness of your own flesh had become intermingled in this motivation, yet the matter nonetheless remains completely the Lord's work. Do not let anyone deprive you of this insight. He who has granted you the beginning will also graciously grant you progress; He who has granted you the will, will also help you to the conclusion.

Indeed things in California look dreadful—abominable, as you describe it. But I really did not expect anything else. That should not discourage us, but rather must encourage us. If the people there were pious, your services there would not be required. The sadder the conditions are, the more your call there is certain. When the apostles came to the cities of

Rome, Corinth, Ephesus, etc., where a truly Sodomite atmosphere prevailed, how disheartened they no doubt were! They were also made of flesh, and it undoubtedly gave them trouble enough. But they began their work in the name of the Lord, and behold, in that mass of humanity which looked like a heap of profligates, soon a number of elect became evident. Now thus follow the holy apostles and you will see the glory of the Lord (John 11:40).

As to your question about the Freemasons, I am of the strong opinion that you should not begin with polemics against Freemasonry. If among them one individual should become evident who learns to love God's Word, do not burden that one immediately with the condition that he dissolve his connections. That you have to reserve for a later time and you have to bear the false fellowship for a time as a weakness. But don't say or preach anything which could be construed as condoning it. Just *be quiet* about it and preach in general that "friendship with the world is enmity with God" (James 4:4).

Above all things be careful not to arrange for the celebration of the Lord's Supper too quickly. Hold those who desire the Lord's Supper off for a while, till you see that you have a small congregation, that there really is a communion there. At first also do not preach about the difference between Lutheran, Reformed, and the United Church, etc., but only about the difference between Christians and non-Christians. Seek to work on the hearts of your hearers and to depict with lively colors the sad condition of those who have no Savior and thus have no hope of eternal life, and at the same time portray the blessedness of those who can say: "Now I have found the firm foundation."[3]

Do not let either a feeling of your own weakness or the seeming lack of results of your work beat you down, but steadfastly pursue your calling. Also consider that there are many who pray for you, which certainly will be heard in due time. Just wait for the help of the Lord. "If He does not help on every occasion, He will help when it is necessary. And even when He delays, He has not abandoned you."[4] And do not be afraid that we are going to let you sit there and force you for the sake of attaining a livelihood to surrender some of the truth and seek paying members at any cost. A neat little sum of money has come in again for you, which I will exchange into a draft and send to you in San Francisco one of these days.

We must outstrip Satan. Pray diligently and strengthen and encourage yourself with the Psalms. Picture to yourself the glorious reward of grace which awaits you if you remain faithful. Even though it may look disheartening, you can say with David: "This is my infirmity, but I will remember the years of the right hand of the Most High."[5] And just consider all the beautiful psalms of comfort. He is coming, before we even know it, and will permit much good to come too.

As often as you may write, please designate what and how much of your news I may publicize, since I am not familiar with your conditions there and do not know whether any of this information could become harmful for you if it would find its way back to California. But in any case write diligently, and I will also diligently answer. In the *Lutheraner* I have also challenged your friends to write to you faithfully, and therefore have published your present address. I arrived here Aug. 28[6] almost completely healed of my bodily weakness. It was no small joy for me, when I heard on my arrival that you had already left. I bless you in my heart and am constantly of the joyful hope that the Lord will prepare your path for you and will not permit your labors to be in vain, according to His promise (Isaiah 55:10-11).

All the brothers and sisters here send the most sincere greetings to you. They remember you in the innermost love. Our whole Concordia is at your side in spirit and salutes you.

Please content yourself with these few lines. Soon I shall write more.

May the Lord take you under His wings of grace and stand mightily at your side, give you rich comfort in all your need, fill you with joy and peace, aid your hand in your labors, and give you the victory over flesh, world, and devil.

Yours in unchangeable love
C.F.W. Walther

This letter is addressed to Rev. Jacob Buehler, c/o Meyer's Hotel, Number 206 Montgomery St., San Francisco, Calif.

To Pastor C. A. Mennicke
Hampton, Rock Island Co., Ill.

St. Louis, Sept. 16, 1861

My dearly beloved pastor,

With heartfelt regret I see from your letter of the 7th of last month how overloaded you are with work and with pastoral concerns. I can hardly restrain my anger when I hear what our congregations in their lack of understanding often demand from a young pastor. May God grant that you will not be crushed under this burden nor worn out before your time.

As far as the excommunication case is concerned, it is my opinion that you should not carry this to the extreme. If there should be danger that the congregation would be shaken in case you would carry through the excommunication as it should be done, then do not do it. Just so you are not urged to commune the one who is worthy of excommunication. One has rather to permit one guilty person to slip through than to endanger a number of innocent people because of carrying out total church discipline, as our old fathers also judged. Excommunication does not belong to the essence of the church but rather to the well-being of a well-organized church. In the Formula of Concord it is even held up to the Schwenkfeldians[1] as an error if one teaches that it is not a proper Christian congregation in which no public exclusion or orderly process of excommunication takes place (Art. XII).

Of course we dare not permit anyone to remove the *teaching* of the doctrine of excommunication or to permit anyone to silence us on this. But you need to explain to your people that you will yield to them because of their weakness until such a time that they will come to better understanding. Up to that time also let the public announcement of an excommunication drop. Here again you have a proof of how necessary it is to include in your sermons material on the corruption which prevails in church affairs in Germany, so that people will cease appealing to the situation in Germany in all their confusion. Furthermore, I am surprised that things are still going the way you say in Rock Island since Selle had a pretty negative judgment about Pastor Ahner's[2] ministry there.

I congratulate you from my heart on the occasion of your marriage. May God lead everything to your welfare, to the edification of your congregation, and to the glory of God.

We have very quietly begun our school year in the seminary with, I believe, 27 students. May God help us further!

In the Lord Jesus,
C.F.W. Walther

To Pastor Johann List
Adell, Wis.

St. Louis, July 26, 1867

My dear pastor, beloved brother in the Lord,[1]

Lack of time, unfortunately, does not permit me to answer your worthy letter of the 15th of this month in any detail. But if I share with you the results of my consideration, I am convinced that you should *not* insist on the exclusive use of private confession.[2] It is a fact that we have already lost many souls and whole congregations through this matter in Wisconsin, since on the part of our pastors there was such an unconditional insistence on private confession. I do not deny that only righteous faithfulness of our pastors has moved them to this position, but what good is it to us if a churchly usage is an excellent means in the abstract for building up the church, when in the concrete it does not bring forth this fruit?

If private confession were indeed by divine command, then we would not have to be concerned about the results but would simply want to be obedient to God and commend the whole matter to Him. But if human beings make regulations, these have value only as long as they work wholesomely according to conditions and circumstances. It is, of course, also true that most of our congregations do not want to hold to private confession exclusively. That is a proof that there is a lack of proper felt needs in our congregations. Only this, when our congregations do not know truly how to treasure private confession and we urge them to adhere to it, then the matter becomes much worse rather than improving. As soon as a majority in a congregation is in opposition to private confession and only endures it against its will, then we can no longer continue to insist on this kind of an arrangement.

We pastors dare not presume to rule over our congregations this way. But if we wanted to force our congregations to adopt something not commanded by God, then we would domineer. That private confession is a salutary custom and that its objective is only the welfare of the souls in the congregation makes no difference. Clerical domineering did not find entry into the Christian church because evil-minded preachers introduced it, but because zealous and pious preachers were of the opinion that they had to insist on what they considered wholesome and that they therefore could not permit the resistance of the congregation to deter them since that resistance had its basis in ignorance.

But I do have to call your attention to this, that you should not permit any change to be based on inadequate reasons. For example, to say that the exclusive use of private confession consumes too much time, this would not be worthy of a Christian. This a pastor may not acknowledge. For Christians are first to seek the kingdom of God, and therefore their time is above all to be utilized in the care of souls. No, the reason that alone must be acknowledged by you for making such a change must be that the majority of members are weak in knowledge and in Christian experience and that they therefore do not understand the benefits of private confession and neither can deduce the benefit therefrom, and that they therefore make use of private confession only under protest. Therefore it would be better to do away with private confession as an exclusive custom before dissension could arise in the congregation and through it finally even open discord and division into factions might occur.

But if private confession is not used exclusively, then it is even more necessary that you insist on Communion announcements and do not yield one iota on this point. I call your attention to the article on this in *Lehre und Wehre*,[3] which I surely need not repeat here. Please look at the October and November numbers of last year. The essay in the October number is of such a nature that it is suitable to be read to a congregation and could be used as the basis of discussion with a congregation.

I am amazed that Pastor Krumsieg[4] inquired whether Methodist baptism is to be considered as valid, since we have taken up this question in lectures on pastoral theology in detail and since this question has also been discussed in our *Lehre und Wehre*. I have no doubt but that baptism in the Methodist church, other things being equal, is valid. I say other things being equal, to indicate that there might be a specific individual case in such baptisms which may not have any Christian validity.

Please content yourself with these few remarks. May God give you grace to do everything well and to assist your congregation even if it surrenders private confession, this glorious heritage of an orthodox Lutheran confession, out of weakness. May God help your congregation to become all that more zealous in the main concern.

Yours in the Lord,
C.F.W. Walther

To His Nephew Johannes Walther

St. Louis, Dec. 11, 1867

Dear Johannes,[1]

I was pleasantly surprised to receive your welcome letter of the third of this month. I can only say yea and amen to your decision to accept the call to Johannisburg.[2] Just a few days before the arrival of your letter I had recommended to Pastor Hanser[3] that Pastor Theodore Miessler[4] in Cole Camp, Mo., would make a good successor for him, and as I reviewed all those names which I could have recommended as Hanser's successor I did not even think of you, whereas at another time I had thought of you and also had mentioned your name. But as I read your letter I was immediately certain that this is the leading of the Lord. From my last letter, in which I evaluated your gifts, you could conclude that I held you to be the most suitable person for Johannisburg.

This is a major jump for you, not so much physically as spiritually, to go from the Wyandott[5] congregation to the Johannisburg congregation; it's going from one pole to another. But I do believe that Wyandott was a good preparation for you for a new field of labor. No doubt it will demand an enormous effort on your part to have to strike a totally different tone. In Wyandott you had to deal with the black devil and in Johannisburg you will find yourself facing the white devil. There you had to contend with rationalism and with Epicurean libertinism, but in Johannisburg you will have to do with judgmental orthodoxism which is authoritarian to the point of heresy, as well as with false spirituality. In Wyandott you had to watch yourself that nobody drove you off the walls, whereas in Johannisburg you will have to watch it that nobody circumscribes you. In Wyandott everything was thought to be too severe, whereas in Johannisburg you will often be suspected of too much laxity. But you are undertaking a blessed work which until now was hardly granted you to an exceptional extent.

Now you must probe deeply into the Word not only to defend the Word but also to use it effectively. Your assignment now will be to deliver thorough doctrinal sermons. That will bring you respect, confidence, and love from everyone. You will therefore have to weigh every word that you will write and then boldly preach, not only to see whether it agrees with Scripture, but also whether it has the flavor of the school of Luther and of the Weimar Bible. Please consider that. You may preach ever so properly, but if your teaching style does not resemble the books to which they are accustomed there, then there will immediately be suspicion against you which must hinder your work and even completely undermine it.

You will certainly not fail in opportunities for private ministrations. There are many people there who do not gladly take one step into the unknown without first getting advice from their father confessor. So it is important to be alert, to pray, and to guard against evil attitudes and impatience and really to study the old writers on casuistry. And especially in your new congregation you will have to guard against hasty decisions, since necessary retractions are dangerous there. Whereas other congregations may consider the pastor as a poor human being who has to dance according to their tune for the sake of money, in contrast to this such congregations as the one in Johannisburg are of the opinion that the pastor must be fit and ready for anything, an oracle who is, so to speak, infallible. They will try you in order to be able to follow you safely, or never to trust you again.

But in spite of all this I believe that you will be in the right place and that you will feel comfortable in your new situation; yes, in many respects you will feel renewed. There are a significant number of outstanding people there who as far as I have been able to ascertain have remained humble.

Who should now be named as your successor is hard to say. It seems to me that if I were to recommend anybody I would simply be sending him into grief and misfortune. But oftentimes much is changed when we once strike the path that first breaks the ice. Perhaps Theodor Miessler would be the most suitable man. He is polished, friendly, yet earnest, has beautiful insights, is energetic, and has a good preaching style. But I doubt whether he would accept such a call.

Now, please be content with these few lines. May God go with you and make you a blessing for many in Johannisburg. Gross[6] and Weinbach[7] will be good neighbors to you.

Cordial greetings to your dear wife from me and my family.

Your loving uncle,
C.F.W. Walther

To Pastor A. Ernst
Elmira, Canada
(Fuerbringer, II, 125—126)

St. Louis, April 10, 1868

My dear brother,

Here is a brief answer to your inquiry. Since synodical affiliation is only a human order, therefore it is beyond doubt that a congregation which is without a pastor can elect a pastor of a different synodical affiliation and can change its own synodical affiliation to the one to which he belongs. I would therefore not have the least hesitation to accept a congregation into our synod which formerly belonged to the Canada Synod but which indicates that it has no confidence in it anymore, all the more since that synod seeks to tie its congregations to itself through those ill-reputed property deeds.[1] In short, the selection of a synod is a matter of freedom.

As incorrect as it is when a synod chases congregations of another synod, and seeks to get them to join without a legitimate reason, so self-evident is it also that one has the right to accept a congregation against which there are no legitimate objections, if such a congregation desires to be received. It then need only indicate to the synod to which it formerly belonged that it is severing its membership. If that synod will not accept that, then such a synod has to be told that this is a main reason why a congregation has to leave its membership therein, namely that such a synod seeks to tie congregations to itself and thus rob them of their freedom.

This will be enough to share with you my firm conviction in this matter.

According to your plan will we see you again in summer, God willing, in Richmond?

This, with a cordial greeting, is the wish of your hurried

C.F.W. Walther

To Wm. Sihler

St. Paul, Minn., July 21, 1876

As much as I dislike to burden you again with a visitation assignment, I have no other way out. From the enclosed documents you will see that charges against Pastor Meyer in Kirchhayn[1] have come to me which are made, in criticism of the decision of the district president, as an appeal for a new investigation. I myself am incapable of undertaking this since after the close of the convention of the Northwestern District and the Synodical Conference I have to hurry home to prepare, after a very short rest, to go to Indianapolis and Baltimore for the conventions of the Central and Eastern Districts. After that I must necessarily begin my teaching duties in St. Louis. At the beginning of November I must again leave to take part in the meetings of the Schoolbook Committee, which may take from 8 to 14 days. Thus I have indicated to the Kirchhayn people that if they absolutely cannot be content with the present settlement they should apply to you with the request that you represent me in the investigation and that you have the final voice in making a decision.

If such a request should now reach you, then I would petition you if at all possible to meet that request. It is said that among those making the appeal there are some good souls who have been deluded, for whose sake it is highly desirable that we meet the complainants positively. It may even be possible that also such among them will be regained who have up to now proven themselves to be rather malicious. May God give you the grace that no one will be lost and that you may succeed in saving what still is salvagable and in protecting the congregation against complete destruction and dissolution. It seems to be a rather bad situation there.[2]

In the hope that I may soon be privileged to see you in joy again, and rejoicing with you in God, I am yours with greetings in the old love.

C. F. W. Walther

P.S. Up till now the Synodical Conference convention has been moving along quite well. It was richly blessed.

To the Board of Elders

Trinity Congregation, Detroit, Mich.

Jan. 13, 1878

To the Highly Respected Members of the Board of Elders of the Evangelical Lutheran Trinity Congregation in Detroit, Mich.

Beloved Brethren in the Lord,

With great sadness I noticed from your honored letter of the eighth of this month that there still are several members of your congregation who insist on attending services at other churches and take practically no part in the congregational services in your church, whereas they appear in meetings of the congregation and take part in discussions, in consultations, in resolutions, and in voting.

Now, you seek my advice. Here it is:

You cannot continue in that way. A congregation cannot continue to be composed for a longer time of two classes of members, of which one group will attend the services but the other group attends services in other churches. Such exceptions can probably be tolerated for a limited time when there is concern for the souls of the people involved and for the peace of the congregation, since love, which is the highest law, in times of need takes precedence over order. But love does not dissolve all order. This it cannot do, since God's Word says: "All things should be done decently and in order" (1 Corinthians 14:40).

The protesting party had received permission to commune in other churches and to absent themselves for a time from the public worship of their congregation, since they had declared that because of the mistakes that had occurred they had lost all confidence in their pastor. This was the utmost that could have been conceded to them in spite of the fact that they had to admit that their pastor taught pure doctrine. The concession was made because the protesters were to be spared from the shame which they thought would be involved if after the conclusion of peace they would again regularly attend the divine services which they had avoided till then. If they now will say that they still do not have any confidence in their pastor and for that reason cannot come and make confession and commune, then their viewpoint is highly problematic since their pastor has admitted where he has not dealt properly and has indeed humbled himself so far as to concede the right to those protesting people to decline his further care of souls in regard to them. As questionable as this may be, this was ascribed to their conscience, into which no one can peer, and the judgment was relegated to the One who sees into the heart, and thus it was permitted to the protesters further to take Communion in other churches till they would want to return to their own church. But the regular attendance at other divine services and nonetheless the active participation in the congregational voters assembly in their own church, this dare not continue any longer. This must cease.

The time in which it may have appeared to be embarrassing for the protesters again to return to their church is long over. If they cannot prove that Pastor Huegli is a false teacher, then they have the holy duty, since they live in his parish, to hear him as their appointed teacher. If they do not want this, then they must either adhere in their hearts to a different doctrine from that which is preached in their church and thus because of their own false doctrine refuse to hear their pastor, or they are enthusiasts who because they view their pastor as unworthy consider his sermons as being anemic, or they are irreconcilable and refuse to forgive, or they are arrogant and want to dominate the congregation.

Therefore these protesters should be confronted with the following questions:

1. Whether they sincerely subscribe to the eighth article of the Augsburg Confession.[1]

2. Whether they can prove that the pastor of their congregation is a false teacher.

3. Whether they can prove that their pastor has been living an offensive life.

4. Whether they can prove that their pastor tyrannizes their conscience.

5. Whether they can prove that their pastor, although he wants to preach and officiate properly, is incapable thereof.

6. Whether they believe that one can separate oneself from an orthodox pastor who is not ungodly, or whether one must do so if he has weaknesses or if he does not possess all the traits which one would gladly see in him.

If they answer number one with yes, and if they cannot come up with any evidence in respect to questions two to five, and if they do not want to be caught in the horrible error referred to under six, then they should be asked whether they will again regularly attend their church. If they do not want that, they should be told that their responses come either out of false doctrine or out of personal hate or out of arrogance, and their problems should be addressed in a friendly yet earnest manner. But if this will not work with them, then they should be told that the very least which the congregation must do is that it will not be permitted in the future to avoid the services of the congregation but to take part in discussions and in voting in the voters assembly. This is my advice.

But consider this well, dear brethren. This is only my *advice*, which I considered myself obligated to give you upon your request. I must therefore request you not to make any direct public use thereof, but, having obtained this advice, to decline to publicize it, and you should deal according to this only when you are clearly convinced that this advice harmonizes with God's Word, of which I myself of course have no doubt. I make this request not because I fear to come out into the open with my advice, nor to take responsibility for the results that may flow from it, but rather I do this so that every person of those whom I do not know will not feel that they are being strong-armed by official authority.

In a completely private way you may, of course, share my letter with the persons concerned, if you believe that this would convince them; but do not do this publicly in order to shame them, and not at the beginning of a meeting with them, but only if the confrontation should reveal that they would finally be willing to yield if they were convinced.

Since I have no time to make a copy of this letter but I do have a concern to keep in mind what I have written, therefore I ask you to take the responsibility of making a copy and sending it to me.

In this matter the elders above all ought to deal with the pastor and to implore wisdom and patience from above.

I greet you in inner love and with the prayer to God that He may turn this sad matter to a good conclusion,

Your brother in the Lord,
C.F.W. Walther

P.S. After I have once more read through the above, I am of the opinion that it would be better if this letter were not shared with those people who absent themselves from the services but that they rather be told that if they want to learn the meaning of the written attempt at conciliation they should get in touch with me.

To an Unidentified Pastor

Concordia Seminary, St. Louis, Mo., July 6, 1881

Beloved brother in the Lord,

On the question whether it is right for a congregation which wants to be Christian to let the state care for its poor and needy sick members, above all the following needs to be considered.

Caring for its poor and needy members is a special duty of every Christian congregation (Acts 6:1-6; Galatians 2:10; Romans 12:13; 1 Corinthians 12:26). For that reason in the time of the apostles this was not only counted among the duties of the pastor as such, that he was to look after the poor and the sick members, but for that reason also the offices of deaconesses and deacons were established and this duty especially assigned to them in the larger congregations in which this concern exceeded the limits of the pastors (Acts 6:1-6; Galatians 2:10; 1 Timothy 3:8-13; Romans 12:8; 1 Timothy 5:9-10).

Since now the care for the poor is a duty of love assigned by God to the church, it is clear that the church cannot hang this duty on the state, just as little as it can do this with other duties, as for example the duty of supporting its pastor. Whoever has a duty must carry it out himself, and not someone else for him, if he is able to do so. If all people were Christians, the state would not need to have funds for the poor and the sick nor institutions for them. But since the people will not out of free will care for the people and the needy sick, therefore the state imposes taxes on its citizens and compels them to establish such funds and institutions because it would be a shame for the state, even if it were a non-Christian state, if it would permit its poor and sick to go hungry and naked and to go to ruin on the streets and if the corpses were lying in the sun rotting away unburied.

Of course also the Christians as citizens of the state must make their contributions to taxes for the poor, but this should not be the case for their fellow believers, who are to be provided for by the church without compulsion, only out of brotherly love. But this applies only to the poor who do not belong to the church and who would otherwise come to naught. The church through such activity is to shine forth also before the eyes of the state and of all non-Christians, showing that the church does not need this enforced tax for the poor, that it does not rely on it, and that it would not even accept in case of special need because those who belong to the church are already well provided for. The enforced outward works of charity the church relegates to the world, which is concerned with people only because of self-interest or because of its own honor or out of self-righteousness or even out of compulsion. For that reason the apostle insists that Christians should conduct themselves so that they are in need of nothing from those outside (1 Thessalonians 4:11 and 12).

That which is not a duty or a right of Christians, but only duties and rights of citizens, is something else again. Therefore we read that the apostle Paul as citizen appealed to Caesar (Acts 25:11) and appealed to his full citizen's rights (Acts 16:35-40). The duties of Christians and of the church and the rights of Christians therefore should not be confused. If the church relied on the poor laws of the secular state, this would be a great shame for the church unless it were done out of enormous need, because thereby the church would be saying that also members of the church have to be coerced to care for their poor fellow members. The church also contributes taxes toward the erection of prisons and even gallows but it does not make use of either of these.

I am herewith returning your letter to you again so that I need not copy out your questions but that you can outline the answers on the basis of my general remarks briefly given.

[Here follow brief replies that Walther obviously made to specific questions not included in Walther's letter. Without the questions, the answers appear rather cryptic and are difficult to understand.]

With cordial love,

Your Christian colleague,
C.F.W. Walther

To an Unidentified Pastor

Concordia Seminary, St. Louis, Mo., March 13, 1882

Intimately beloved friend and brother,

With deep emotion I read your letter of the tenth. This has brought me to my knees to grieve before God with groanings and tears about the speedy deterioration of spiritual life in our old congregations. The difference is becoming narrower and narrower between a congregation in a state-church system and one in our system of free congregations with their apostolic constitutions under God's inexpressible grace. And what can we expect of our new congregations if the older ones show them such a poor example?

I am in complete accord with the printed leaflet you enclosed. To your first question, whether there is any one point in the leaflet on which we have gone too far, which would therefore not accord with one's conscience, I must say forthrightly no, there is not. For it is not denied that there could be someone who provides hospitality for travelers who stands in a truly God-pleasing calling, even if he serves strong drink. For strong drinks are not in themselves prohibited and under certain circumstances can be enjoyed with thanksgiving. But it is another matter whether the proprietor of a grocery store may turn his store into a tavern for local people. He would thereby make his store into a pesthouse for others, and for his own people it would be a house where God could not dwell with His blessings. We here have succeeded by the grace of God to enforce the principle that no congregation member may be a saloon keeper or a grocery store proprietor with a tavern. One member who refused to receive instructions we have therefore excommunicated. And this same person, as far as I know, finally went to pieces after violence and murder occurred in his establishment. And this is a frequent result when a tavern keeper refuses to continue to serve the drunkards who demand more and more drinks from him. But I am beginning to lecture, which is totally unnecessary for you.

Your second question asks, "According to your opinion, are we going too far in our congregation?" This question I no less answer with a decisive no. In my opinion, you could not ask for any less. Any kind of a lesser demand would only make evil all the worse. For thereby the conducting of a "drunkard's den" or a tavern with or without being attached to a grocery store would be legitimized. This might for a shorter time be conducted rather circumspectly, but later on, like an avalanche which rolls into the deep, it would bury everything in its path. No, it remains certain that running such establishments of temptation and delusion is serving the devil, with whom we dare not make any compromise and to whom we dare not capitulate.

Naturally after such an evil, or much more such corruption, has already taken deep root, and after the consciences of members have been dulled, one dare not begin by excommunication or suspension. The objective must always be shown to the people involved so that later on they cannot say that what has formerly not been rejected can now not be rejected. But those dulled people must see that the objective is to save them and not to drive them out of the congregation with a hasty ultimatum. It is relevant here to remember "exhort with all *longsuffering* and doctrine" (2 Timothy 4:2 [KJV]). One dare not take recourse to sharper methods till the milder approach has been proven useless and till people want to rest on those futile milder approaches like soft pillows. At the beginning when this battle is begun, the example of St. Paul must be our guide, who admonished each one with tears (Acts 20:31) and who wrote to the deluded Corinthians with many tears (2 Corinthians 2:4). In the beginning one has to avoid all stormy and bitter harshness, and the heart of the congregation has to be softened through the most loving presentation of the situation to which they have come and where they will go if this penetrating evil is not turned away. The members of the congregation have to attain a bad conscience and to understand that they will assume a larger fault and responsibility than the tavern keepers already have, if the congregation will not show itself to be like a righteous mother in dealing with her children fallen into error and if the congregation were to follow in Eli's footsteps.

In the third question you asked finally, whether it would be improper, in case the congregation would not take the steps against those grocery

84

store proprietors, then to make the above declaration. To this I answer, certainly not. But you will not want to threaten to do this immediately from the beginning. Threats do not effect a healing but only serve as law working repentance. They may therefore not be used till all other approaches have proved fruitless. For that reason St. Paul only threatens toward the end of his Second Letter to the Corinthians (12:20 and 21; 13:1-4).

The main damage is in the lack of knowledge and lack of alert consciences. You are not yet dealing with godless people who act completely contrary to better knowledge and conscience. I pray that God would preserve you from seeing the Word bring an odor of death, give rise to dealings leading to death. Go at your difficult work, then, with a confident heart. Probably, or even most likely, we hope, it will go much better than you think. But of course it is better that your membership be reduced, which God may forbid, rather than the whole congregation be led to corruption.

Let this suffice. I have many letters awaiting my humble replies, so that I do not know how I can manage it all.

With greetings to you,

Your colleague in joy and suffering in the Lord Jesus,
C.F.W. Walther

Walther as Churchman: Administration of Synod and Interchurch Relationships

To Wm. Sihler
Pomeroy, Ohio
(Fuerbringer, I, 6— 15)

St. Louis, Jan. 2, 1845

Dearest brother in office and in the faith,[1]

I cannot tell you how great my joy was when I received your precious letter of December 11 on Holy Christmas Eve, just a few days after I had received a similar letter from Pastor Ernst.[2] God be lauded and praised for this great grace that He moved you, dearest brethren, to reach out to us with such great love. May He grant that the relationship thus established between us may become very firm and be a rich blessing for us and for the whole church especially in this our new homeland.

For a long time already I have groaned in the inner man that I have to stand here so alone, and this has at times become almost unbearable for me. For, oh, how great is the danger here that isolated congregations will only develop into new sects! True, according to my convictions no congregation is tied to another in such a way that the two must have a common church government in order to possess all the rights and gifts of the church. But how can we hope that we may be preserved in the fellowship of one faith, one mind, and one speech if we despise outward ties with those who now make the same confession before the world, when such a union is possible? We, who in unbelievable blindness formerly permitted ourselves to be led by Stephan, have special reason to seek out those of orthodox faith in order to be assimilated also into their outward fellowship. Besides, we would give the enemies cause to consider us a special sect and to treat us as such. And God knows that we ourselves under Stephan had nothing else in mind but to prove ourselves completely faithful to the true Lutheran church. But there was nothing which caused us to fail in this very thing more than our stubborn exclusiveness. The more dangerous and corrupting this became for us the more we now yearn for the careful preservation of catholicity and the avoidance of every type of separatism.

86

Therefore you are most welcome, dear brother. With great joy I offer you my hand. I do this in conjunction with my colleague here, Pastor Buenger,[3] who works with me in the same congregation. I am sorry that I cannot also at the same time give you the thinking of the other pastors united with us in the same faith here in the West, but I will send your letter as also that of Pastor Ernst to them and ask them to express themselves toward you. I do not doubt that they will all heartily rejoice, as I do, in the increasing hope of a union with you.

You present several questions for my response, and also Pastor Ernst did so. I believe I may assume that the points the letter raised were presented no less by your desire. I therefore take the liberty to enclose in this letter to you the answers desired by Pastor Ernst and to ask you to share it with Pastor Ernst as soon as possible, since I am right now very short of time. You certainly will forgive me this presumption.

The first question: "What is the situation in the city of Wittenberg[4] on the Mississippi, and with the congregations in Altenburg,[5] Dresden, Frohna, etc. in the Saxon colony?"—Answer: *Wittenberg* is located rather unfavorably. Though it was first supposed to be the midpoint of our settlements for the immigrants in Perry County, it has remained the weakest of all the places. It contains several stores and shops and some professional establishments. The little congregation there is an affiliate congregation of Frohna. Four miles inland from the Mississippi is *Altenburg,* where Pastor Loeber[6] works. This is the most spread out and has the largest population and is growing more and more into the kind of place that Wittenberg was supposed to become. Here they are building a fine stone church, to be completed in the course of next summer. Here there is also a teacher, our dear Mr. Winter[7] from Plamena near Halle. The villages of *Dresden* and *Seelitz,* one mile distant, form a single parish with Altenburg. Formerly Seelitz was the parish of Pastor Buerger[8] who emigrated from Lunzenau in Saxony, but who resigned out of conscience scruples three years ago and wanted to return to Germany, but then permitted himself to be named as the pastor of a separated part of the congregation of Pastor Grabau[9] with which he became familiar on his journey.[10] He is still there. From Altenburg three miles further inland, towards the county seat of Perryville, there is the little village of *Frohna,* where Pastor Keyl[11] is serving the small congregation in church and school. Five miles southwest of Frohna is the *Paitzdorf* congregation, served by our dear Pastor Gruber[12] from Reuss in the Altenburg territory [in Germany]. Two small congregations which have existed here for some time have joined it (the one in *Perryville* and the one on the *Whitewater,* Jackson County).

The first-named congregations all had to work through many difficulties, but God helped them thus far, so that now there is no longer any lack of the basic needs of life. For a while also the confusion of minds was great, into which the members got when the Stephanite deception was discovered. There were splits, tension between congregations and pastors, and the like. But since God gave us grace, so that the light of the pure doctrine has broken forth all the more brightly when the darkness in which those people suddenly found themselves was the deepest, so now the finest relations prevail between shepherds and flocks.

Second question: "What is the situation in the congregation in St. Louis,[13] with its church building and its school?"—Among all the congregations this one has outwardly advanced the most. At the time of my brother's ministry here, it was poverty-stricken. But God has graciously looked after it, so that the congregation now has its own fine brick church in this growing city so important to the west, which comprises about a thousand people. In the church there is also a large space in the basement, as is customary here, in which the first parish school and the voters' assemblies are conducted. Since my official duties have increased very much, F. Buenger, former candidate and schoolteacher, was placed at my side as a second pastor. He still takes care of the teaching in the first class in our first school and also serves a small German Lutheran county congregation, 12 miles from here, as an affiliate. Teacher for the second class is Buenger's younger brother,[14] and he also serves as the teacher at a second, smaller parish school in the northern part of the city. The number of our schoolchildren averages 130 to 140, of whom about one third are such whose parents have not yet joined our congregation but only attend our public services. The number of our voting members (male adults) is presently 120. In the year 1844 I baptized 70 children in this city; I had about 1,600 communicants.

Third question: "Is there hope that a seminary for pastors and teachers could be established in St. Louis or in some other place in the settlement?"—The basis for such an institution was laid in our first year in Altenburg.[15] At first the former candidates Brohm, Fuerbringer, and Buenger and I taught in it. However, as the three last-named were called away, Brohm with the beloved Pastor Loeber took care of the school, and almost without any support from the poor congregations. After also Brohm left, called as pastor to New York, the congregations here and in Perry County finally adopted this important undertaking, even if with modest resources. Candidate Goenner[16] was named by the joint congregations as college teacher two years ago. He really only teaches the philological disciplines, since the students get instruction in other fields from pastors Loeber and Keyl. The school up to now had more the form of an academy, but there are two students who now are being inducted into the real academic studies. There are eight students in all. I will ask Rector Goenner to give you a detailed report about our school. It might be possible that you could arouse interest in Germany for it, for we need some charitable help if we don't want this school to remain sickly and weak. It would be especially desirable to move the school to St. Louis.

Fourth question: "How are the congregations of pastors Fuerbringer[17] and Schieferdecker?[18] Would they not be willing to enter into closer relationships with the brethren in Ohio?"—About those dear brethren I can tell you that they labor under great difficulties but not without fruit. Their congregations (Fuerbringer's is 37 miles from here,[19] and Schieferdecker's is 20 miles) present an increasingly optimistic prognosis of becoming a good Lutheran growth stock, especially Schieferdecker's, in spite of its small size. The same holds true of the congregation which our dear Master Wege[20] serves as German Lutheran preacher in Benton County, Mo., 250 miles from here.

Fifth question: "With whom do the Saxon pastors comprise a synod, or are they alone by themselves?"—Among us pastors (Loeber, Keyl, Gruber in Perry County, Schieferdecker and Fuerbringer in Illinois, Wege in Benton County, Mo., Brohm in New York, and myself and my colleague Buenger, and Pastor Geyer,[21] just now taking a position in Watertown, Wisconsin Territory), there is a unity of faith and confession, an agreement in our views of conducting the ministry, and so great a conformity in liturgy and the like as there could possibly be. We carry on a continual correspondence in which we share our experiences and mutually advise, admonish, comfort, discipline, and encourage one another. There is among us a relationship of the innermost friendship. Also the congregations organized from our fellow emigrants are in active fraternal contact.

But with all this no real ecclesiastical organization has come into being. Our main objective thus far was only to be mutually founded on pure Lutheran doctrine. We have above all sought to strive after a constant oral and written exchange of ideas and thus to help each other stay in step as we progress out of the Stephanite delusion and move forward to the clear truth. Through the discovery of the Stephanite deception we were driven into the writings of Luther. All of us have, next to the Word of God, studied almost exclusively the writings of Luther, and we believe that through the guiding of the Holy Spirit by means of this incomparable treasure we have now first come to proper clarity. We had become suspicious of all our understanding; thus everything was subjected to the strictest reexamination.

Up to now our goal was a thorough reformation in doctrine and practice, and that was what we believed we had to pursue. But we do not want to follow a false spiritual tendency. We see vividly that without an outward uniting of the orthodox Lutheran pastors and their congregations, the unity of the Spirit and thereby the unity of doctrine cannot be preserved, and much less will anyone's talent be used for the common good. I can therefore answer your question by saying that we are working towards a common church government.

Sixth question: "Would it be possible together with our brethren to form a church organization?"—I hold this to be not only possible but also most desirable, and extremely promising for our common good. In fact I hold it to be unavoidable for conscience' sake, if a union can in any way be attained. But I must remark that the whole West is filled with German demagogs who do all they can to make every form of a synodical organization hated, and even well-intentioned people do not remain untouched by them. There is here thus a certain shying away from this kind of institution, for people are afraid of priest rule. On top of this is the problem that especially our congregations of emigrants are running scared of anything which might give suspicion of being a hierarchy, since they suffered so terribly under Stephan. Therefore we would have to discuss the question first how the desirable church affiliation could be introduced without arousing the suspicion that the shepherds have in mind a way to dominate the flocks, or that the arrangement could easily lead to this.

I, for my person, am prepared to make every possible sacrifice in order to bring about church union. Just for this purpose I dared (in spite of my great lack of the necessary gifts for this) in God's name to send into the world such a leaflet as the *Lutheraner* is and to present it to the church in America, to do at least my little part to call together those who are correct in the faith.

Here your third question also has bearing, as to whether we have any ties with the present Lutherans in the Buffalo area and in Wisconsin. With sadness I have to report that a tie-in had in fact been initiated but that it was shattered since Pastor Grabau's position was at the time based on errors which he expressed in a pastoral letter *(Hirtenbrief)* which he sent us for evaluation.[22] His main errors consist in this, that he holds ordination to be a *divine* ordinance, ascribes conscience-binding authority to church orders, restricts contrary to God's Word the right of congregations to call pastors and decide matters. In contrast he elevates the ministry in several respects to a higher position than the Word of God, our Confessions, and Luther's writings do. The pastors who hold with Grabau against us are Rohr in Canada, and Krause and Kindermann in Wisconsin.[23] But

90

through Pastor Ehrenstroehm a conference was recently arranged, to be held next spring in Wisconsin, in which possibly the last attempt will be made to establish doctrinal unity through face-to-face discussion and on that basis to establish common church government.

The Seventh Question: "Would it not be possible that new arrivals could receive ordination either in St. Louis or, through delegates belonging to that synod, at their assigned station?"—This question is related to the solution of the sixth question. Up to now each one of the pastors among us, though standing independently, has availed himself of the prerogative which he has by virtue of his call into office to ordain publicly in his congregation any orthodox and properly called candidate upon his request.

The Eighth Question: "Are there in and around St. Louis people who would like to study, and are teachers being prepared there?" This is answered under three.

The Ninth Question: "What provisions would the brethren in St. Louis advise to preserve German?"—In our situation here we know of no other means except our little college. Besides, there seems to be much less danger *here* that the German language will be crowded out in our congregations that there is in the East and the Middle States. The Lutheran congregations here are exclusively German and have no need of English services. The greatest danger here is the lack of knowledge and indifference connected with the poverty of the scattered congregations. Since it is possible for the Methodist preachers, provided richly with means of support, to carry on gratis in the little congregations for quite a while, they are the ones who reap the harvest. Also the Evangelicals[24] here find it more possible to hold a congregation together, since they gather all people who call themselves Protestant. When I was asked to send a congregation a German pastor, the matter more than once misfired on the condition which I had to make, that I could not recommend any of the so-called united preachers.

Ah, Illinois, Missouri, Wisconsin are sad fields of labor. A Lutheran is heartbroken when he sees how Satan has barred almost all doors. Here there would be enough, under the most fervent mutual prayers to the Great Shepherd of the sheep, for a Lutheran synod to deliberate. Oh, that it would soon, soon come into existence through Jesus' help!—I am not acquainted with the congregations between here and Columbus.

The Tenth Question: "Would friends in St. Louis be willing to take over the historic German school of Grimm for their own strengthening? Would they be willing also to encourage others to do this?"—I must confess that I am not familiar with the indicated work, and I ask for further

Walther and his wife Emilie nee Buenger (courtesy Concordia Historical Institute).

The five cousins of the Buenger family, taken about 1870. Walther's daughter Julie is seated on the right (courtesy Concordia Publishing House library).

Lehre und Wehre.

Jahrgang I.   Januar 1855.   No. 1.

Zur Lehre vom heiligen Predigtamt.

Von Pastor C. Zuttringer.

Die Frage von Kirche und Amt ist unbestritten eine Zeitfrage. Sie bewegt nicht bloß die lutherische Kirche, sondern auch außerhalb derselben stehende Gemeinschaften. Das Resultat dieses Streits wird aber doch kein anderes sein, als daß die evangelische Lehre von Neuem als gerechtfertigt aus Gottes Wort erkannt werden wird von Allen, welche die Wahrheit ernstlich suchen. Die rechte Kirche hat längst entschieden über diese Streitfrage. Was wäre das auch für eine Kirche, die achtzehn Jahrhunderte lang nicht im Klaren mit sich gewesen, was sie selber sei und ihr Amt! (Matth. 28, 20. 1 Tim. 3, 15. Joh. 16, 13.) Es kommt nur darauf an, daß man das Geld der reinen Lehre auch wiederum recht schätze und auf solche Weise je mehr und mehr im Bewußtsein sich vertiefen lasse. Wegen des innigen und unzertrennlichen Zusammenhangs der Artikel von Kirche und Amt mit dem vernehmsten von der Rechtfertigung aus Gnaden in Christo Jesu durch den Glauben konnte es nicht anders kommen, als daß der ganze Kampf der Reformation neben diesem hauptsächlich jenen galt. Was unsere Väter uns als Erbteil hinterlassen haben, das lasset uns immer klarer in den Verstand und immer lebendiger in das Herz aufnehmen, nicht in blindem Köhlerglauben, sondern aus eigener Gewißheit durch den Heiligen Geist, auf die Zeugnisse seines Bibelworts gegründet.

Auch der würdige deutsche Pfarrer, Johann Friedrich Wucherer, hat über Predigtamt ein Büchlein veröffentlicht. Er verspricht durch dasselbe „einen ausführlichen Nachweis aus Schrift und Symbolen, daß das evangelisch-lutherische Pfarramt das apostolische Hirten- und Lehramt und darum göttliche Stiftung sei." Dasselbe ist auch uns von vornherein gewiß. Das öffentliche Predigtamt in der Kirche Gottes bis an den jüngsten Tag ist göttliche Stiftung und nicht wesentlich verschieden vom heiligen Apostelamt. Des verstorbenen Dr. Höflings Anschauungsweise, gegen welche Wucherers Schrift vor Allem gerichtet ist, ist nicht die streng lutherische. Aber indem Wucherer

1

The masthead for the first issue of *Lehre und Wehre*, published in January, 1855 (courtesy Concordia Publishing House library).

Christ Episcopal Church, on Fifth and Chestnut Streets in St. Louis, where Walther's Trinity congregation worshipped until the church below was dedicated in 1842 (courtesy Concordia Publishing House library).

The first house of worship of Trinity Evangelical Lutheran Church, St. Louis (courtesy Concordia Publishing House library).

Zeugniß.

Daß Herr *Julius Johannes August Friedrich* gebürtig von *Huntington, Ind.* seit *1. September* 18 *84* bis *20. April* 18 *87* in dem hiesigen Concordia-Seminar der deutschen evangelisch-lutherischen Synode von Missouri, Ohio u. a. St. dem Studium der Theologie mit *großem* Fleiße obgelegen, sich dabei eines *tadelhaft christlichen* Wandels befleißigt und in dem vorschriftsmäßig mit ihm angestellten öffentlichen Examen pro Candidatura zu Uebernahme des heiligen Predigtamtes als *sehr gut* vorbereitet sich erwiesen habe: solches wird demselben unter Anwünschung göttlichen Segens hierdurch nach Pflicht und Gewissen bezeugt.

St. Louis im Staate Missouri den *21. April* 18 *87*

Das Lehrercollegium:

The last diploma signed by Walther as seminary president on April 21, 1887, for graduate Julius Friedrich (courtesy Concordia Publishing House library).

The faculty of Concordia Seminary, St. Louis, taken sometime between 1887 and 1892. Sitting (from left): C. H. R. Lange, M. Guenther; standing: G. Stoeckhardt, F. Pieper, A. L. Graebner (courtesy Concordia Publishing House archives).

95

Walther receives the doctor of divinity degree in 1878 from the theological seminary of the Ohio Synod (courtesy Concordia Publishing House library).

Another view of Walther's study, where many of his theological and pastoral works were produced (courtesy Concordia Historical Institute).

Concordia Seminary in 1883, where Walther served as professor and president to the end of his life (courtesy Concordia Publishing House archives).

97

Walther's carriage, presently located at Concordia Historical Institute. An illustration of this carriage also serves as the logo for this series.

Walther's south St. Louis home, as it was draped at the time of his death in 1887 (courtesy Concordia Historical Institute).

98

Der Lutheraner.

„Gottes Wort und Luthers Lehr' vergehet nun und nimmermehr."

Herausgegeben von C. F. W. Walther.

Jahrg. 1.   St. Louis, Mo., den 7. September 1844.   No. 1.

Bedingungen: Der Lutheraner erscheint alle zwei Wochen einmal für den Subscriptionspreis von Einem Dollar fünf und zwanzig Cents für die auswärtigen Unterschreiber, welche davon die Hälfte vorauszubezahlen und das Postgeld zu tragen haben. — In St. Louis wird jede einzelne Nummer für 6¼ Cents verkauft.

Vorbemerkungen über Ursache, Zweck und Inhalt des Blattes.

Die deutsche Bevölkerung des Westens von Amerika wird offenbar mit jedem Tage größer. Mit derselben wächst hier zugleich die Anzahl derjenigen, welche sich zu dem Glauben bekennen, den einst Luther den Deutschen gepredigt hat. Es stehen jedoch hier die Glieder keiner andern kirchlichen Gemeinschaft so verwaiset da, als die der evangelisch-lutherischen. So viel ihrer auch hier sein mögen, die sich noch Lutheraner nennen, so leben sie doch so zerstreut und sind von allen Mitteln meist so ganz entblößt, daß sie an vielen Orten kaum im Stande sind, in einen Gemeindeverband zu treten und einen Prediger ihres Bekenntnisses zu bestellen, der ihnen diene. Die deutschen Lutheraner sind daher hier in nicht geringer Versuchung, den Glauben ihrer Väter zu verlassen; entweder nach Kirche, Gottesdienst u. dergl. gar nichts zu fragen, oder in anderen hier bestehenden Gemeinschaften Befriedigung ihrer religiösen Bedürfnisse zu suchen. Unsere theuren Glaubensbrüder in diesem Theile unseres neuen Vaterlandes bedürfen darum allerdings der Ermunterung, ihrem Glauben treu zu bleiben; sie bedürfen der Warnung vor den Gefahren des Abfalls, deren so viele ihnen hier drohen; sie bedürfen Waffen, sich gegen diejenigen zu vertheidigen, die es ihnen streitig machen, daß der Glaube der rechte sei, den sie von Jugend auf aus ihrem Catechismus gelernt haben; sie bedürfen den Trost, daß die Kirche, zu der sie sich bekennen, noch nicht verschwunden sei, daß sie daher keineswegs Ursache haben, bei irgend einer andern Gemeinschaft Zuflucht zu suchen.

Dieses gewiß von vielen empfundene Bedürfniß, und die Ueberzeugung, daß es unsere Pflicht sei, unsern hiesigen Mitbürgern darüber Rechenschaft abzulegen, was in unserer Kirche geglaubt und gelehrt, und nach welchen Grundsätzen sie von uns gehandelt werde; dieß hat den Unterzeichneten bewogen, in Verbindung mit mehreren seiner Amts- und Glaubensbrüder in Missouri und Illinois, ein Blatt unter obigem Titel herauszugeben. Dasselbe soll nehmlich dazu dienen: 1. mit der Lehre, den Schätzen und der Geschichte der lutherischen Kirche bekannt zu machen; 2. den

Beweis dafür zu liefern, daß diese Kirche nicht in der Reihe der christlichen Secten stehe, und nicht eine neue, sondern die alte wahre Kirche Jesu Christi auf Erden sei, daß sie daher noch keineswegs ausgestorben sei, ja, nicht aussterben könne, nach Christi Verheißung: „Siehe, ich bin bei euch alle Tage bis an der Welt Ende." Unser Blatt soll ferner 3. dazu dienen, zu zeigen, wie ein Mensch als ein wahrer Lutheraner recht glauben, christlich selben, geduldig leiden und selig sterben könne; und endlich 4. die im Schwange gehenden falschen, verführerischen Lehren zu entdecken, zu widerlegen und davor zu warnen, und insonderheit diejenigen zu entlarven, die sich fälschlich lutherisch nennen, unter diesem Namen Irrglaube, Unglauben und Schwärmerei verbreiten und daher die übelsten Vorurtheile gegen unsere Kirche in den Gliedern anderer Parteien erwecken.

Vielleicht nicht wenige, wenn sie dieß lesen, werden uns entweder die Fähigkeit absprechen, das Ziel, das wir uns selbst gesteckt haben, zu erreichen; oder sie werden fürchten, daß unser Blatt den Geist der Unduldsamkeit athmen, und somit das Verschiedengläubender unterhalten und vermehren werde. Auf das erste Bedenken haben wir nur dieses zu antworten: Wir erkennen selbst geringe lebendiger, als irgend jemand, wie viel uns abgeht, den Beruf des Herausgebers eines christlichen Zeitungsblattes in seinem großen Umfange zu erfüllen; wir wissen aber, daß es in göttlichen Dingen nicht auf große Gelehrsamkeit und Beredtsamkeit ankommt, seinen Brüdern nützlich zu sein, sondern auf rechte lebendige Erkenntniß der seligmachenden Wahrheit und auf ein einfaches Zeugniß von derselben. Uebrigens haben wir in der Absicht, in diesem Blatte die geistreichsten Lehrer unserer Kirche, insonderheit Luthern, selbst reden zu lassen, und wir meinen, daß schon allein diese mit dem Blatte dargebotenen Gaben dasselbe so gehaltvoll machen werden, daß sich der Leser das Unsrige wenigstens als eine geringe Zugabe gefallen lassen kann. Was das zweite Bedenken betrifft, so wird es gewiß bald gehoben werden, wenn die Leser nur einige Blätter mit Aufmerksamkeit und ohne Vorurtheil werden geprüft haben. Wir sind selbst eine geraume Zeit von mancherlei Irrthümern gefangen gewesen, und Gott hat mit uns Geduld

gehabt und uns mit großer Langmuth auf den Weg der Wahrheit geleitet; dessen eingedenk werden daher auch wir gegen unsere irrenden Nächsten uns beweisen und uns alles sündlichen Richtens und Verdammens durch Gottes Gnade enthalten. Wir werden nicht sowohl die irrende Person, als vielmehr ihren Irrthum angreifen. Wir werden uns auch nicht als solche geberden, die allein rein lutherisch sein und die Wahrheit allein besitzen wollen, sondern nur Zeugniß geben, daß Gott auch an uns Großes gethan und uns zur lebendigen Erkenntniß der alleinseligmachenden Wahrheit gebracht hat.

St. Louis, Mo., im August 1844.

C. F. W. Walther,

Pastor der deutschen ev. luth. Gemeinde ungetrennter Augsburgischer Confession hier.

Zeugnisse Luthers:

Welches der Hauptartikel der christlichen Lehre sei.

In seiner herrlichen Auslegung des Briefes an die Galater schreibt derselbe: „In meinem Herzen herrscht allein und soll auch herrschen dieser einige Artikel, nehmlich der Glaube an meinen lieben Herrn Christum, welcher aller meiner geistlichen und göttlichen Gedanken, so ich immerdar Tag und Nacht haben mag, der einige Anfang, Mittel und Ende ist. Und wiewohl ich solch viel Worte davon gemacht, empfinde ich dennoch gleichwohl, wenn ich dieser Hohe, Tiefe und Breite dieser unmäßigen, unbegreiflichen und unendlichen Weisheit kaum und gar nehrlich ein geringes, schwaches Anfänken erreichen, und kaum etliche kleine Stäublein und Bröcklein aus der allerköstlichen Fundgrube habe an das Licht bringen mögen. Dieser Artikel ist der einige feste Fels und die einige beständige Grundveste alles unsers Heils und Seligkeit; nehmlich, daß wir nicht durch uns selbst viel weniger durch unsere eigene Werke und Thun (welche freilich viel geringer und weniger sind, denn wir selbst) sondern durch fremde Hülfe, nehmlich, daß wir durch den eingebornen Sohn Gottes, Jesum Christum, von Sünden, Tod und Teufel erlöset und zum ewigen Leben gebracht sein."

The front page of the first issue of *Der Lutheraner*, Sept. 7, 1844, soon to become a catalyst for the union of confessional Lutherans in America (courtesy Concordia Publishing House library).

information. I hardly need mention that all of us are all thinking most earnestly of doing everything possible to preserve the German language here and to counter the evil leaven which with the English language so easily mixes itself into the pure doctrine and polity of our church.

The Eleventh Question: "Would it be agreeable to you if we would regularly see to it that you would get the most important church literature?" This question has happily surprised me. You would move us to profound thanks, for we do not yet have ways to acquire such literature directly.

In respect to the unfortunate Stephan, I have had no opportunity to apprise myself of his present situation or his feelings. As far as I know, he now lives in Kaskaskia, Ill., where it is said he still functions as a pastor among the Germans there. Up to two years ago we still made attempts to bring this deeply fallen man to a knowledge of his sin, but till then it was all futile. In a hardened and arrogant manner he denies everything of which he was very clearly convicted. He continued to declare himself a martyr.

I hope it might be possible for you to visit us in St. Louis sometime. I would see to it that the pastors associated with me in Missouri and Illinois would assemble here at the same time. Might it not perhaps be possible that you and the dear pastors and brethren in the faith associated with you might take part in the conference scheduled for Wisconsin next spring?[25] If you could not personally take part, you might be in touch by correspondence. For this purpose I stand ready, if you so desire, to send you the *Hirtenbrief* of Pastor Grabau mentioned above.

I am writing the above to you in the utmost haste, which I hope you will forgive me since I am at present sighing under an enormous work load and still did not want to let you go without an answer.

I send my greetings to you and all of yours cordially and fraternally; and I pray God, who has begun the good work of concord, that He would also further it to the honor of His name and for the blessing of many souls.

Your humble brother in the Lord Jesus Christ,
Carl Ferd. Wilh. Walther, pastor

To Wm. Sihler
Ft. Wayne, Ind.
(Fuerbringer I, 57—60)

St. Louis, May 10, 1849

Dear Friend and Brother,[1]

Your welcome letter of the 30th of last month as also the one from

Prof. Wolter[2] of the 28th I received two days ago in the same post. Of particular joy for me was the news that the rumor of a revolution in your congregation was unfounded. Your reasons for having the students requisitioned by me wait till the synodical convention outweigh the reasons for their more speedy placement into the ministry, especially since one of the vacant congregations, which needed to be taken care of most immediately, could be provided for by candidate Buttermann,[3] who here came out of his Unionistic faith[4] into the Lutheran conviction and who has been a source of great joy for me. It is the congregation in Chester, Ill., about 60 miles south of here on the banks of the Mississippi. The congregation which next ought to be provided for is the one at Dutchmann's Hill. But I hope that Strasen[5] together with a neighboring pastor will be able to look after its most pressing needs until after the convention and thus preserve it for our church. A third congregation has come into being in a St. Louis suburb called Bremen. [Footnote by Walther:] A fourth congregation is the one which Rev. Schliepsick[6] was forced to leave, the well-intentioned members of which want to join a neighboring congregation so that together they can support a Lutheran pastor. [End of footnote]. This congregation [in Bremen], which has promise of becoming an important post, as small as it may be now, has to have special consideration.

I am therefore inclined to urge that Lochner[7] be called there. If this should come about, then Lochner's present position must be filled with a competent man, since his people are naturally a bit spoiled by the fine gifts he possesses.

But above all, Town Eden[8] in the Buffalo area must be considered. Keyl[9] has written me about a possible preacher named Dulitz,[10] that he came to the knowledge of the truth and that he has shown himself very adept and decisive. Since he has a good education, I thought of him for Eden. But Dulitz has not turned out well. We must now consider taking care of Eden quickly through one of our seminary students. I thought of Volkert,[11] but there is one matter that still stands in the way. Brohm[12] has declared that if a theological professorship here should be preferred him, he could not accept. If he would insist on this, then I think we should consider Craemer.[13] Now if Volkert were a man who could at least to some degree replace Craemer in the mission [the Indian mission in Frankenmuth, Mich.], then the position of a theological professorship would be important enough to make Craemer a professor even in the case that Volkert would not entirely replace Craemer in his mission service. I consider Craemer to be entirely the right man to train young people to become genuinely German and genuinely Lutheran preachers. One could wish that he had an even more thorough dogmatic preparation, but the *docendo discimus* [we learn by teaching] finds its application in him all the more, the healthier the core of his knowledge is. Please give this some consideration. If you come to a conclusion, please write to the Eden congregation (through Buerger[14]) and give them a *definite* assurance as to *when* they can get a pastor. Buerger complains that the congregation is getting impatient, and affirms that it has no other demand than to get an *orthodox* and *faithful* worker. Such a person there would not come into any personal contact with Grabau.

Now I come to a matter which I write last, because it is very painful for me. It will *most likely* be completely impossible for me to take part in the forthcoming convention of our Synod. For more than a month we have had a cholera epidemic here, and every week it is more destructive. It was not until yesterday, however, that I had the first case of death in my congregation on account of the plague. A healthy, lively girl of 16 died after 14 hours of illness. But in the city in general the plague is raging to such an extent that, wherever one is, one constantly sees the hearse coming and going. Whole families have died, and especially some parts of the city (where the Germans and the Irish live) are so hard hit that the residents live in constant fear and dread. Some die after two or four hours of the disease, right after they had felt their healthiest and strongest. The sick usually retain consciousness to the last moment, and thus there is always a little hour of grace to hear God's Word and to be fortified with the Holy Sacrament.

Now, St. Louis today is so spread out that if the plague once gets the upper hand in the congregation, one pastor could not possibly meet every need. To this is added the danger, that one of the pastors will also be swept away by the pestilence, for it does seem that it is catching even if it was not so in the past. Luther impresses it emphatically on pastors in his little work, *Whether a Pastor May Flee from Dying* (which I am thinking of republishing) that *they* above all dare not abandon the lambs in such need. So as much as I will lose thereby and as much as I thereby place a burden on you, you will see yourself that I cannot with good conscience sacrifice my immediate duties toward the congregation entrusted to me in favor of my love for our Synod.

The members of my congregation, some of whom live in considerable terror of this frightful judgment of God and who right-well know the duties of a Lutheran pastor, would take it very ill if I would leave them in such need. And still more would I be blamed by those who might have to die without spiritual comfort during my absence. And some might even, with the world, think that I was with joy taking advantage of the synodical convention as a good opportunity to get out of the dangerous situation, and that in the most difficult time, for with the increasingly hot weather the raging of the plague has been noticeably increasing. It is expected that in June and July it will reach the highest level.

I share this information with you in haste, to prepare you for the situation that, as it looks, you will at the synodical convention have to take over all my functions as president. My presidential report, of course, I will send in with our delegate. The other pastors who have decided to come from here will not be hindered from going by the cholera since this pestilence is raging almost only in the cities, mostly in the large ones. Those who want to come are Lochner,[15] Fick, Schieferdecker, Biltz, and probably Strasen.

If I do not come,[16] I will certainly be among the brethren in spirit and will fervently beseech God to enlighten them and bless their deliberation to His honor and the weal of His church. If the pestilence should sweep me away also, may the Lord grant me a gracious moment for a blessed departure from this miserable life into His heavenly kingdom. Remember me in your intercessory prayers, a really poor and miserable sinner, and tell our friend Wolter that I sincerely request his prayers for me.

May the Lord strengthen you and grant you rich comfort from the overflowing well-spring of His glorious Gospel.

Your often deeply troubled
Walther

To Wm. Loehe
Neuendettelsau, Bavaria, Germany

Concordia [Seminary, St. Louis, Mo.], June 5, 1852

Honorable sir, esteemed pastor,[1]

Under the assumption that Wyneken[2] had already written you, I was going to wait with writing you till after the synodical convention. But since I hear that Wyneken has not yet written you, I cannot wait that long.

First of all, please accept our most sincere thanks for all the love and care which you evidenced for us when we stayed with you. The best gratitude will be provided by God Himself through His blessing which He will bestow on a peace enterprise now made possible.

On Feb. 2 we arrived safely.[3]

Great was the joy here upon the report of the result of our journey and of the peaceful accord reached with you, most honored pastor.[4] Certainly countless prayers of righteous Christians received the assurance that they were answered. Also from other sources, such as the Ohio Synod,[5] we have received unsolicited testimony of the wholesome impression which the news evoked when it was known that we had not broken with you but rather had tied the ties more firmly, so that I dare hope that the most recent controversy with this and similar synods which want to be confessional here has been fought through and this will be the last. After the close of our next synodical convention, Wyneken and I are thinking of journeying to Columbus[6] to pave the way for unity, not an outward one but a unity expressed by a mutual fraternal spiritual exchange between us. With the people here the situation is for the most part quite different from that among many of the half-Lutherans in Germany, for many of them are not people who because of material considerations have not gotten off their duffs, but they have never progressed any further because the light is just beginning to shine for them.

Upon our arrival we found the Grabau[7] faction engaged in a very bitter fight against us. And it seems the reports of the results of our delegation only stirred them up further. They have almost exclusively been engaged in trying to prove that those people who separated from them and whom we accepted were all godless people of whom we could only be ashamed and whose acceptance at best proved the godless nature of our principles. If we only knew of a way to peace which we could take without offending our conscience, how gladly we would take that path! But as long as the peace negotiations are *all* to be opened with admissions of guilt only on our part, we cannot take the initiative. We have received into membership only such people who according to our deepest conviction were excommunicated by our opponents contrary to the Word of God or who were to be served with the means of grace by the opponents only under condition that they would denounce us and accept principles which we held to be erroneous. Now many are turning to the Grabau party whom we have had to discipline because of their unfaithfulness to the Lutheran faith and who now, instead of confessing their past error, take revenge on us by joining in the pronunciation of excommunication over us because they felt the prick of our testimony against them.

Now to turn to the matter about which you had the courtesy to write me. In respect to the disposition of the teachers seminary[8] to be established by you, I must say that I felt somewhat dejected at first by this news, but only because of our dearly beloved Schaller,[9] who was not only himself highly elated but whose whole congregation likewise with great enthusiasm had adopted the idea of daring to hope for a flourishing, proper school in their midst in Detroit, under their nurture. These human considerations, even though not unholy, soon gave way to more proper considerations, about which you had given me insights. Therefore I now submit gladly to the fact that our plan sustained an alteration, and even more so since, according to other news of yours, there is now the prospect that our northern colonies in Michigan[10] will expand and become a second Pennsylvania in a short time. . . . I now feel quite different about Michigan and the great work which is developing there. I experience a surge of joy at the irrepressible hope that there American Germanism and Lutheranism may finally establish a buttress and wellspring from which the same can and will revitalize itself also in other places.

According to God's providence nothing further has been done in respect to the assignment of Siekelmann.[11] And before they arrive, we will not take any action in respect to the placement of Fleischmann and Pruotti,[12] whose arrival you announced in your worthy letter of April 7, which arrived here on May 24. We will first discuss things with them, and carefully consider the instructions you have given them. We will not take any unilateral action in matters which are of interest to you without having clear directives from you, except for matters which you have freely entrusted to us. From now on it will at any rate be a holy and precious duty for our synod to walk hand and hand with you and the friends associated with you wherever this is possible and to view all our general concerns as one body, which we would not be able to do without you.

I have been stunned by the position which the Bavarian supreme consistory is taking more and more. I especially feel sorry for Dr. Boeckh,[13] and the dearer this man has become to me, the more I grieve to see how in him the word of the Lord is being fulfilled: "To everyone who has will more be given; but from him who has not, even what he has will be taken away." The best aspect of this matter is the hope awakened in us eventually to see many of our dear brethren, possibly even you, here sometime. For the sake of my beloved Germany, I naturally cannot hope for this, but if God in His anger would cast away the seal ring, how would I dare ask, "What are You doing?" And how happy I will be if God would resolve that here . . . the space of His tents would be widened and the carpets of His dwelling would be extended and, to deepen the stakes, we might break out in expansion to the right and to the left.

It has been a great joy to me to hear that not only in Mecklenburg and in the dukedom of Bremen-Werden a collection is being taken for our college, but that you too are gathering gifts for this purpose. Because of ever-more-pressing lack of space in our present facilities, we have in God's name begun the erection of the second wing[14] in the hope of assistance from Germany, since our congregations, on the one hand, are just now finishing paying off the expenses incurred in the building of the first wing and, on the other hand, precisely the most willing ones must bring significant sacrifices to cover their own current expenses for a church and school as well as for general church purposes. The expenses for the new building will come to $4,000, to which will be added another $1,000 for digging a new well and for the erection of a utility building, wagon shelter, and other related things. We will praise God if we only get enough so that we will not immediately again have to have collections in our congregations. God knows that we have undertaken such a large construction project not because of arrogance but out of necessity. I am therefore confident that our hope will not be put to shame.

You, most respected pastor, will have seen some things in the *Lutheraner*, from the time when we were absent, which may have troubled you. This material was included in the *Lutheraner* to my great astonishment and contrary to my will from a private letter which was sent here. I hope because of your great love that this too, as so much in the past, you will be able to forget.

If in the near future you should happen to meet the esteemed men Bruer, Hommel, and Stirner,[15] I ask you to convey my fraternal greetings.

In 14 days we will journey to Ft. Wayne for our synodical convention. There I hope to be able to meet and to talk to the brethren Fleischmann and Pruotti, who will be there in the company of Brohm,[16] and to take them to St. Louis.

With most sincere love and respect,
Your most humble
C.F.W. Walther

P.S. For many in Germany it may be of interest to know that in the last session of Congress a law was passed which would make it possible for every head of a household, who either is a citizen or who can under oath establish that he is in the process of naturalization, to obtain 160 acres of government land provided he has no land of his own.

To Ottomar Fuerbringer
Wisconsin
(Fuerbringer, I, 82)

To O. Fuerbringer, in care of Rev. F. Lochner, Milwaukee, Wis.

Concordia [Seminary, St. Louis], June 10, 1852

My dear brother-in-law,[1]

I have just received the report that the best way to travel from here to

Ft. Wayne will take you over Chicago and can be completed in four days. In 20 to 22 hours one can travel from Chicago to Ft. Wayne by railway and plank road. I feel compelled to make haste to urge you and beg you to come to this synodical convention. You could arrange it that you would arrive in Chicago early on the Monday before the convention begins and then continue your travels from there with us Missourians.

It would be very painful for me if you were not present and if we would miss your contributions at the next convention, especially as an old friend and close relative of yours and also all the more in the interest of our hard-pressed church. We need you urgently, to put it briefly. Besides that, your presence this time will no doubt have a significant impact on the formation of the synod in the election of new officers for 1853, especially since you rendered tremendous service to the synod recently and your love for the common good has been shown. I say this without guile, for in these things I look only to the furthering of the kingdom of God. You will understand me.

In sincere, faithful love,

Your
Walther

Perhaps to Pastor Johann Kilian
Texas

Concordia College, St. Louis, Mo., March 17, 1855

Dear brother in our precious Lord Jesus,[1]

I am unable to express what a refreshing experience it was as I opened your precious letter of the 21st of last month and saw therefrom that you are now in America, and namely in Texas, about which I have long had some disheartening concerns, since men have settled there under the cover of the Lutheran name but actually concerned with building nothing else but the unionistic Babel. Herewith I want to express a heartfelt welcome to you in the name of the Lord.

Since I know that you belong to those who have brought their souls as an offering to the Lord Jesus Christ (Acts 15:26), therefore I have the confident hope that you will never regret having made this land your last place of residence in this world. The harvest here is great, but the workers are few. We are actually carrying on a war here, for the small Lutheran Zion is compelled not only to fight for its very life against Papists, Calvinists, Zwinglians, Methodists, Baptists, Unionists,[2] Episcopalians, Swedenborgians,[3] etc., etc., but it has even within itself many elements

107

which have to be overcome. But I do not harbor any fear that the heat of battle which you will meet here will deter you. If you believe with us as you do, that the treasure of true doctrine has been entrusted to our precious Evangelical Lutheran Church, that this church is the pennant bearer of Christ, how could it alienate you to see that this church is the main point of attack for Satan and that the church has to bear both the trowel and the sword at the same time?

I had delayed a few days in answering you in the hope of being able to find the time for a much more detailed report on our local church conditions. Unfortunately this leisure time has not been found. Constantly new and necessary activities, which I have to carry out first, prevent me from writing in detail.

March 28th

After I had written the above, I was called away and since that time have hardly been able to find a quiet quarter hour anywhere. So that I will no longer delay this letter, which can serve as a sign of life for you from us here, I will conclude it here by imploring your brotherly consideration, and with the promise to write much more in detail as soon as possible.

The requested testimony, I trust, you have already received. I take the liberty of sending you the copies of *Lehre und Wehre*[4] which have already come out, which is a newly founded theological monthly journal. Since as editor I receive a few copies, I am able for this year to send you some of these, since I can well imagine that your income must be fairly sparse. Pastor Buenger in St. Louis, who is my colleague and my brother-in-law,[5] takes joy in sending you a free subscription to the *Lutheraner* this year. You had expressed a desire to have some book in which you could be informed on the situation of the local Methodists. For this purpose I am sending you the little pamphlet by Dr. Sihler, *Dialog of Two Lutherans Concerning Methodism.* I hope this will serve a good purpose for you.

To give you an opportunity to become acquainted with our synod and its organization and stance. I am sending you a copy of our constitution and several of the annual reports. I also enclose a copy of the printed collection of correspondence of the Saxon Lutheran immigrants with the Grabau faction from the time when they still stood alone.[6] To understand this situation, it would be good if you would read Pastor Grabau's second *Synodalbrief.*[7] I will attempt to secure a copy for you. There is as yet nothing like a common church or congregational order for our congregations in Synod.[8] Our situation is so new that it does not permit regulating by any kind of written canons. We are following Luther's principle that the church order be first put into practice and tested, and then be written down and elevated to the level of church rules.

Your offer to help on the staff of the *Lutheraner* was a matter of great joy for me. From the issues which are being sent to you, you will soon recognize the assignment which the *Lutheraner* set for itself, but you will also see how far we are from attaining the objectives. You will see especially the lack of manpower, the lack of people who can really speak to the common man in his own language. I do not doubt but that God has given you a special ability in this respect with which you can fill a need on our staff. The first volumes, of which I am able to send you a few samples, had the objective in focus a bit more clearly and there was more unanimity of thought and we were able to achieve more graduated progression. Later on, when the *Lutheraner* found itself in different circumstances, it presented now this, now that, as the momentary requirements overtook it, and presented doctrine in thetical and antithetical fashion. Besides that, there is the additional factor that in the last years I fill an office[9] which alone surpasses my talents, since, as is self-evident, I consider myself only as an American emergency church worker. I beseech you therefore urgently to dedicate a part of your certainly very limited time to assist us on the staffs of our journals. Here in America, where people read much and where much is written and where everything is so decisively expressed, periodicals are an extremely important tool of the church, and those who work in this area can be assured that their work will bear rich fruit, provided they serve the truth.

I regret very much that you are working so far distant from us and therefore we hardly dare entertain the hope ever to see you here in our midst. If God would graciously extend my miserable life for another few years, which of course otherwise I would hardly dare wish, I would hope that I might have an opportunity to meet you in New Orleans. We have two pastors of our synod there, namely Pastor Carl Metz[10] at St. John's congregation (working there since the 11th Sunday after Trinity 1854), a former student of our Concordia Seminary, and Pastor Wilhelm Fick Jr.[11] at Zion congregation (since the First Sunday in Advent 1854), a former student at Goettingen[12] but without the Goettingen slant, rather with a good Lutheran insight. Possibly therefore New Orleans might be the third place where with God's help we might come together to conduct a small conference.

I hope you will not take it amiss when you see from the *Lutheraner* that I took the liberty to report a few items from your valuable letters to our readers in Synod. I found it impossible to withhold from my dear brethren the joy which they would experience when they heard such unexpected news from Texas.

Once again I beseech you to have patience with this miserable scribbling done under great distractions. And I commend you and your dear congregation to the grace and rich blessing of our Lord and Savior Jesus Christ, as well as sending greetings from us and our brethren.

In the Lord Jesus Christ,
Your brother and fellow servant,
Carl Ferd. Wilh. Walther

To Pastor F.W.T. Steimle
Brooklyn, N.Y.

St. Louis, Jan. 25, 1861

My dear Pastor Steimle,[1]

I had intended to answer your welcome letter immediately, but was only waiting for such a time when it might be possible for me to answer in much greater detail, as I thought might be necessary. But I have not been able to find that kind of time, for I am constantly stuck in this crush of time schedules. But in concern that you might interpret my total silence as indicating that I was not interested in your affairs and what has motivated you so deeply, I now will write you at least a few lines as per your request to express my thoughts on those things which you wrote me.

You declare that from now on you will take the whole matter of your Christianity and your stance in and to the church with decisive seriousness, may it cost what it will. Who would not rejoice at this news? If the angels in heaven rejoice over one sinner who repents, how much more ought we fellow sinners to rejoice when one fellow sinner, a fellow redeemed, and a brother in the ministry who had already believed in the Lord, resolves to serve the Lord with renewed, heightened, purer, more determined faithfulness! You wrote that from now on the Word and only the Word will be decisive for you and will be your only directive, whatever it may require of you in doctrine, in life, and in your official duties. This is certainly a blessed resolve.

But strangely, at the same time you confess to me that you have come to the conviction that the visible Lutheran Church is the church in the proper sense of the word and that nowhere else is the church to be found. In vain do I look through your letter for a Scripture passage which might have urged you to this conviction. Therefore I absolutely fail to grasp your turnaround. The more decisively you want to walk according to the Word of God, the less you can harbor that kind of thought. For according to the Word of God, the church is the body of Christ, and every member of the church is a member of Christ, the invisible, spiritual, heavenly Head; the church is subject to Christ, sanctified, purified, glorious, "without spot or wrinkle or any such thing," but "holy and without blemish" (Ephesians 5:23-27). I therefore completely fail to grasp how your resolve to walk meticulously according to the Word of God can be reconciled with your new concept of the church. I fail to grasp how you cannot see that when Scripture nevertheless calls visible, pure and impure fellowships (in doctrine, faith, and life) churches, this expression occurs according to the synectoche [a figure of speech] according to which the whole bears the name of its best part and is thus called so only improperly.

Or did you not look at Scripture on this point nor *presuppose* that the Confessions are in accord with Scripture? Even in the light of this, I do not grasp your point. In the seventh and eighth articles of the Augsburg Confession the church is called an "assembly of all believers and saints," namely if one wants to speak about it in the proper sense, as the eighth article says. But have you ever *seen* an assembly of saints? I strongly doubt that, for you would have had to receive a special revelation from God, which I do not believe. For you see that group of people of whom you *believe* that therein is a part of the assembly of believers, according to the marks of the church, but this last you cannot see.

Then add to this the seventh and eighth articles of the Apology of the Augsburg Confession, and then every doubt as to what according to Lutheran doctrine the church is must be dissolved. It seems to me that we Lutheran preachers, when we search for the real sense of the Augsburg Confession, would do well to search for it in its authentic explanation, the Apology. Oh, read the Apology on this point, and if you read it without colored glasses, you will soon be cured of your papistical notions of what the church is. Then for the defense of the seventh and eighth articles of the Augsburg Confession add passages like those in the Apology pertaining to the Mass, where it says: "God nevertheless preserved His church, that is, some saints under the papacy, so that the Christian church did not totally perish." There you see how those saints, living scattered here and there in the midst of the papacy according to our Confessions constituted the church and that it was sustained through them.

Add to that what the Smalcald Articles, III, 12, and the Small and Large Catechisms under the Third Article, and finally what the Preface to the *Book of Concord* says about "those *churches* which have up to now *admittedly not come to agreement* with us,"—where according to the context the Reformed are to be understood, which still are called churches.

If you want to make the visible orthodox church into the one holy Christian church, today therefore the visible Lutheran church, then you are from that instant on devoid of weapons against the Roman Catholics and you will consequently be compelled to become Catholic. For either there was no visible orthodox church before Luther, or the church was at that time overwhelmed by the gates of hell, which is impossible, or the papistic Roman Church was it. Since according to your present principles you deny the first two sentences, you are compelled to accept the last, and thus will become a papist. That you certainly do not want to do. Well then, so become a Lutheran and accept the true Christian doctrine of the Lutheran Church on the church, which it sets up as an article of faith, as the communion of saints, which by the marks of the Word and the sacraments is recognizable as existing, and by the *pure* Word and sacrament is recognizable as a pure orthodox church.

If you have such a great longing to learn Lutheran doctrine, to cling to it, and faithfully to teach it, I would urge you to read Luther's writings. It cannot be otherwise but that in *Luther* the *Lutheran* doctrine is the purest, the brightest, the most complete and original (according to the Scriptures). It is plain stupid to continue to argue about Lutheran doctrine, and to follow one's own presumptions, and not to turn to Luther himself. And that is my summary and general advice to you in your present critical circumstances. Buy the whole collected works of Luther, if you don't have them yet, and read them day and night. If you do this sincerely, not as Luther's teacher but as Luther's student, you will soon become divinely certain and happy in your faith and then in your standpoint within and toward the church.

As you write, you are just as concerned with teaching properly as with living a godly life and seeking the one thing which is needful. Oh, my dear brother, how can you then fail to see that only the concept of the church as a *fellowship, assembled in the Spirit, of those who are born again and renewed* corresponds to the nature of living Christianity, whereas the mechanical concept of the church as a fellowship of the orthodox, whether they be converted or unconverted, will necessarily lead to a dead Christianity, that is, to unchristendom and to a fleshly emphasis which says: "This is the temple of the Lord, the temple of the Lord."[2] This concept will make Pharisees out of people and make them into such Jews as the Scriptures describe in John 8:33; Matthew 3:9; Romans 2:17-25, cf. verses 28-29. If you want to implant earnest searching for salvation with fear and trembling, as also zeal for purity of doctrine, then you have to return to the doctrine of the church as a spiritual fellowship; if not, you will lay the foundation for a dead *opus operatum*,[3] and instead of leading people to inner [renewal] you will lead them to an outward [faith] without regeneration and renewal.

You express concern that our synod is stuck on defense of pure doctrine rather than the exercise of true godliness and the planting of real concern for the welfare of souls. It may appear to you that way if you only see what we do in the area of polemics. But if you would become acquainted with our congregations, then you would see that we do not only by God's grace wield the sword but also with heartfelt faithfulness work with the trowel,[4] and constantly seek to live in true repentance from a whole heart and also seek to lead to this in all faithfulness and zeal those who are entrusted to us. That there may be a few among us who know no other element than the contention for pure doctrine, who have not experienced true repentance, that I do not dare to deny, for God knows this alone. But this is the unanimous direction of all our preachers, that we want to attain salvation and to help people to salvation only on the path of sincere repentance. My dear brother, one must not judge people according to appearances. Many a person may seem unbending when he speaks up publicly, although in his own prayer chamber and in his own heart he engages in constant fervent spiritual striving and a fervent prayer life. But this, like the church in general, is removed from the eyes of shortsighted people, for the kingdom of God (or the church) does not come in outward form, but is within us.

Please do not believe that as I write these lines I was motivated by the lust of conquest of which we are so often accused, that I was angling for you and writing in the hope of getting you to fill our ranks. As highly as I consider all those who support the truth, so earnestly I wish that these would *not* all be concentrated in one spot, but be scattered about like "the salt of the earth." Those who think we want to kidnap people know us as little as they know themselves. As often as a person or a whole congregation from another synod wants to join us, I am frightened. I know that when conscience motivates us this way it is not good to reject the applicant outright, for thereby another whole flood of abuse would be poured out over us. Would God that all the other synods would rise above us; I would be so little jealous because of it that I would rather thank God for it from a full heart! Proofs that I actually have dealt on the basis of these fundamental principles and in this way of thinking I could adduce in great numbers.

The Lord be with you. Please let me hear from you very soon.

Your humble brother in the Lord,
C.F.W. Walther

To Ottomar Fuerbringer
Frankenmuth, Mich.

July 8, 1865

My dear Fuerbringer,[1]

I think back with joy on the precious hours which I was able to spend with you in Milwaukee this past month. It was almost as if the days of Eichenberg had returned.[2] And oh, how necessary it is for me in these sad times to know that I have brothers in this world who will not abandon me to stand alone.

The reason why I write these lines to you now is the heartfelt desire which I would like to express to you, that you might be kind enough to be present in the first stage of the convention of the Central District in Cleveland this year. I do not ask this so much because according to the resolution of the general synod at the last convention the district presidents are to meet regularly and enter into consultation with the general synodical president each year in which the synod does not meet. Rather I ask this of you because I and all the local seminary professors are very much in need of the advice of the synodical representatives. Our new state constitution has been adopted, and I am still undecided whether I can take the oath of loyalty which is required by it. And in case I am unable to take this oath I need your advice as to what I should do. So I ask you, let me prevail on you to come to Cleveland and to make the arrangements so that in any event you can be there on Aug. 19, the Saturday before the Tenth Sunday After Trinity, for which day only the forenoon is designated for the convention.

Please consider that this matter is not only of great importance for the peace of my own conscience but for my whole life, which I hope may not be too long, as well as being important for our whole synod. If I do not get any advice on this, then there is no other recourse but to resign my office, for if I cannot take that oath in good faith, then I will not take it at all, and if I do not have any directives to move the institution, then I must resign my work here.

I know full well how great an offering I demand of you hereby, but I hope that your love will recognize that even though I am not worthy of such a concession on your part, yet I am very much in need of it. Do not think that the matter can be solved without you. I tell you that I am especially in need of your expression if I am to resolve this matter. And a written analysis is also quite inadequate here. This you yourself probably will already have noticed when we discussed this matter once before.

114

May the Lord be with you and your family. Please grant your severely afflicted old friend the favor of an affirmative reply.

Your
C.F.W. Walther

Possibly to Pastor C.A. Mennicke
Rock Island, Ill.

St. Louis, July 17, 1865

My dear pastor,

I am compelled to ask you to take an assignment which may be fraught with many difficulties. From the enclosed letter you will see that there are a number of members of the Iowa Synod congregation in Dubuque who have separated from that congregation and turned to us. They say they have taken this action because they can no longer endure the hierarchical tortures of their pastor. The first of the signatories is known to Professor Craemer. This man, Adniel Schmalz, was at one time a member of the congregation in Ft. Wayne, and only moved to Dubuque because of Pastor Dietz,[1] who left the Missouri Synod and joined the Iowa Synod because of conscience. Professor Craemer gives Mr. Schmalz the testimony that he is a true and upright Christian of whom he would never believe that he would be guilty of sectarianism. Because of Mr. Schmalz we therefore have a good inclination to these people who have separated. In addition to this there is the fact that it is well-known that the sugar-sweet gentlemen from Iowa[2] have a strong inclination to interpret the office of the ministry in an imperial way and thus play the Lord of the parish.

What we now ask of you is that you travel to Dubuque as early as possible and look up Mr. Schmalz, and then also at the same time go to see Pastor Bredow[3] and ask him whether the people have been under church discipline or not. If they have been under church discipline, ask him why. But before you go to see Bredow it would be good that you would share with all the people the Iowa Synod's stance on doctrine, that they do not have an unqualified acceptance of the symbolical books, that they do not hold the pope to be the Antichrist, that they make articles of faith into open questions, that they have people among them who justify chiliasm, etc., and that this is the most important reason to separate from this synod. If the people understand this and you find that they do not stand under proper church discipline, you have to look after these people after you have shared that information with Pastor Bredow, preach to them, and promise

115

them that either you if possible or another Missouri Synod pastor will provide for their spiritual needs.

But if the case should be that one or more of these people have been under church discipline, then you may not give them Communion till they have satisfied their former congregation. Then also they should be received into membership if they are convinced of the false position of the Iowa Synod. It will also be necessary that you inform yourself of the content of the annual report of Pastor Bredow which is referred to in the letter and that you read the refutation. As I said, your assignment is hard, but God will lend grace so that without guile as the doves and wise as the serpents you may deal with this so that everything will redound to the honor of God and to the welfare of those souls.

You may in no way pull back from this. You are not only the closest one who can do anything; you are also the most suitable one by the grace of God. Think of it, the Lord says: "Him who comes to Me I will not cast out." Therefore we must follow the Savior, even when we anticipate nothing but insult therefrom. Also think of this, that it is important that we put a little barrier to the Iowa enterprise. Under a show of right they represent a false Lutheranism and with their assertion on the authority of the ministry they lay a yoke on the conscience of Christians which is thoroughly contrary to the Christian freedom of the children of God. This we dare not simply watch passively. The Iowa pastors take our people even if they are in church discipline and mislead them to false doctrine. How much more then must we be willing to receive upright Christians who come to us because they are under the yoke of false doctrine.

It may pose many a difficulty to you to go to Dubuque. But we are asking you for the sake of Christ to try to overcome these difficulties. Your work certainly will become even more important not only for that handful of people there, but probably for many others who are groaning under similar difficulties.

Please preserve the enclosed letter and send it back to me in due course.

I commend you and yours to the Lord and send greetings from
Your friend and brother,
C.F.W. Walther

P.S. As soon as you know whether and when you will travel to Dubuque, please send Mr. Schmalz a notice. The people there will no doubt pay your travel costs, but if they would not, these will have to come out of the treasury for inner missions.

To Prof. F.A. Schmidt

Decorah, Iowa

St. Louis, Jan. 9, 1866

My dear professor,[1]

Just now delegates of Trinity congregation came to me to inform me of the congregation's resolution that a sort of memorial booklet is to be published in which among other things all the sermons preached on the occasion of the dedication of the church are to be included. They ask me to request you that you would kindly send me your English sermon so that it also can be included in the memorial booklet. I am hereby fulfilling their request and urgently beseech you to respond favorably to the congregation. This matter will no doubt cause you some work and will even further restrict your already limited time, but I am relying on your love that you will make the sacrifice. As they say, the advice of a king one can neglect, but the advice of God one should praise.

You probably read the malicious remark of Lohmann[2] on the occasion of the notice in the *Watchman*[3] to the effect that now also the Missourians understand that the pure doctrine can also be preached in the English language. That man deserves to have his fingers rapped a bit. Without doubt he is angry that the Missouri Synod through your *Watchman* is entering a field of labor which his kind thought they had a monopoly on. Should you not get in touch with Wetzel?[4] According to Brobst[5] he is in Mt. Solon, Augusta County, Va.

Eight days ago Sunday the faithful Pastor Birkmann[6] was buried. So one after another goes home. Soon the second generation of our pastors will stand alone. Yesterday I received the news that Pastor Vogt[7] will call on me tomorrow to reestablish his old relationship with the Missouri Synod. According to Pastor Muckel's[8] witness he has always conducted himself uprightly and has erred only out of confusion. Pastor Reinsch, who came to us from the Iowa Synod, has been called to Milwaukee to take Crull's place.[9] Crull resigned because of his throat ailment and has now returned to New Orleans to his parents. Tomorrow Henry Craemer[10] will leave for Cleveland to function there as an assistant for the sick Wyneken.

Right now my nephew Robert Engel[11] is visiting here, who was a former Saxon pastor but who had to resign his office because he had written a love letter to a girl although he was already married, at a time when he was overburdened with work. It is truly regrettable for him as a person. He is as good as useless for our church since this case has become known in our circles. He is unusually well grounded in doctrine and besides is a philologist and an accomplished dialectician. Thus the devil takes those few who have the gifts and the desires to serve the church and makes them useless.

May God grant you strength, light, courage, and joy in your taxing work, especially also for the energetic execution of your publishing venture, the *Watchman.*

Please greet your dear wife, as also your beloved colleagues Larsen,[12] Brandt,[13] and Sievers.[14] In the Lord Jesus,

Your friend and brother,
C.F.W. Walther

To Pastor H.C. Schwan
Cleveland, Ohio
(Fuerbringer, II, 37 – 39)

St. Louis, May 15, 1866

My dear pastor,[1]

I write the following in dutiful response to your honored letter of the 9th.

I am not at all of the opinion that Mr. H. Craemer[2] should be posted to Crete, [Ill.]. A place where there is a parochial school teacher is not a post for a young energetic man, while a large number of our worn-out pastors still sit in the dust of the classroom and are thus not able to use their best energies in their main responsibility. Besides that, there is this, that our dear Craemer is especially suitable for our old father Wyneken. He should keep him. I cannot see that Crete is more important than Cleveland; it is only a more pleasant position as an independent pastor compared to the vicarage in Cleveland. Now I believe that Henry is just the kind of person who is more willing than others to look at the need of the church rather than his own pleasant position. Therefore we should be glad to have him in Cleveland. If he is taken away from there, then I do not know anyone else to recommend for that post. And Wyneken must have a vicar. Craemer should be hurriedly examined, ordained, and installed, and the people in Crete should be informed that they applied too late. As far as I know, President Buenger[3] has recommended several people to the congregation in Crete, but they preferred to have a young unmarried man to call.[4]

I am really shocked by the news that Wyneken wants to resign. Is that dear man in his right senses? What kind of an example would that be?

Wouldn't that be teaching all godless and stinking covetous people in our congregations how they should deal with those who have become sick and ailing in the service of the church? If Wyneken would do that, there would be a cry of opposition heard through the whole synod. How gladly would not our synod contribute an orderly share to his dear congregation for the support of this worn-out faithful synodical servant, if Wyneken would become an emeritus—in fact, it would press such help on the congregation. This is all self-understood, for Wyneken sacrificed his health not in Cleveland, but first on his mission trips and then on his synodical visitation trips.[5]

Even before your letter reached me, a call to Liverpool arrived for student Lothmann,[6] which he also accepted. So he is no longer available for Cleveland.

That Pastor Fleischmann[7] has completely on his own given up his affiliate congregation and that because of this there will be a new pressing need for another pastor has saddened me very much. You already have enough trouble with the requests for preachers which come to you, and we here, where people seek the source of a supply of pastors, have even more difficulty. This need continually aggravates other changing accidental needs.

Today also Pastor Hamann[8] was here to explain that his doctor has forbidden him to preach and has urgently directed him to take an ocean voyage because of his liver ailment (probably also affecting the lungs). One can see by looking at this dear man that he is like a worm-eaten apple. Thus we need another vicar again. This probably will be Pastor Biedermann,[9] who after his relocation in the vicinity of Cape Girardeau, Mo., ruled there only 24 days. The congregation there (formerly served by Pastor Doederlein,[10] a former Iowa Synod man who came over to us) blew up, and suddenly a large congregation was reduced to a small group of 15 members which can hardly support Biedermann with his family, especially since because of his health he is unable also to teach school.

You are completely right to complain about the lack of reports of visitation trips to congregations in Synod. Would God that this were also the case with Fuerbringer.[11] There has not been a single sound coming from him. I fear that I do not know what I am going to report about his visitation activity, and yet I dare not remind him of his duty and thereby arouse a sleeping lion, just among us. Otherwise I am on a good footing with him now. As I hear, he also does not want to attend the convention in October. What do you advise me to do? Furthermore, what do you recommend for topics of study? As reported, among others also Dr.

119

Krauth[12] will visit us. That man is turning out well, but the decisive testing with the Pennsylvania Synod is still in the future for him.

Heartiest greetings to your honored wife from me and my wife as well as from Mrs. Tschirpe, who is living with us for the present. My sincere fraternal greeting also to our precious Wyneken and to our dear Craemer. The Lord be with you!

Your
C.F.W. Walther

To Prof. F. A. Schmidt
Decorah, Iowa

St. Louis, Jan. 16, 1867

My dearly beloved brother in the Lord:

When I read the first number of the new volume of your *Lutheran Watchman* yesterday, it struck me like a rock that I had not yet answered your welcome letter of October 7th of last year. I got this out immediately and read it again and determined today to let everything else rest and first answer your letter. That I first get to it today, I could list a large catalog of reasons, but to what purpose? Please believe me when I simply tell you, that partly—and indeed in the very largest part—circumstances prevented me, and in part it was a lack of energy and of my own will, and not any lack of inner love for you. Now to the answer.

It is a total impossibility to create pastors. We are barely able to supply congregations of the synod which become vacant. This year we do not have a single student in my department who can be sent out, since at the end of the present school year we have only such students in attendance who have been in this institution only one or two years. We hope that this will be the last year in which such a hiatus will occur. The flow of students from Ft. Wayne[1] will from now on be a regular annual event. There is a similar situation in Craemer's department, that is, the practical department. In that department there will only be several students available but these few students are already committed. It is a pity. From all directions we hear the cry, "Come over and help us," but there is a lack of people who are willing or able to say, "I will be your messenger."

Your complaints about the difficulties in the Norwegian Synod[2] I have in no way misunderstood. You are, I am convinced, no dark pessimist. I can also hope that you will keep your eyes open and continue to serve as a salt, and I pray to God that He may preserve you not to fall into the slumber of the young maidens, for this would be a great misfortune although it could happen very easily since in other synods the conduct of affairs is so lackadaisical that where only a few people are [spiritually] alive some other synod may appear very lively by contrast. But this can have a paralyzing reciprocal feedback.

But, my dear brother, do not permit your depressing experiences to take your courage and your love away. God has placed you in a post which may not be very pleasing to the emotions, but one which has more promise for fruit and for salutary influence. So, persevere there till the Lord will direct you otherwise. Consider that God cannot accord us poor sinners a greater honor and grace than that He shapes our poor lives so that when they are past, they are not like flowers that wither, the places of which no one recognizes, but they leave behind in the future of the Kingdom of God signs of powerful results which reach into eternity. That is something incomparably great, to be God's coworkers even beyond the confines of a small local congregation. Continue then as good Missouri leaven among the Scandinavian brethren. If it should seem to you at times as if you were crowding this one or that one uncomfortably, then just seek to sweeten that with your love. Your work is not in vain in the Lord.

Your *Watchman* accords me great joy. I am sorry that you have to complain that others are abandoning you to carry the heavy burden all by yourself. There are no doubt too many who have the zeal but have very limited abilities. If they are not on a treadmill like an editor is, who has to keep going or go under, they find all kinds of excuses, indeed compelling reasons to do nothing. But for God's sake do not for that reason take your hand from the plow. God has given you a very precious tool for uncounted blessings in the form of the *Watchman*. Do not permit anyone to wrench it out of your hand. The work is great, heavy and bitter, and the wages of the false brethren is thanklessness, but the true church blesses you on high and God has already given you the crown of faithfulness. Do not talk so much about your own weaknesses. Those you can complain about to God, but to human beings use a fresh and joyful approach as David did against Goliath. You come in the name of the Lord to avenge the blasphemies against the army of the Lord and to comfort the true Israel. Therefore from your pocket fetch yourself stone after stone for your sling and fear no enemy spears even if they were as large as a weaver's beam.

That Sihler and I did not appear in Reading[3] has had a negative influence on you, as I could imagine. But consider how long we already had stayed in Buffalo.[4] We would have had to spend one week in idleness in the east if we had wanted to await the beginning of the convention. Thus we thought that that kind of a sacrifice was too much, since we firmly believe that it was more important that we show our good will rather than hope for any possible wholesome results. We were convinced that what happened would happen, that we would be heard out of kindness, that we would be sent off with politeness and declarations of affection, and then that would be done as was resolved, namely, an imposing organization would be called into being to impress those and to stop the mouths of those from whom they had come forth.[5]

Americans cannot by any means come to feel comfortable in the Lutheran spirit of simplicity which desires nothing but to do the will of God, to follow His Word, to confess His truth, to rescue His honor, and to safeguard his conscience and then permit God to rule. Americans think that a victory of the truth is nothing impressive if it is not manifested in some impressive sensate embodiment. I fear much that the final deception will be worse than the first. All those hollow synods whose consciousness was not affected by the signing of so many confessions without modifications now have a great opportunity to show that nobody can accuse them now of being unlutheran. They are now going to take a big mouthful of confessionalism even though they haven't even read the confessions once—to say nothing of having examined them to recognize their conformity with Scripture—and least of all have they digested them or practiced them.

Now I must confess to you that I feel something like shame within myself that I did not go to Reading and that I have let you and Mueller[6] sit there alone. Possibly I was mistaken in judging what my duty was in this respect. But at the same time I can hardly deny a sort of secret joy that I was not in the battle. It is a frightening thought to me to think that I would have had to sit in the same pew with those smart aleck Iowans,[7] those worldly wise mockers (Ps. 1). Basically we should now permit the gentlemen of the convention, with a few honorable exceptions, to have a good conscience. Your essay in the *Watchman* of January 1 has pleased me greatly. I will ask Craemer to translate this for *Lehre und Wehre*.[8] In the *Lutheraner* which came out yesterday I have somewhat reminded the Iowans of what they are and how they have stood hitherto, after they had made themselves out to be so "sternly Lutheran."[9]

In the Buffalo[10] domain, as I hear, things are in turmoil. Everyone is preoccupied with the process of dissolution. Hochstetter,[11] Renold,[12] Weinbach,[13] Zeumer,[14] Leemhuis,[15] Doehler,[16] Groszberger[17] and Kanold[18] are decisively Missourian; adherents of von Rohr are the older Mueller[19] and his son, Maschop[20] and Schadow;[21] uncertain are Wollaeger,[22] Meiszner[23] and Runkel[24] in Cincinnati, Bauer[25] in Toledo; Eppling[26] is semiGrabau; real Grabauites are the old man himself and his son John, Winkler,[27] Gram,[28] Tuerk,[29] Graetz,[30] and Schroeer.[31] Thus the situation is in fact a sad one, and yet in comparison with the past, it is now truly glorious. The light shines into the darkness, and behold, wonderful forms emerge. The printed protocol of the meetings is very unsatisfying, for only the resolutions could be printed, otherwise it would not have been possible to secure attestation from both sides. The protocol at least establishes what was emphasized, what was conceded, and what was adhered to, so that the opponents cannot retreat if they do not want to repent. The discussions which these resolutions provoked were really the only cause of pique in the whole matter. Possibly Hochstetter may publicize this in his book reviews.

Please excuse my wide digressions and my flightiness in this letter. Greet your wife sincerely, also the precious brothers Larsen, Brand, and Sievers. May the Lord be with you, with your whole calling, with your office, in your heavy work, and with

Your intimate friend in the Lord who Himself is the Truth,
C.F.W. Walther

P.S. If you write me more in detail, you need not apologize. Your letters are always beneficial to me, among all the mass of correspondence I receive.

To Pastor Ch. H. Loeber
Thornton, Cook Co., Ill.
(Fuerbringer, II, 86–89)

St. Louis, March 25, 1867

Dearly beloved and honored pastor,[1]

Just in these last days I have been overwhelmed with work which cannot be postponed, and so I first get to answer your dear letter of the 12th today.

I have been quite pleased to note the heartfelt joy which you felt in respect to the victory of the truth which was celebrated recently over against the Buffalo Synod people.[2] In fact, if one looks back to observe what has happened among the Buffalo Synod people who now humbly extend the hand of apology and of brotherly fellowship to us publicly, one is astounded and cannot but acknowledge that divine truth has an incomparable power over the hearts of men. Only may God preserve me from ascribing to my miserable person any part of this victory, although God certainly does not begrudge me as well as you the strengthening of faith which this development has provided and the refreshment I find in it after long years of concern, fear, worry, labor, and bitter disgrace. Would

God that your blessed father were still living![3] He was the first one who exposed himself in this fight to the poisoned arrows of a dishonest foe. How he would now rejoice with me over the glorious outcome of a fight that seemed hopeless, at least as far as the opponents were concerned!

Of course, we won only the majority but, as far as I know the personalities involved, truly the salt in the opposition party. And although Grabau may turn heaven and earth to assert himself, together with his few faithful followers, a Winkler, Hahn, Gram,[4] and his son, yet he has suffered such a serious setback that he can never again recover and will thus be able to do only slight damage to those outside his synod. Morally he is dead, and his system which constricts consciences and kills off all evangelical church life has been publicly put to shame. Pastor Von Rohr with his son,[5] with the Maschops, Schadows, and Muellers (in Freistadt), which is really a pitiful company, only make themselves a laughing stock when they want to salvage Grabauism without Grabau for the world and for the church. Certainly if America would only recognize that which serves for its peace, it would have all the prerequisites for becoming the land of the final renaissance of true Evangelical Lutheranism. But it looks cloudy enough.

It is truly lamentable that your dear congregation still does not want to join Synod. This shows how far people's confidence in the ministry has sunk, after they have sighed so long under the rule of egotistical rationalists. I would not especially belabor the congregation on this account, but would at the most ask them each time when the synodical convention is about to begin whether the congregation has not yet convinced itself that it is its duty to participate in this fraternal endeavor for the common concern for the kingdom of Christ. If that doesn't help, I would not do anything further and would only call the attention of the people to the fact that if they again should be without a pastor, they would hardly get one from Synod in view of the great shortage of pastors, and then they would either be without a preacher or they would have to find some vagabond on their own.

I consider it absolutely correct not to continue forever to admit those people to Communion who live in the parish but do not want to join the congregation. I would admit them only for a limited time. This is a different matter than joining a synod. The latter is of human law, the former by divine law. Participation in Communion sponsored by the congregation is indeed the highest privilege of a member and is participation in the innermost fellowship with the congregation, yet is not actual joining. To this belongs, also according to the Word of God, the actual affiliation with the congregation in its function as the higher tribunal (Matthew 18:15-18),

124

as well as participation in its meetings and not only those in which the Word of God is proclaimed through the public ministry, but also the *mutual* admonition, observance, and provocation to love and good works (Hebrews 10:24-25). God obviously wills not only the invisible but also the visible church, as Baptism and the Lord's Supper already show. He wills not an unregulated, random, occasional gathering together, but rather regulated congregations with church tribunals. Whoever does not want anything to do with these latter things, sets himself against God's clear will, or if he only wants to use these benefits but without participating in the work, he is a self-seeking individual who, spiritually speaking, refuses to eat his own bread. Others are to work for him, to provide, to contribute, to stand at the breach, and to counsel, but he himself wants to be only an idle observer, enjoying it all without work.

One also has to consider that, in such a case, withholding Holy Communion is not something absolute, it is not declaring that such a one is unworthy, it is not a ban, but only a suspension, as is the case with one who becomes aware of the fact that his brother has something against him (Matthew 5:23-24). It is not a question of exclusion from offering a gift, but rather has to do with the necessary preceeding fulfillment of a condition for a God-pleasing offering. But in any case, the church order always ought to leave the pastor some leeway to prolong the time according to certain circumstances and certain spiritual conditions. For love must always be the empress of all church order and law, but conversely freedom may not be used as a cover for wickedness, in this case for greed, for improper conduct, and for injury inflicted on the church.

Please content yourself with this brief letter. Thank God that the Lord has permitted your dear spouse to recover again from serious illness. Greet her most cordially from us.

Looking forward to a joyous reunion soon on the occasion of the district convention in Chicago, I remain, in sincere and inner love,

Your friend and brother in the Lord Jesus,
C.F.W. Walther

To Pastor H. C. Schwan
Cleveland, Ohio

Ft. Wayne, June 30, 1869

After discussing the matter with my colleagues and with Dr. Sihler, with Pastor Stubnatzi, and with the local college professors,[1] I have come to the conviction that it would not only be highly desirable but in many aspects even necessary that this year's convention of our synod be held beginning the first Wednesday in September, instead of the second Wednesday in October. If in our institutions we make a three-week break after one month of school, it will do great harm especially to the newly entered students.

Besides this, it is first of all highly desirable that Dr. Preuss,[2] who shows himself more and more as a man of orthodox orientation as also of thorough learning and of eminent teaching ability, begin his teaching work immediately with the new school year. Second, it is highly desirable that our synod should enter in on the plan that a professor of theology from the Wisconsin Synod[3] be established in St. Louis, and a preparatory school teacher of our synod be appointed to the Wisconsin Synod institution in Watertown, that thereby both synods become truly blended together. If our synod, as I hope, will accept this proposal, then it would do great harm if this new arrangement would first be inaugurated a rather long time after the beginning of the school year. Our dear Wisconsin brethren have taken such a positive attitude in their last convention that we must thank God for having blessed us with this development.

Our proposed amalgamation with the Wisconsin Synod, in my opinion, can hardly be overestimated in importance. With this development there would be inaugurated a unification of German Lutheran churches in America as it should be. The feedback in regard to the General Council[4] and even the churches in Germany would certainly follow. But above all it is important to strike the iron while it is hot. The devil and his tools will do everything to choke off this new development at the very beginning.

Furthermore, after we have solicited reactions from others, we find that it is not difficult for our dear farmer members to attend a synodical convention already in early September, since this is the time between the harvest and putting in the winter crops. Also our local congregation here [Ft. Wayne] is willing to make arrangements for hosting the synodical convention earlier than it was originally planned.

In case you could accept my proposal, I ask you that you notify Professor Craemer[5] as quickly as possible, so that he can publish the proper notices for presenting this in the next number of the *Lutheraner*.

The notice for the change of meeting date for the synodical convention I enclose herewith. It is up to you either to sign this or to add your own notations. The matter of Dr. Preuss and Baumstark,[6] as important as an immediate solution hereof may be, I have deliberately not mentioned in public announcements.

Yours most obediently,
C.F.W. Walther

To Ottomar Fuerbringer
Frankenmuth, Mich.

St. Louis, Nov. 1, 1870

My dear Fuerbringer,

A few days ago I received two official documents from the Ohio Synod informing me that the Ohio Synod[1] in its last convention has ratified our earlier agreement unanimously without any strictures, and second, that the Ohio Synod established a committee which is soon to meet with representatives of the Missouri Synod, the Illinois Synod, the Wisconsin Synod, and with the Norwegians, at a place to be named, to draft a plan to enable those synods to work jointly in the matter of the preachers seminaries, which plan then would be proposed to all synods for adoption.

I have given my consent to this last proposal and also promised to charge our District presidents to express their opinions on this. This request I hereby direct to you and at the same time I beseech you, if you agree, to declare whether you would find it suitable to convene the projected conference either during the week before the First Sunday in Advent or in the week before the Second Sunday in Epiphany in St. Louis or someplace in Ohio, and whether you would appear in person, and in case you would not be able to do so, whom you would send as your representative.

I hold this letter as being very important, and I am convinced that if we succeed in this, it will be a great blessing for the work of the Lord.

Excuse my haste.

In sincere brotherly love, your
C.F.W. Walther

To Ottomar Fuerbringer

St. Louis, Feb. 21, 1872

My dear Fuerbringer,

While we here had to be thinking of making preparations for the synodical convention to be held in St. Louis beginning on April 26, it suddenly struck me like a hammer against my head that you might possibly again be of the opinion not to attend. Therefore I am tearing myself away from all my work and urgently invite you to come this time and to be a guest at my home, where you will meet fellow guests Stephanus Keyl and his family, my son Ferdinand, my son-in-law Niemann, F. Lochner, and possibly Brunn,[1] who is also invited—all people among whom you will certainly feel comfortable. Also, we will do what we can to make your stay as bearable as possible. Please consider, my dear old friend, if you do not come to Missouri this time, to this very important stage of activity, then you probably will never come at all. All our relatives here would be very happy to have you in our midst once more, and we would be sad if you stay away. It would also make a painful impression on the synod if you were again absent.

I well know that certain impressions that you have received earlier have filled you with a certain aversion to the general synodical convention, and I do not intend to argue with you whether these impressions were caused by others or not. But I think we are here dealing with interests that go far beyond our feelings. I believe you owe it to yourself as a Christian, to yourself as a member of the synod, as a pastor, as a district president. You owe it to the kingdom of God to overcome this reticence. I know that you complain that you always feel physically unwell at these meetings. But even in this you ought to make a sacrifice to the Lord and His kingdom.

You may believe it or not, but it is true that nobody holds anything against you quite so much as that you are so withdrawn. Every indication of your coming out of this is good for us all. You will not take it ill if I as your old but humble friend, if I the younger of us, now assume the position of teacher. Think of it. Every Christian must deal so that everybody else could do likewise under the same circumstances without harming anyone. With God there is no respect of persons. If everybody would immediately withdraw from public life when he has had negative experiences, how could society exist? Don't say, "Things will go okay without me." As true as it is that God does not really need us, yet God, according to His great goodness, wants to make us His media; and who are we to refuse to let Him use us? And to counter every argument you might feel in your heart, are we not also obligated to do everything to prevent some harm which might result from nonaction?

In brief, I am convinced—forgive me if I say it right out—that you will sin if you follow your feelings and your heart and stay home while we here deal with a matter which is yours as well as ours, if you look after your special duties at home while we discuss, resolve, and in part carry out the most difficult, the most responsible matters with much anxiety, fear, care, and labor for the general good. Don't let us forget that both of us have one foot in the grave. Let us therefore labor while it is day, for "night comes, when no one can work."[2]

More I will not write. I only implore you that you not be angry at my forthrightness. You would do me an injustice, for only my love for you, my old friend, to whom I am also attached in other ways, makes me so bold as to pour out to you in the name of God my whole heart. God knows how precious you are to me, and therefore for everything in the world I would not like to be guilty of letting you not fulfill any duty that rests on you or that anybody should be suspiciously judgmental of you.

Well, then, I repeat my request: Come![3] Overcome yourself and all other obstacles that can be overcome, and you will see that you will have here days not of care but of edification, no doubt together with some work and responsibility. We will make you feel at home as much as possible. I will gladly see you accept a preaching assignment, but I do not want to pressure you on this matter. But in case you would be inclined to do so, write me immediately. Greet your family cordially.

Your old companion in sorrow and joy,
C.F.W. Walther

To Wm. Sihler
Ft. Wayne, Ind.

On board the Belle of La Crosse
at Camanche, Iowa, July 11, 1873

My precious Sihler,[1]

After longer inner tensions, I finally resolved to take a trip on the Mississippi in order, God willing, to regain my strength through fresh air and complete intellectual inactivity. I had exerted myself so hard intellectually at the last conventions that after the Northern District convention was ended and also the pastoral conference which followed thereupon, I suddenly lost my memory for the period of the last 20 years. Suddenly I no longer knew where I was or that Lochner, with whom I was staying, was pastor in Milwaukee, that I had there attended a convention, etc., although otherwise I was fully conscious. This condition prevailed for about half an hour, after which my memory gradually returned.

The doctors whom I consulted stated that this kind of attack was very serious at my age. Two of the doctors without mutual consultation gave me their opinion that if I do not cut down my intellectual activity, softening of the brain will result. That attack, they said, resulted from insufficient blood flow to the brain. Thus it became clear to me that I had to take my condition seriously. As ready as I am, believe me, to devote the rest of my powers to the service of the church, yet I believe I have no right to continue in my previous manner after such a serious warning. The thought of an eventual softening of the brain with its tragic side effects is naturally a frightening one for me. I would rather remain useless till my death but have my proper senses than to remain active for a short while but end up with a loss of my senses.

At first I only wanted to travel to Rock Island and then hurry on to the convention of the Synodical Conference. But I can see that longer inactivity is necessary. Therefore on the way I decided to go on to St. Paul and thus to abandon my hope of participating in the Synodical Conference convention, even though I do so with a heavy heart. Therefore I request you to excuse me from the meeting. It will probably not be necessary that you make any reference to my prognosis, since this would provide an unnecessary joy to all my many enemies. If God should according to His inexpressible wisdom deal with me as the doctors say may be possible, the opponents will in due time learn of it, if this should happen. But in the meantime I shall be praying to God to preserve me from that, above all for the sake of my enemies, of whom I know that inasfar as they are inimical to me, they are also inimical to God and His truth.

Absent in the body, yet I will be present in the important meetings in spirit. May God grant both wisdom and voice to you, to make a penetrating presentation of your theses.[2] Before my departure I had already gathered "witnesses" for the first eight theses, which I have entrusted to Pastor Brauer,[3] my substitute. He will, I hope, present them at the proper opportunity. I also have given theses on parish.boundaries[4] to Brauer, which possibly could be read and very briefly discussed. I have had 250 copies made of your theses. Brauer will also bring these along.

May the Lord Jesus Christ be among you and bless your deliberations, that the Synodical Conference like a mighty tree may strike deeper roots and also bear richer fruit. Sometimes I almost become frightened when I think of the many considerations which certain precedents here and there concerning our confederation awaken. It will not hurt that our counterparts in our synods be somewhat earnestly reminded of the responsibility which rests on them because of their unification with us. Please give them all my most humble and cordial fraternal greetings. I implore your and the brethren's gracious intercessions. God willing, I will most likely not return home until toward the end of next week. If I feel emotionally stronger, I think I may still attend the two forthcoming district conventions this year. God be with you and with

Your
C.F.W. Walther

To Missionary C. M. Zorn
India

St. Louis, Mo., Feb. 20, 1875

Beloved and honored brother in the Lord,[1]

Finally I get to responding to your welcome letter of Sept. 20 last year. You probably are not awaiting an answer from me anymore, and I am practically ashamed to try to serve you with this response at this late date. If it were worthwhile, I would even give you a list of the duties which rest on me, provided that you would look on my miserable person, loaded with work—if this were conducive to arousing your forgiveness that I am only today responding to your request, and that in such a poor, inadequate manner. Every hour that I have apart from my official duties which cannot be delayed I have to steal, and even then I am almost always disturbed by people who want to speak to me if it is not yet a late night hour. Besides that, for a major part of each year I have to make trips for Synod. But enough of this. Let me just appeal to your considerate love.

The essays which you and brother Zucker[2] have sent for my opinion I duly received and have read them again and again. Both essays have given me great joy. I had not thought that such a brilliant witness could exist in India. In both essays there is evidenced the spirit of a thoroughly Biblical, evangelical and Lutheran stance. Doctrines which are for the most part displaced, or at least set into the shadows today, as for example justification, the doctrine of the Word, the doctrine of the sacraments, the doctrine of free will and of the election by grace, are brilliantly displayed herein like crystals. Your presentation of the papacy is straight-on the best which I have read in recent times. As I read this, my heart laughed within me. Your faithful adherence to our precious church and her pure-gold confessions has refreshed me. As far as the essay of our dear brother Zucker is concerned, I do not know what I should still mention. The same I would say for your essay also, if you had not formulated yours in the form of scientific theology. But since this is the case, you also draw forth from me a suitable critique.

As I was reading your essay the second time, I took the liberty to make notations of those things which occurred to me. If I enclose these comments herewith, I beseech you cordially not to entertain the thought that I want to elevate myself above you and show forth my pride in this kind of criticizing. Only your earnest request that I critique your essay made it possible not to put good constructions on it but to proceed according to the basic assumption of Augustine: "Hold to the intent, but correct the language." Possibly I have misunderstood you here or there. Often it might have been desirable on my part to make more detailed expressions of my comments. But if I am not further to delay my answer, you will have to satisfy yourself with this little bit.

Now a few general remarks. It seems to me you have not sufficiently freed yourself from the newer abstract means of expression. In Germany one does not count as being educated nor as being intellectual nor as being a sharp-witted thinker if one has not adopted the mode of speech which stems from abstract philosophy. But on this point it seems to me it is a matter of denying oneself. This kind of language clouds matters, whereas nobody ought to speak as clearly, as simply, as a soul without guile, as concretely, as a theologian, for he must deal with truths on which the very salvation of men hangs.

The other general remark which I permit myself to make is that I cannot condone that you do not simply make Bible passages your point of departure but base your discussion on certain fundamental assumptions from which you then draw longer deductions. Also this I do not consider to be the method in which theological themes should be treated. For with that method only a sharp thinker can follow your discussion, and furthermore, by that means we do less to firm up the faith than to overwhelm the reason of people. You use John 1:5 as the basis of a discussion but only through an ingenious use of this text do you achieve a Scriptural foundation for the elaboration of your theme. That is interesting; in fact, that overwhelms one. That arouses admiration, but it does not confirm one's faith. The principle which ought to be the point of departure of the Lutheran theologian is not a single passage or a single doctrine, but is rather the whole of Scripture. Again and again the Lutheran theologian has to come back and work from this basis.

In sum, my opinion is that if the Lutheran Church is to come to full bloom in India, all the teachers there will have to take the simple speech of Luther and simple mode of thought of our fathers as their model and conform to those.

I am really afraid that when you read the above, and my remarks which I enclose herewith, you will be thoroughly disillusioned in your anticipation for soliciting my participation in your valuable work. And I almost regret already that I am so brash as to express my thoughts in criticism of you. Only a thief gives more and better than he has. And only this and nothing more was in my mind when you summoned me, this poor person, to make a critique.

Go ahead and throw my hurried lines into the fire. I shall not be angry with you for that. If I have not been able to serve you, yet you have served me, because both those essays have strengthened me in the faith. Only this one thing I ask of you, do not withdraw your brotherly love for me but also include me and our important work here in America in your intercessions, just as I will not cease to remember you and your enormous work diligently before the Lord.

Your fellow participant in tribulation
and in the patience of the Lord Jesus Christ,
C.F.W. Walther

To J. C. W. Lindemann
Addison, Ill.

Indianapolis, Aug. 8, 1876

My dear director,[1]

The angel speaks in the book of Tobit: "It is good to guard the secret of a king but gloriously to reveal the works of God" (Tobit 12:11) This agrees with the rules of literary work and without doubt speaks strongly for the view that those who have experienced the history of our synod or who have heard about that history from those who have experienced it should be asked to sit down to write a history of our synod before they depart this life. It seems to me to be unquestionable that you are a person of extraordinary qualifications for writing such a history. Nevertheless, I shrink back from joining those who would burden you with this task. You have recently been in great danger of becoming completely unable to work because of overwork, as you yourself probably also observed. Therefore I am afraid of tempting God if I were to challenge you to assume the above mentioned undertaking besides your enormous official duties.

But even apart from this, I consider it almost too difficult and too dangerous a matter that a history of our synod should be published as long as the pioneers are still alive. It should no doubt be written in their lifetime, but not published. There is no doubt that there are some, or perhaps even many, who are kept from joining our synod through false misrepresentations which they have of our synod, or they are kept from drawing closer to us because of the maligning of our church that goes on. But I am certain that those who are of God would not begrudge the effort if it is really important to read and study our publications in order to enable them to make their own independent judgment about us. I would not object if you were to gather materials for describing the history of our synod and even begin to work through these materials, as long as you would not be goaded into this work but could do it in love, or as we say in German, in all leisure. This is my answer to your question after right contemplation.

Another thing. Is it not a resolution of Synod that representatives of the teachers conferences are privileged to send representatives to the meeting of the School Book Committee at their own cost? If this is so, we should not overlook it. But already in a different vein, it seems that possibly we should not reintroduce these representatives. After such representatives have once felt their dignity, they can be easily miffed if they are not invited again. This might become the reason why they might, without being aware of it, look with some prejudice at any given book that is published, and thus resist the introduction of such a book. Please write to me about this with just a few words. Next Monday evening I shall be traveling from Cleveland to Baltimore, where I am invited to lodge with H. Hanser.[2]

The Central District has with a substantial majority rejected the proposal to begin construction work in Springfield.[3] Also several other matters have made the last sessions very unedifying for me and have weighed on my heart. But otherwise everything came off quite well. Please keep the second-last remarks to yourself and only let them serve as a brief groan from me.

Your aged and poor father and brother in the Lord,
C.F.W. Walther

Probably to Ottomar Fuerbringer
Frankenmuth, Mich.

St. Louis, Nov. 22, 1876

Dear friend and brother in the Lord,[1]

What you have written to me about the relationship of several of our pastors in Wisconsin to Pastor Zorn,[2] I had already heard from letters of Pastor Kleinhans[3] and Zorn himself. This matter is very crushing and humbling to me. As far as I understand this matter, the reason for it lies partly in stubbornness and partly in the wretched attitude prevailing.

That Zorn does not speak as we do can only alienate a person who is not understanding, but that he believes as we do is without doubt for me. A man as original as Zorn is like fresh blood in the arteries for us who have gone through a demanding school and therefore do not have the courage to move about as freely as he does. But for Zorn it is good to enter into our disciplined relationship. Characters like Zorn bring their own dangers. But the sniffing for heresy with such people, when they get wind of it, only works the opposite of what it seeks to achieve, and it has in it a good measure of pharisaism.

I have already heard of Pastor Stecher,[4] that he belongs to the faultfinders in the most evil sense of the word. I would very much like to know the names of the others who, I hope out of good intention, but with limited understanding, are agitating the inquisitors of heresy. Zorn does not know me if he is worried that such gossip about him, as has already broken out, will turn me against him.

[The rest of the letter to this district president is concerned with technical points of casuistry, and is therefore omitted here.]

C.F.W. Walther

To a District President

St. Louis, Mo., Dec. 7, 1876

Highly honored Mr. President,[1]

I took the liberty to present to you the question whether, as president of the synod, I was empowered to name a committee which would work with the committee of the Ohio Synod, already elected, on the question of the Ohio Synod propositions relating to the amalgamation and in part the demarcation of both synods and discuss a plan of union and where possible sketch such a plan out.[2] At that time I was inclined to answer my own question in the negative. This was not so much because I was aware of any kind of limitation on the president of Synod, but rather because of the spirit and the principle which has prevailed among us, a violation of which could easily give rise to some offense.

After the requested answers of all the presidents of our districts had reached me, I see myself compelled to notify you that I was confirmed in my opinion that it is not in my area of responsibility to establish the kind of committee referred to above. Among others, President Wunder[3] wrote: "As far as your first question is concerned, I am of the opinion that the president of our synod should not do anything till Synod in official convention expresses itself on the proposal of the Ohio Synod. According to that proposal, such far-reaching changes are to take place in our synodical life! A large number of congregations which had resolved after some serious struggles to join the Missouri Synod would now be directed to join another synod. Furthermore, these congregations are not to receive *Der Lutheraner*, from which they have been obtaining their spiritual nourishment and their weapons, as a synodical organ. They are now to join a synod which uses a different hymnal and a different agenda. If the praesidium would, at the next convention of Synod, present propositions accepted by a committee consisting of members of both synods dealing with the execution of the plans for changes submitted by the Ohio Synod, this would appear as if the decision of the Missouri Synod was influenced from above. When our synod was divided into districts, there were discussions for years about the purposefulness of this step. Should we now be more hasty when we deal with the dividing of Synod into different self-contained synodical bodies? It would seem to me as if the dear Ohio Synod has been moving forward a little bit too rashly. It would have been sufficient for the time being if it had presented its opinion and had made a proposition without wanting to negotiate with us about the execution thereof, and if it had granted its congregations, especially those which as proposed were to join a new synod, time to consider it and to express themselves on this, whether they really wanted to join the Missouri Synod. The suspicion could easily arise as if the synods were selling the congregations and dealing with them without inquiry whether they were satisfied." So this notion has been completely driven from my thoughts and I must now conscientiously act according to it.

Besides this, President Strasen[4] wrote: "Since the plan of Ohio, as it seems to me, is only to introduce an outwardly new course of action, therefore I am of the opinion that this discussion should not be held without inviting the western synods friendly to us to participate. Yes, it seems that there is even more to it, especially when I read points P, J, D, of the Ohio Synod plan, namely that if those synods would consider this step as being presumptuous and would be disquieted thereby, then we would either push them aside or, after concluding the unification with the Ohio Synod, only leave the way open for those other synods to join after that. And besides, there is another point according to my opinion, namely that the goal to which we are striving, as our whole synod is aware, is the establishment of state synods. But whether it is a general conviction that now the time for an amalgamation has already come is very questionable to me. Not so long ago one could hear outstanding members of our synod say that we would be dead before that goal could be attained. Might it not therefore be considered strange in our synod if that proposed committee would be established? Would it not be advisable to take the matter presented to the Synodical Conference in its report of 1876 together with the proposed plan of the Ohio Synod and discuss this in all our district conventions, as also have it discussed in those synods which are friendly to us, and then in fall of next year let this committee meet? In that case the synods friendly to us in the west would also be able to take part in such a committee and would probably go with us." Also these considerations seem to be well founded and have strengthened my own reservations. In short, I am now for the view that the proposed committee first meet next fall after each one of our districts has voted for it and has selected its members.

The honorable synod of Ohio has gone ahead with its example and therefore it will not consider our hesitancy as a rejection of the course of action for a unification and a territorial demarcation which we have already entered upon.

Two other things I want to mention: Outside of President Wunder, no other president questioned the formal right of the synodical president concerning the proposed action, but there was not a one who was completely in accord with the propositions of the honorable Ohio Synod under point B.

Thus I find myself compelled no longer to withhold the communication of our conviction from President Loy,[5] but I am prepared if I should be convinced of another opinion to change my stance.

Commending this extremely important matter to the Lord of the church and greeting you in affection and inner brotherly love, I am

C.F.W. Walther

To Pastor C. F. Th. Ruhland
Nieder-Planitz, Saxony

St. Louis, Mo., Nov. 25, 1877

Heartily beloved friend and brother,

For weeks I have been preoccupied day and night with nothing else but the need of our Saxon Lutheran Free Church,[1] above all the need in which you find yourself. Oftentimes I get very little sleep because of this. I go about agonizing for you and am hardly in a position even to carry out the most urgent duties of my calling. My comfort in this need is Luther, especially the letters he wrote at the time of the submission of the Augsburg Confession. Oh, what a hero of the faith becomes evident there in much,

much greater distresses of the church! In contrast, I am revealed as a miserable dwarf in the faith. But I must also share with you that even my mustard-seed faith again and again comforts me and makes me joyful. But enough of this. I have only a few free minutes, and therefore to the task.

You desire to return to America again in spite of all the dissuasion from us. Therefore I finally have also come to the conviction that we dare not continue to resist your wish any longer. After everything that you have written to me and to others, it does seem as if it might appear that we were offering you up if we were to continue to oppose your return. It is indeed true—and I speak here before God—that you have proved by your deeds that you were the most suitable man among all of us to found the difficult work of a Lutheran Free Church over there. As fully as I have been convinced of this gift which God has bestowed on you above all others, with His help to carry out such a gigantic task, so much you have, as people unanimously testify, far exceeded not only the expectations of all others but also my own. Let this testimony be given to the glory of God. But it almost seems as if God appointed you only to prepare the golden ground in labor and strife, and then to direct you to a less demanding activity in His kingdom here on earth after you have absolved your duties there.

When I now lay down my arms over against your requests once more to reopen for you the gates of your old spiritual homeland, I dare not withhold from you the fact that in my conscience there is a condition attached thereto which you alone can fulfill and on which the whole local pastoral conference agrees with me.

We are namely of the opinion that you should not leave Germany without first having made a final attempt to see whether an understanding cannot still be reached between you and your synod on the one side and Hoerger and Krauss and, if possible, also Wagner on the other side.[2] It would be terrible if among those over there who confess the truth which God has also revealed to us here an irreconcilable breach remained. What kind of unholy intention Satan has with this cannot be completely imagined. I shudder when I think of it. But if you come back before an understanding has been reached between you and Hoerger, then we cannot hope for any kind of a peaceful conclusion later on. As long as we here do not judge you as the one who bears all the fault, so long we will also remain an unfriendly opposing group for them.

Therefore our thought is this, and please do not be shocked by the demand: You have to become the Curtius[3] who will cast himself into the ecclesiastical breach or, to speak without the figure, you will have to take up once more at the point of the conditions which Hoerger so insolently demanded in May of last year when you extended such a friendly

138

invitation, namely his demand to let the matter be judged by all the brethren there—some facts, of course irrefutably according to God's Word. I do not doubt even for a second that you will emerge from this judgment fully justified. My only doubts concern the question of whether Hoerger will be willing to go back to his own conditions to achieve a unification; and in case he would do so, whether that will lead to peace. But how much could be gained if we succeed! Also the last suspicion would disappear that the fault of the breach lies with you, and we could then with a joyful conscience recognize our separation from Hoerger and decisively oppose him and not be concerned about what could result therefrom, in the certainty that all harm resulting from such a breach would be on Hoerger's conscience.

But also as far as Wagner and Grosse are concerned, the former's essay has indeed not persuaded us that you and Brunn had interfered in an alien office, but it has made it impossible for us to oppose Wagner's charges with more than our moral persuasion. The appearance as if you and Brunn,[4] without our protest, in fact, with our consent, had only for the sake of the drive to expand been applying a precious truth that both you and we here have always recognized with great earnestness and have validated against others, that weighs on us heavily here.

We therefore have struck upon the thought, especially since Wagner seems to demand this of us, that possibly it would be good if our synod would send two representatives over there who would mediate between the two sides, providing that both sides would *in writing* confirm that this is their desire. Since I myself, as one of the accused, cannot belong to such commissioners, therefore our conference has contacted all district presidents with the request to write to our German confessional partners to make an inquiry about this matter, and if everyone over there would consent, then to elect a mediating commission and to empower them and without delay send them off.

What do you think of this? And, if you do not reject this proposition, who in our synod, according to your opinion, would be suitable for this kind of a mission? I have been thinking of men like Schwan, Gross in Buffalo, Staender, and Allwardt. Sihler (who himself is probably too old for this) calls attention to Stubnatzi,[5] who has proved himself for a number of years to be such a remarkable ruler in the church (if I may use that kind of an expression), even in very difficult cases, that one is astonished what all is in that small prosperous-appearing man.

Now may God grant that all this above may not cause you to sink into pessimistic thoughts. Do not permit the kind of thoughts to enter your heart as though we here secretly backed your enemies or as though we were inclined to engage in unholy church politics so as to attain a compromise contrary to the truth or to what is right. Since I sent that letter to Hoerger, which he in a highly indiscreet manner shared with Wagner, and which the latter publicized in such a shamelessly indiscreet manner, Hoerger has not received a single line from me. The last time I wrote to Wagner is even further back, if I am not totally in error, and I have not written at all to Krauss since his return to Germany although he has forwarded detailed reports to me. The way those gentlemen use private letters, one really becomes fearful to give them anything black on white. [Footnote by Walther:] I respect you very much and thank you sincerely for the discreet use of my letters to you. You could have put me into a position of great embarrassment if you had published many of the confidential parts of those letters, and this to your own benefit. May God reward you for this fraternal faithfulness. [End of footnote.] So, what we want is nothing but that you do not permit the malice that has been exercised against you to keep you from doing everything possible which is reconcilable with your conscience to prevent the blame or even only the appearance of blame for a split among the orthodox pastors and therefore also to justify the church fellowship with which you are so intimately connected.

As far as the self-preoccupation of proud spirits in respect to the peace of the church is concerned, I always have the illuminating example of Luther in his relationship over against the arrogance and restless spirit of Andreas Osiander in Nuernberg (after Luther's death, in Koenigsberg). Osiander soon revealed himself to Luther as being a dangerous man. But since he still showed himself as being one in doctrine, Luther was careful not to provoke him. He even let it pass that in Schmalkalden Osiander criticized Luther's sermon, when Luther became ill, although without mentioning Luther's name ([Walch] XXII, 1043 ff.; Erlangen, Vol. 59, 252 ff.). Luther had a difficult time calming the Nuernberg pastors, who were suffering because of Osiander. Walch shares a wonderful letter of Luther to Osiander in which Luther tries to quiet him in the most gentle way (XXI, 1467 ff.). So Luther prevented Osiander from coming out in public with his false doctrine while Luther was alive. If we could publish a good biography of Luther, if we only had more help, it would be a good warning for pastors.

Oh, my heartily beloved friend, think of the wounds from which the poor church now is bleeding, and think of the overwhelming grace and patience of the Lord, which He bestows on all people as also on us, and do everything you possibly can to win those who with us confess the truth, so that when the devil thinks he has a point for rejoicing, at least we will not have provided it for him. In heaven you will receive from God such a great reward of grace for every cross, for every groan which you have had to utter and for every tear, that you will be able to say with Luther that you will reprove yourself for ever having wept one tear or uttered one groan (On Genesis 39:5-6).[6]

But I must now close. Please interpret my inordinate blabbering in a good way. May God grant that my miserable letter will not make your heart heavy, but lighten your burden. Above all greet your wife and your dear children and tell them that I hope once again in this life to see them if the Lord will grant us another year. Please remember me also graciously to my most honored benefactress Miss von Haugwitz. I commend you to the comfort and the wonderful help of the Lord.

Your sincere friend, brother, and fellow cross-bearer,
C.F.W. Walther

To Pastor J. G. Sauer
Ft. Wayne, Ind.

To Pastor Sauer

Concordia Seminary, St. Louis, Mo., March 23, 1881

Most intimately beloved friend and brother,[1]

Your dear letter has joyfully overwhelmed me in many respects. First of all, that you in such a friendly manner invite me to be your house guest during the time of the sessions of our synod in May. I accept this gracious invitation from you with the most heartfelt thanks. You were even so good as to let me choose my fellow guest. Since in these last days before the beginning of the convention of Synod my son-in-law will be here as a member of a commission,[2] and since it would be highly desirable for me to have longer discussions with the president of Synod[3] in those days, therefore I make bold to utilize your authorization and to suggest the latter as my fellow guest.

A second reason for a joyful surprise in your dear letter was the news which you shared with me about the current position of Professor Stellhorn[4] on the election controversy. This news removes a heavy stone from my heart. I have recently been filled with deep distress at the thought that, when Professor Stellhorn goes to Columbus,[5] he will there make use of the opportunity to abandon all considerations and to step up as our opponent. It would be dreadful for me then to be forced to fight with a man whom I consider as highly as Stellhorn and who till recently was so close to me. Oh, how I would rejoice and how I would thank God on my knees, if

Professor Stellhorn would rather assume the office of a mediator and if God would bless his mediation so that Professor Loy,[6] who opened the attack in such an intransigent manner, would again pull himself in and yield to the possibility of a reconciliation!

Unfortunately I don't see any possibility of any dealing with Professor Stellhorn before his move to Columbus. I am now in a position where, other responsibilities excepted, I must utilize *all* my time to bring my students to the objective, and thus have time neither for written nor for verbal discussion with Professor Stellhorn. It is terrible that Professor Loy has attacked us with such lack of restraint, so that we are compelled to counter more forcefully if we do not simply want to fall completely into the hands of our enemies and thus deny the cause of the truth. I wish Professor Stellhorn could picture himself in our position and be provoked by our polemics, which are not directed at him. I can do nothing but to appeal to God that He would turn this matter so that a permanent schism which cannot be healed does not arise.

This time only this much on this point.

Please greet your respected wife from me and tell her how I rejoice that, God willing, I shall be her guest.

In the Lord Jesus,
Yours most intimately,
C.F.W. Walther

Walther the Schoolman

To the Dean of the Theological Faculty
Goettingen, Germany

St. Louis, Mo., Aug. 1, 1855

Honorable Sir, especially highly revered Dean:

Your excellency's valuable correspondence of June 5 this year is at hand. With deep humility I see that the honorable theological faculty at Goettingen[1] is inclined to name me for the honorary degree of doctor of theology on the occasion of the forthcoming 300th anniversary of the Augsburg Religious Peace.

I consider myself completely unworthy of such a high honor. For the Lord's sake I cannot deny that here in America, where the church had to lift itself out of chaotic circumstances, my own humble but well-meant efforts have not been quite without results. Yet my theological knowledge is so spotty that although in a land of emergency workers I might occupy the place indicated for me possibly not without doing some good, only with the greatest embarrassment would I bear a dignity which would elevate me to the ranks of the theologians, albeit the lowest place among them.

The forthrightness which I owe you, honorable sir, all the more since the friendliness which you show me is undeserved, demands of me that I also mention that my acceptance of the honor you intend for me would put my conscience into conflict over the standpoint which your venerable faculty takes in respect to the Evangelical Lutheran Church, to which I and the Missouri Synod belong out of the innermost conviction. Therefore I make bold respectfully and humbly to decline the proferred distinction, which I trust your excellency will condone in view of the circumstances alluded to. And kindly accept my most obedient request to condescend to accept my most sincere thanks.

Commending myself humbly to your excellency's further kindness and in the most supreme reverence of your excellency, I remain

Your most obedient servant,
C.F.W. Walther
Professor of theology at Concordia College, St. Louis

To Prof. Gustavus Seyffarth

New York City

Dec. 29, 1855

To Rev. Professor Seyffarth[1]
in care of Rev. O.T.E. Stohlmann,
105 Mott St., New York

Highly respected sir, dear professor,

Your valued letter of the 17th of this month is at hand. I cannot tell you with what joy I received it. Your detachment and silence for a longer time had caused me the most painful dread. I had already begun to fear for your life in this country of swindlers and murderers. My helplessness was so much greater since I could think of no way to get any certainty about your situation or about your present whereabouts. Besides this, there was your silence. But finally I wrote to Pastor Brohm in New York to ask him to find some way to get some information as to your fate. God be praised for hearing my prayers and intercessions, that my trepidations did not become realities. May the Lord now also help further, that in His time we may have you in our midst here.

As far as our local college is concerned, the situation is as follows. There are two departments: one a theological seminary with nine students, and a *Gymnasium* with about 50 students. In the seminary department Professor Biewend[2] and I teach. Biewend is at the same time director of the college. Goenner, with the title of rector, teaches the first class in the college and is soon to have a helper, with the title of conrector, who is to teach the lower classes. If we succeed in filling this position, then our only need will be one more man for the seminary. Our greatest need is a professor for the historical discipline. How I would praise God if you would be willing and able to come to take over Biblical isagogics, archaeology, and church history! But there is such a lack of financial means. For the time being we would be able to pay you only a very modest salary. But we would gladly be satisfied with an arrangement under which you would devote only the smallest part of your time to the seminary, so that through literary work you would be able to generate the missing part of your income for the assurance of your livelihood.

But, most honored sir, if this last point alone would be the factor which would make it impossible to gain your services for our institution, then I would first want to devise some way to overcome also this particular hindrance. When Wyneken and I several years ago were again in Germany, the supreme consistory in Bavaria gave us the promise of

144

substantial help for our institution. Since Dr. Harless[3] now stands at the head of this *Collegium*, I have no doubt but that he would make good on his word if we would now appeal to them for support for the establishment of a new theological professorship for the historical discipline.

Therefore I make bold to pose the humblest question to you, to inform me kindly as soon as you can as to your thinking on this—whether you are inclined to grant our institution one hour daily and besides that in other ways to find some means of livelihood for yourself, whether you are inclined to serve our church here, or whether we can count on it that you would be in a position to dedicate more time and effort to our seminary here. The latter possibility would naturally be above all in accord with our wishes and requirements. But even the first possibility we would consider a supremely gracious guidance and providence of God for blessing our church. In the meantime I will pray God that His will may be done and that He will lead everything to redound to His honor and to your contentment and best interest.

I believe I can give you the joyous confidence and assurance that your talents really would not be wasted, but would be dedicated to the service of the Lord, if you would be willing to dedicate a part of your talents to our institution. Our laborers in the Word have an evident and wholesome influence on the people here and on the total formation of the church, which I say only to the honor of God, who has made something out of nothing. We also seem to be just now in an interesting epoch in the development of our church here, and on this assumption I will issue an invitation in our theological periodical in the first number for next year for a general conference in which we would be able to discuss the ways and means to lead to a unification of all Lutherans from the synods here. If this would meet favorable response, I would hope for much success for a healing of our fragmentation, and I see in your coming here a good omen for our present endeavors.

I commend you and your honored wife to the unchangeable faithfulness of our God.

Your most obedient servant in the Lord,
C.F.W. Walther

To Prof. Gustavus Seyffarth
New York City

Concordia College, St. Louis, Mo., March 25, 1856

Highly honored, dearly beloved professor,[1]

Your worthy letter of the 21st of the previous month has reached me, although very tardily. I received it just as I was on the point of undertaking a trip. The local Protestant Christians here have founded a political paper since the other political papers in the west are openly organs of anti-Christianity, and they hope with this new paper to displace those other papers in the homes of the Christians and in a general way to provide in the upstanding families a Christian outlook on current events and to effect a conscientious use of civil rights and privileges among the people.

Up till now it has not been possible to find a suitable editor. This paper, which has been in existence for one year, had an editor who wanted to write for the satisfaction of the Christian people but who was not able to achieve this. Therefore the paper has had a precarious existence. The local Christians here hardly felt like identifying themselves with their own creation. In spite of this, thousands of dollars were spent in order to keep the ship afloat in the hope of getting a better pilot. But all our efforts to secure the services of a Christian editor remained fruitless. Therefore we resolved to offer the position to one of the pastors of our synod who serves in Canada,[2] since we had testimonies as to his competence for the fulfillment of our objectives. But when we offered a written contract, we were met with a refusal. So it was evident that this possibility held out no promise of success. Thus I was commissioned to travel to Canada to try to persuade the designated pastor as well as his congregation of the importance and the urgency of this matter. Thus I made that journey and, after surviving great and numerous difficulties, have returned again with the good news that in a few days our new editor will put in his appearance and undertake his office here.

We hope that also you, in case you will come into our midst, will be persuaded of the importance of this affair and every once in a while favor this newspaper with a few pearls from your rich treasures. Since the paper is large, it must appear as a daily, for only in this way can it compete and fulfill its stated purpose under God's gracious blessing. But therefore it needs a lot of stuff.

I have taken the liberty, most honorable sir, to write you in somewhat more detail so that I would have an excuse for delaying my answer so long. For as inexpressible as my own and my friends' joy was when we received your last assurance that you have the intention of joining us here and have even held out the possibility that you would probably be here very soon, yet so large is our concern that through my silence I may have caused you some second thoughts about putting your intention into practice, which intention no doubt the Lord, our faithful intercessor, has put into your heart.

I live in the firm conviction that with your appearance at our institution a new era will begin for it. I have never considered my miserable self to be a professor, even though I am pictured as such here. I am nothing but a very desperately needed emergency worker in my own area, but I have recognized clearly how important this post is which has been assigned me. I was called to it to establish the foundation of a project the idea of which I see before me rather clearly but which I am not in a position to build, to say nothing of being able to carry out this plan. Day and night I hope for an architect. All our former attempts to find such a one and to secure such a person in Germany have gone fully askew. But the Lord be praised eternally that He has provided for our needs in an almost secret way without our thoughts and without our doing anything. We would have considered it a presumption to even think of securing your services, since our institution is still in its infancy.

Before the next convention of our synod, which will not take place until 1857, hardly anything decisive can take place. But then I hope the synod will relieve me of the office of president of the joint institution, that is, seminary and college, under the latter of which we really mean *Gymnasium*, and confer that office on you, since I live in the confidence that you for the sake of the love of Christ and of His dear people will be willing to take on this burden.

Since I desire that you should have living facilities in keeping with your wishes, I invite you that after your arrival, which God grant may be soon, you make your home with us and take your meals with us until we can find a suitable residence for you. The best travel route which you can take, according to my recent experience, would be New York to Buffalo, from there to Cleveland, and then to Indianapolis, Terre Haute, and Alton, Ill., then to Illinoistown, which is on the eastern bank of the Mississippi opposite St. Louis. This is the shortest and surest way one can travel completely by rail. In St. Louis if you would be so kind as to inquire at the porcelain factory of Pechmann and Gauche, 8 North Main Street, they can direct you to my residence. Mr. Pechmann is a member of our congregation and will consider it a joy and honor to escort you to my place. The school is located about five miles from the center of the city, although it is still at the present in the incorporated boundaries of the city.

Your book boxes have arrived, but they will not be released [from customs] until the content has been certified. This matter cannot be handled till your desired arrival.

May the Lord bring you to us soon. For this I constantly pray to God.
Your most obedient,
C.F.W. Walther

To Teacher Theo. E. Buenger
Chicago, Ill.

St. Louis, May 7, 1861

My dear brother-in-law,[1]

Thanks, sincere thanks for your friendly and loving invitation. But we are not able to accept. I, as pastor, cannot leave this precious congregation in such times as the present. We may soon be compelled to admit in our conscience that it is necessary to utilize all our powers which we have to counter the plans of Satan. My family, which I had to get out of the danger zone, I have sent out to the Kerckhoff[2] settlement in Missouri, since our state can be easily isolated from the free states and it might be possible that I could be separated from my family for a longer period of time. I am a Missourian and therefore will never be moved to separate my fortune from that of my state unless I am forced. This state has so far protected me in life and property, so in the time of need I will not become unfaithful to it.

There is great excitement here, but it has not come to actual physical violence. But since the state militia has concentrated here yesterday, it is possible that any moment a frightful catastrophe could erupt. The worst is that our congregation itself, because of various viewpoints of the political situation in the state, is split in two. Very slowly our congregation members themselves began to read the constitution of the United States and of the state of Missouri and thus to compare this state of affairs and to form their own convictions. Up to now most of them have only been influenced by the Boernstein[3] politics. How they therefore judge, you can well imagine. Boernstein lives as a captain of the Union troops in the Marine hospital with his regiment, opposite the college. These gentlemen really are not inclined to visit the college and to take care of this once and for all, for they know that as Christians we stand on the side of the state government, in which we live and stand, since we are "at all hazards" subject to that authority, which has power over us.

Therefore we are not in a position to accept any kind of token of your love for us and we only ask in these dangerous times that you pray for us, which we no doubt need very much, since God knows what kind of frightful uprisings may occur in these next days, which have been engendered through 30 years of abolitionist agitation.

Greet your family, the brothers Mueller and Wunder, Conrector Schick[4] and your colleagues, and remind all of them to remember our precarious position before God's throne. God be with you and with yours!

C.F.W. Walther

To Pastor J. M. Buehler
California

St. Louis, May 21, 1861

My dear brother,[1]

If you are angry with me that I have been silent so long, I certainly have richly deserved it. But if I confess to you how sorry I am, and promise to make amends, I hope that you will also absolve me. I could adduce many things for my own defense, but, not to make my repentance suspect, I will be silent.

You will be anxious to learn how things are going here. I can hardly share anything very joyful with you. After our governor[2] rejected the president's request to send troops for the fighting in the south, the Union forces have gathered significant military strength here, comprised mostly of local Germans under the command of Boernstein,[3] Frank Blaer,[4] and others. The whole arsenal and the surrounding area, down to and including the Marine hospital, is simply swarming with Union troops.

Since it seems that the battlefield would be fixed here under the very windows of the college (even Commander Boernstein, lying in the Marine hospital, putting his hands on a cannon, swore to shoot up this secessionist nest, as he loves to call our college), and since the governor presented a prospect of a military bill in the legislature, we have felt conscience-bound to close down the institution till further notice, and dismiss all the students and pupils to return to their homes, partly so that nobody here would have his life endangered by our hesitancy, partly that the students from the northern states would not find themselves in the embarrassing situation of being drafted by the state military to fight against the northern forces.

So already for three weeks the college is empty and forsaken. The rector and his family are in Perry County, the conrector and his family in Chicago,[5] my own and Saxer's family is staying with Kerkhof, and Lange's family with Voigt,[6] and Saxer and I are living here alone and solitary like two eccentrics in the attic. Mennicke[7] went to Rock Island, to succeed Selle[8] if the latter was moved to Fort Wayne; Mangelsdorf[9] is pastor in Belleville; Baumstark,[10] a student from Germany who came with me, went to Quincy and will no doubt become the pastor there. The only older student still left is Mueckel,[11] who will also very likely soon enter a field of labor.

What else has happened in St. Louis you probably have read in the newspapers. The land and the city is beat down, suppressed by a heavy military government. This government has at least brought one good thing, namely that we have the prospect of protection for life and property for the time being. The cleavage between those Americans who are southern sympathizers, which naturally comprises the majority both in the city and in the country, at least if you take into account the conditional Union people[12]—the rift between them and the Germans is really frightful. The foundation for real animosity has been laid, which will probably never be worked out and will only await the day of free action, that is, the day of revenge.

Our congregation is split. The largest part seems to be Republican in sympathy. We, the teachers and pastors (exclusive of the rector), are considered as secessionists because we are opposed to having our Lutherans freewillingly serve in the Union military or take the oath of allegiance to the administration to serve as volunteers in the Home Guards. But we are nonetheless naturally for the Union. But in a way we cannot see why the state does not have the right of secession according to the United States Constitution and according to their own constitutions; and partly we have declared that if a state secedes from the Union, naturally the individual citizen will not revolt but will either emigrate or will subject himself to the seceding state government, according to the Bible passage: "Be obedient to the power that has authority over you."[13] It does not say "Has the right over you." But in the heat of the argument here it is impossible to have a quiet and rational word with anyone who is of a different persuasion. We will simply have to wait till this drunkenness which has afflicted every aspect of life here, it seems, will be slept off. How painful this situation is for us, namely that our own Lutherans are in the political domain completely led by atheistic newspapers which determine their attitudes and from which they naturally absorb much more than politics, all this you can well imagine.

As you will have noticed from the *Lutheraner,* there has been a constant dribble of funds coming in for California. But since the $100 you have received from Pastor Steger[14] was only an advance (a loan), this amount first has to be deducted from the current receipts and paid back. Therefore at this time there is only a little over $80 available for equipping a second pastor. But what is that? Besides that, there is the question of finding a suitable man. The most suitable one was without question Bartling,[15] but he has taken a wife and therefore will not be about to go. If he would be able to go, where would we find the money to pay for both of them? Pastor Schmidt[16] in Baltimore seems, according to the most recent reports, compelled to move on from there, since the two Haenels[17] have left his church. Schmidt, too, I thought, was a suitable person from California, but in his case the same difficulty confronts us, since he is married. Mueckel is a good man, but whether he would fit in with you I do not know. What do you think of this? Steger seems to be so firmly entrenched that we cannot consider him.

What you need is a man who has a mission spirit, that is, the spirit of joyful sacrifice, flexibility, and a sincere love of people, and who has a well dispositioned sociability as well as humility, all traits which will enable a man to conform to a fellow worker. But such personalities are not as frequent as one might think. When one thinks of the totality of our synod, it is a joy to look out over the whole army of the servants of the Lord. But when one considers them individually, one sees a snag here and a difficulty there. What are your thoughts regarding persons of whom you may believe that you could well work together with them and from whom you might hope for some divine blessings in your circumstances over there?

Your reports always are extremely beneficial to me not only because I see therefrom that the work of the Lord there continued to go forward but because each report is a new evidence for me that the Lord has granted you joy in your calling, love for the souls that have been entrusted to you, and wisdom, zeal, and patience in your present circumstances. Even though you stand completely alone, yet you can sow the Lord's seed. My heartfelt wish and my earnest prayer to God is that the Lord may maintain you therein and also continue further to bless your work.

From all your remarks I can see with joy that through the sweet Gospel you have opened the hearts of many to your message. It is unnecessary that I should remind you that you must also diligently apply the salt of the Law. I do not mean that you must engage in legalistic diatribes, scolding and making of demands, but that you explain the great demands of the Law and unlock the Law's profound meaning and point out its spirituality as well as emphasizing its seriousness in its threats, so that the hearers may be brought to the point that they do not view the Gospel merely as a palliative for some painful sores, but view it as the cure for cleansed wounds. If the Law is not sharply in focus (which can be achieved in a quiet way without table pounding and boisterous presentations), then eventually the joy of the Gospel will be lost and the seed is sown on stony ground and the time will arise when the believers, meeting temptations and tribulations, which the world, the flesh, and Satan will never permit to be absent, will fall from the trees like unripe wormy fruit and perish.

On this point Luther is a splendid model. As comfortingly as he preaches, each of his sermons is also a storm warning over all outward Christians, which one first notices when one really begins to actualize

Luther's hearers in a lively way. At our last district convention we saw again, with joy, how profoundly Luther also grasps the Law and how carefully he thought it through, and we were encouraged also in this to follow him as well as we poor inadequate teachers are able to do. We will, of course, never achieve more than a weak limping after Luther, for Luther did not learn those things like we must but experienced them without preliminaries through his own experience and absorbed them through deep meditations so that it looks so original with him as if it had all been immediately revealed to him. Oh, what tribulations does it take and what mistakes before we gain such insights! What great and certain and precious truths lie hidden in Luther's simple words! He carries within himself, I am tempted to say, an inexpressible idea, not a truth which can be attained in a speculative way through formulations. Therefore Luther first says this, then that, and all kinds of things about some question and often repeats what he said before with very few alterations, till he hopes to have conveyed the living concept which lies within himself and to have made it alive in his readers and in his hearers. There is something of the apostolic in that man. Oh, how our church mucks around in all areas of learning in order to discover new things, and the full cisterns of Luther's insights we let stand there!

Please content yourself then with this short letter. I wrote this while the cannons were thundering in the vicinity. They are trying to pound into us Missourians again the dependence on the glorious Union and on the Stars and Stripes. May God grant that the cure may be effective. But I have to admit that this article of faith does not seem especially firmly established here. Well, then, at least when the kingdoms of this world will fade away, may the church remain in one faith and in one love and in one hope. From the church one cannot secede without losing eternal life. But the church does not shoot anyone dead, but makes alive. The church does not coerce anyone, to force anyone to remain in her, but she beseeches and exhorts, even with tears of love and with a fervent zeal. Now, we want to remain loyal to this worthy maidservant. Even if she appears uncomely and sunburned, she is still the king's daughter and truly beautiful internally (Psalm 45:14).

May God fill you with the comfort of His Holy Spirit. May He make your lips fervent, and aid you in expressing His great deeds and to experience His deeds for Christ's sake, who is your intercessor and mine, and every sinner's Savior. Amen.

Your
C. F. W. Walther

152

To Johannes Walther
Walther's Nephew

Concordia [Seminary, St. Louis], Aug. 11, 1862

My dear Johannes,[1]

The following is to inform you that, according to the militia law of Missouri, the students as well as the faculty of an educational institution which is chartered and incorporated by the state are free from the duty of active military service. Therefore also the pupils of our Concordia Seminary have free access to this exemption, since we have a charter dated Feb. 23, 1853. Therefore not only is every student enabled to return to the seminary without fear of being pulled into the military, but this may be the only means for many of them to avoid conscription, if they come to St. Louis and move in to the old study halls, where they will naturally find a welcome reception under the circumstances. I ask you to make this information known to the Concordia students in your neighborhood, students Schmidt, Graeber, etc.

God be with you.

> Your old uncle,
> C.F.W. Walther

P.S. From the enclosed clipping you will see that other institutions are also making use of the indicated privilege. I would enclose legitimate papers but, as I know, these would be valid only for the state of Missouri. Is Pastor Richmann still with his people, or if not, do you know anything about him?

To J. C. W. Lindemann
Addison, Ill.

(Fuerbringer, II, 39—41)

To Director J. C. W. Lindemann, Addison, Ill.

St. Louis, May 16, 1866

My dear brother,

Your dear letter of the 12th, which I just received, hit me like a veritable thunderclap out of the clear blue sky. If I had no knowledge of the strange circumstances into which the poor children and servants of God can stumble, what you wrote me would have perplexed me completely. In fact, it might even have made me dubious about you or your colleagues. But God has led me not always in bright sunlight but often in the dark vale of heavy affliction, so that I believe I can transport myself into your position and into your feelings.

To put it briefly, I have no doubt but that you are stuck in a very heavy affliction, and if you are seeking comfort in the hope that you can escape from your difficulty by being released from your present office, you are simply in error. No, no, dear brother; the dear Lord has called you there, and there you have to stay. Although it may seem in your own mind as if the evil foe had led you there because you are buffeted on all sides and everything seems to go wrong, yet this is only an appearance. Where Satan holds sway, there "his goods are *in peace*" and it looks as if there the dear angels are residing. But in the house of Job, where God resides and the dear angels are watching, there the devil is loose.

I must of course assume that you also have your weaknesses, and possibly these consist of precisely those attributes which give the others a small victory; but without doubt those with whom you are dealing have the same attributes, and bearing the burden of their brother becomes wearisome for them. Where you are convex, those others are not exactly concave so that you always fit together. In brief, you are a human being and they are human beings, and so it is not to be wondered at that people like Paul had "a sharp contention" with Mark and Barnabas and Silas at times. But God carries on His work through men with whom it sometimes seems as if one would go to the right and the other to the left and the third one would hold back, *and yet the work progresses*. Why? So that we may see that we are only God's masks; we can really only spoil His work. But still God does not carry it on without us, but through us and at times only with us and in spite of us.

Please do not misunderstand me. I have no intention of presumptuously making a judgment and ascribing any kind of fault to you, and certainly not the larger fault in this present misunderstanding. I only wanted to say that even if you were partly at fault this would be no reason whatsoever for you to give up your present office.

As far as I can see, you are especially gifted for our teachers' seminary. As far as I know, the whole synod is unanimous in this. But that you are so constituted that other people easily feel hurt by you, this is not proof that you are in the wrong place.

So for the time being you should abandon all thoughts of being relieved of your present yoke, except through a blessed death. Far from using my small "personal and official influence" to help you in this way escape from your present difficulty, I will rather use both personal and official influence to keep you nicely in your present post. I am of the firm conviction that the clouds of despair which now weigh on your spirit will again be dispersed and that you will again work in your present calling with joy and contentment. But also be patient with the weaknesses of your colleagues and do not permit disharmony to develop between you so that you cannot freely look one another in the eye. Do not let up till the misunderstandings are removed and whatever sins were committed are sincerely forgiven.

Temporarily only so much on this point. May God give me grace when I hurry to your midst, that I then may mediate as an impartial person in case any little splinters are still sticking in anyone at that time.

Mr. Diez[1] has at my suggestion given up the idea of going to Addison, as you already know. I have not yet dared to inquire about Mr. Brauer[2] in Baltimore. I am afraid that the Baltimore people will cry murder if we would call him away from there. When I come to Addison, we can discuss this matter together and then initiate something.

Please content yourself with this miserable scribbling, as I have just taken a few minutes robbed from other duties. I commend you to the enlightening, comforting, and guiding mercy of our faithful God. May He guide us into the best ways.

Yours in the Lord,
C.F.W. Walther

To Dr. Wm. Sihler
Ft. Wayne, Ind.
(Fuerbringer, II, 217—21)

St. Louis, July 10, 1871

My dear Sihler,

In the 6th of July issue of the *Missionary and Lutheran* there is an article signed by "G." in which the writer claims to have visited our institutions in Ft. Wayne, St. Louis, and Addison and also finally to have taken a look at the Watertown school. In that article the actual outward deficiencies in our local institution are portrayed, although in fairly loud colors, against which one would hardly want to say much. For we here in many ways have to get along in a rather destitute manner and are sustained only by the hope that when the debt of the Ft. Wayne school is paid off Synod will tackle the problem of developing better accommodations for our students too. At the same time the faculty of our St. Louis seminary is accused in that article of making Watertown[1] our favorite. Indeed it says in that article in respect to Ft. Wayne: "The superior officer[2] is doing all he can to cripple the institution which needs his cheerful countenance."[3] This is associated with a case of discipline in which I am alleged to have been dissatisfied with the discipline that was exercised there. Then it says further: "This" (namely that Watertown seems to want to become a rival of Ft. Wayne) "feeling seemed to bear heavily on all the professors at the latter place and even on many of its citizens, and it was in this spirit that the call made to Professor Achenbach[4] to a congregation in Illinois was received. While the Professor very reluctantly accepted the call, he did so as having been dictated by higher powers, and that his services as teacher were no more wanted."[5]

In this article we here, namely myself, am set forth in a very poor light. I may well admit that I should have done more for Ft. Wayne than I have. But accusations such as the one referred to above I do not deserve. I was indeed the one who expressed himself at the second-last synodical convention against Ft. Wayne, but only against the locality, because I was of the firm conviction that Ft. Wayne was unhealthy, namely the place where the college buildings stand. If this is a proof of a lack of love for the institution, I do not understand it. When, however, Synod resolved to let the institution remain at Ft. Wayne, I did everything I could to work for Ft. Wayne. I sent out a circular to all congregations trying to persuade them that they could support the work of God among us in no better way than through offerings for Ft. Wayne. At every synodical convention I drew on all my eloquence to solicit gifts and students for Ft. Wayne. When the question arose, whether the construction plans there should be continued, although the amount required by Synod was not in hand, it was I who assumed the responsibility for continuing the construction contrary to the resolution of Synod, and this out of love for the institution and out of recognition of its necessity and its very high significance for our work. It was I, also, who tried to get the Central and the Eastern Districts to agree to assume responsibility before Synod itself for the continuing construction at Ft. Wayne. It was I who adjured Rector Schick[6] not to resign, because I did not want to lose his excellent ability for our dear college. Are these proofs that I have been working to cripple the Ft. Wayne institution, or is this exactly the opposite?

It is true that in the last years I have not made official visitations there.[7] But why? I besought Director Saxer[8] to notify me when I would have to come to take part in the examinations. He did not answer me. I still went, but arrived too late. The main course of the examinations was over. As soon as I began to discuss with Mr. Saxer the health conditions in the institution, he became so agitated that I had to abandon this and could not deal with him further. I stood between two fires. Professors Schick and Lange[9] expressed their displeasure that I first spoke against retaining the institution in Ft. Wayne and then worked for it (namely after that had been resolved by Synod). Director Saxer felt that since I had not given up my reservations about the location of the institution, I therefore was an enemy of the same. I noticed very clearly that I was an undesirable person. For that reason, and only for that reason, I considered it disadvantageous to visit Ft. Wayne as inspector. Why should I sacrifice my precious time in a job of which I saw beforehand that it would be totally in vain? God knows how gladly I would have come, if I could have had the slightest hope to be of use to the institution.

When the wretched disciplinary case of Kraemer's 20-year-old son arose, I could not persuade myself that Director Saxer had proceeded properly in this case, and I still cannot do so today. Director Saxer promised me to write to Kraemer and admit to him that he, Saxer, had probably not proceeded properly. If he had done this, I would have been completely satisfied and could have concluded therefrom that he was reconciled to me. And even if he had not done what he had promised in Cleveland, if he had written to me fraternally and explained to me that he could not reconcile it with his conscience to confess an overly hasty action here, I would have been satisfied, for I well know that as Christians and as Lutherans we need not all necessarily arrive at a unanimous judgment as to how we must proceed in a discipline case. But since Mr. Saxer has stubbornly remained silent and has not taken account of the fact that I, although his opponent in this matter, am yet his old friend, his brother, his colleague, and also the responsible supervisor of the institution, so I saw all the more clearly that my activity in behalf of this institution was for the time being futile.

To judge from the article in the *Lutheran and Missionary*, it seems that you in Ft. Wayne have shared with a stranger who is an opponent of our synod, of its doctrine and above all of its practice, our family squabble and that you have accused us here, namely me, before him. If this is so, this indeed belongs to the most bitter experiences of my life—now, I hope, soon to be ended. I would not have believed that this could be possible.

Should not my whole former life hitherto be a witness that as long as I do not fall from grace it would be completely impossible for me to make the institution of another synod my favorite and to attempt to destroy our own institution through it? I have rather been of the opinion, and am so now, that it is of advantage to the church if there are as many good academies as possible, and the whole synod has shared this feeling with me, for which reason it went in on the Wisconsin Synod proposal to post a teacher to the Watertown school if the Wisconsin Synod would also post one to St. Louis. But I have never even for a second doubted that our Ft. Wayne school would always claim its superiority, and I have considered the idea that Ft. Wayne would sustain harm through Watertown as a laughable matter, if you will pardon my expression. I have advised no one to send his child to Watertown but have permitted it when it happened because of concern that Ft. Wayne was not healthy. As far as I know there is no one in our synod who wants to have his son take the full philological course in Watertown. Rather, as far as my knowledge goes, it is the plan of all parents, when their sons are ready for the upper classes, to let them complete their education in Ft. Wayne, because all of them are convinced that Ft. Wayne surpasses all other institutions in this country and because they prefer Watertown over our own institution only out of health considerations for the younger boys.

As far as calling Professor Achenbach away is concerned, I was involved in this only to the extent that I took part in nominating him for that position. And this I did with the supposition that he was anxious to make a change because of reasons of health. This Professor Achenbach will of necessity testify to from a letter which I addressed to him in this matter. If he accepted the call to Illinois "reluctantly,"[10] at least it was not I as a "higher power" "who dictated to him the acceptance of the call.

Now the question is what is to be done in view of the article in the *Lutheran.* Obviously I cannot answer it. But if there is not reply, this will give a bad impression. After I have borne so many things for our dear synod and have had to let myself be held in suspicion, be scolded and reviled, I am no doubt able to bear this burden also. But the question is whether the cause of the Lord and common justice for me this poor sinner does not require a declaration to set the facts straight. I will leave this up to you and the faculty. Please greet all members of the faculty from me fraternally and tell them that I am not angry with any of them but only groan for years under the pressure that they are angry with me and morally hinder me from carrying out my duty to the institution, namely personally.

The respective number of the *Lutheran,* I assume, you yourself have. If this is not the case, then I am prepared to send you my copy on request.

Hopefully you will all come to Indianapolis if God does not hinder you. There I hope, God willing, to speak to you further.

Your old friend and brother in the Lord,
C. F. W. Walther

158

To Wm. Sihler

Ft. Wayne, Ind.

St. Louis, Dec. 14, 1871

My dear Sihler,

Your dear Son Gottlieb[1] just asked me whether I objected if he visited Dr. Preuss,[2] saying you had advised this. I answered him I could not permit him to do this and that I was convinced that you had given him this advice only because you were not sufficiently familiar with the circumstances. I hold that if students go to visit this poor man, they can of course not challenge him outright, since this would first of all have a very harmful effect on Preuss himself and arouse in him the thought that he had sympathizers among the students, who are not certain of the matter at issue nor certain of their own faith. Secondly, I have a concern that it is tempting God to let a young inexperienced person fall into the hands of one who has fallen from the faith, who has up to recently been respected as an orthodox and learned man. Finally, I am fearful, if it were permitted students to see Preuss, a huge offense could develop in the congregation.

As reported, Dr. Preuss has recently been engaged by the Catholics to edit a political paper for them. The end of the song will no doubt be that Preuss will become Catholic, unless God will intervene in an extraordinary manner. Preuss would then utilize his fine knowledge and abilities to defend the Antichrist. It is true that Preuss is an enigma. He has always showed himself to be greedy for money and yet he has left a lucrative position with us.

It seems to me that in the past he had committed more than he has confessed to us. And instead of doing true repentance and cleansing his conscience through the blood of Christ, he has sought rest in orthodoxy without being convinced by the Spirit, to defend everything orthodox which can be defended according to his own reason. The longer he stood in this position, the more active his conscience may have become and accused him of being a hypocrite. When all this misfortune came over him, the agitated conscience may have been escalated to a tortured conscience. He himself said that he indeed believed but that he sinned again and again. He said that although believing in Christ, for example, on shipboard he had been certain that if the ship had sunk, he would have gone to hell. He himself insisted that he did not come to deny justification by faith through exegesis, but rather through experience, that his sins were even now yet being punished by God, whereupon then he sought the reason for this denial in the Word of God and also found it. It is remarkable that Preuss only resigned when his plan was crossed up that he would later work on the *Abendschule* alone and to make it independent of synod.

We have done what we could to bring him to his senses and free him from the snares of the devil. But everything was in vain. He knows as well as we do how our church interprets those passages which he quotes for himself, for formerly he has done it himself. It is a lost cause here to try to give better insight to remove misunderstanding. God will have to change his will, otherwise there is no help for it. If you personally could deal with him, you might possibly hit that spot in him where he still can be reached. That a student should deal with him is dangerous, and in any case completely useless.

You can well imagine in what sadness we find ourselves. I have had little sleep since the revelation of the fall of this unfortunate person, and during the daytime my concerns seem as if they shall break my heart. But my comfort is that the Lord rules His church. He will know why this frightful cross has been put on us. Perhaps this great fall from the doctrine of justification was necessary, so that many a one who is lukewarm on this doctrine and has become lazy would awaken and become vibrantly aware of the preciousness of this treasure. Our enemies will have a good laugh, and they will especially get at me, since I had defended Preuss although I never publicized anything for which I had not received prior sanction from my colleagues and from the vice-presidents of Synod. But I know well how necessary a heavy cross is for me, if my poor soul will finally be saved. May God soon grant me my end in this world, so that I may not finally also grow feeble and despair and thus lose what I have attained. Join in prayer in my behalf.

Your essay will appear in *Lehre und Wehre*,[3] since it seems to me that stylistically it is not easily understandable enough for the common man. You do not object to this?

The local Board of Control has provisionally called Professor Schmidt in Decorah as Preuss's successor. If the Norwegians should thereby be motivated to make Schmidt their Norwegian professor here, we would no doubt have to permit this to happen and then seek a different person. I have already thought of Schick[4] and Lange.[5] What do you say to this? Brohm[6] is opposed to Lange. Brohm's opinion is that Lange has no gift of teaching, and I myself do not know whether he is able to give instruction in Hebrew exegesis.

The Lord be with you and yours, whom I greet, as also the teachers at the college and Pastor Stubnatzi.[7]

In the Lord Jesus, your
C. F. W. Walther

To Pastor Hugo Hanser
Baltimore, Md.

St. Louis, May 30, 1872

My dear brother,[1]

In all haste, I only inform you that I have conferred with the other members of the faculty and shared your letter with them and that every one of them has had the experience that the students coming from Fort Wayne[2] have for the last years with few exceptions had nothing less than[3] a Christian attitude and motivation for the theological calling. The impressions which I regularly receive of the first-year students from that place are such that I almost completely despair. Yet God up till now has given His grace that most of them, after the Word of God has been brought to bear on them constantly, finally are overcome by the power of the Word. As I hear, Lindemann[4] himself challenged the students to share with him the experiences they had in Fort Wayne, and they admitted that an unchristian spirit has been prevalent, one that was dominated by human laws and human fears. I have spoken to the teachers there repeatedly, but they have never been willing to admit that this was so.

I am unable to comply with your request to give you special hints for the forthcoming investigation there, since I have not been put on the committee by Synod, and furthermore, I have noticed for a long time that the exercise of my supervisory duties has been poorly received. I want to say just confidentially to you that, besides this, men like Wyneken[5] and Schwan[6] have done what they could to make me ineffectual.

May God support the committee to carry out its high and responsible assignment so that a comfort as well as a blessing may redound to the church. While you are there, we here will be kneeling in prayer.

In the Lord Jesus, your saddened but hopeful
C. F. W. Walther

P.S. With the above complaint about Wyneken and Schwan I by no means intend to imply that these brethren have opposed me with conscious deliberation. However, a certain inexplicable antipathy against me was always expressed in every possible circumstance. Without doubt the devil is behind this, for he well knows that harmony among the servants of Christ will be harmful for himself. May God help us poor sinners through this all. Without doubt I myself, without wanting to do so, also bear great fault.

To Pastor F. Sievers

Frankenmuth, Mich.

St. Louis, Jan. 6, 1873

Dear and honored friend and brother,[1]

Only today do I get to answer your letter of the 29th of December, since I did not want to answer only on the basis of my bare awareness that there are no people that I know suitable for your district school. Therefore I made further inquiries. But even now I cannot recommend anyone to be appointed to your school.

Mr. Brackmann, former teacher at our citizens' school,[2] was not only completely competent for such an office, but was also willing to assume such an office. Although he was not deep in knowledge, yet he was throughout an upright Christian and Lutheran. But he has a wife and three children and would not be able to make do with the salary of $250 which he would receive as a district school teacher. Moreover, I feel heartily sorry for this man. He is in a painful situation. He is now recovering from a nervous disease connected with dizziness and is without employment and thus without support. His abilities are exceptional. He is good in philology and in history, and he is competent in the English language, both speaking and writing. Only his methodology leaves something to be desired. And yet his pupils, both boys and girls, always learned something from him. But an institution such as our citizens' school, in which everyone wants to become a polyhistor within one year, according to the wishes and expectations of the parents, surpassed the demands which were made of him and which he could meet. Thus in a polite manner he was pushed aside and now actually suffers financial embarrassment. He is a man of a simple heart, easily led. Would you possibly know a position for him? God grant that I could help him find a position and thus also a means of livelihood.

As far as the mission enterprises of our dear Baierlein[3] are concerned, I am of the opinion that we do not dare to hold out great promises for them. Baierlein seems to me to be a man who starts many things but is unsteady, although his competency is certainly significant.

Your dear sons[4] give me heartfelt joy. They are diligent, conduct themselves in a way seeming for a Christian youth, are much beyond most others in the finer customs, and seem to be making progress.

Be content with these few lines. The letters from Neustadt[5] you will permit me to publish in *Der Lutheraner* without the names. When this has been done, I shall send them back to you with thanks.

The Lord be with you and yours.

C. F. W. Walther

To J. C. W. Lindemann
Addison, Ill.

St. Louis, Aug. 7, 1878

My cordial, most intimately beloved, sincerely highly honored brother Lindemann,[1]

You have given me a bad scare with your letters of the 6th and the 5th of this month. What in all the world happened? It is not true that you are not up to the demands of your post, for by the grace of God you alone are up to it. You are above all the one through whose faithfulness and skill God has given us and still preserves for us such a blessed teachers' seminary. It is highly desirable that we have on the faculty of our teachers' seminary a classically trained man who can read the journals containing divine wisdom in the Latin language and test them according to the original text of the Word of God. In fact, this is in many aspects of relative necessity. That the director have precisely this kind of training is not absolutely necessary.

Therefore for God's sake do not assume the responsibility for having your call nullified. God does not tolerate our fooling around with these things. If others are ready to assume this kind of responsibility, then let them. If they succeed, then you have to suffer this in humility and patience. But till that happens, stay put where God has posted you, since you desire to have a peaceful conscience. You had better abandon that nice little dream of the quiet life of a literary man in a small town far removed from all those people who make life miserable for us. As much as you would be suited for this and as much as you would create a great benefit for the people in this kind of role, you are not called to this, whereas if without your doing and with God's permission people were to cashier you out of your office, which I do not at all fear, then you would again be available for the ministry in which God has sealed your work. Your gift to write books for the people would therefore not go lost.

To help you according to your proposition to shake off the heavy yoke which weighs on you is asking too much of me, as you yourself seem to feel. May God in His grace preserve me from that. According to my conviction you are at the right post. And may God sustain and strengthen and bless you in that post till your death, if the world is worth it, and then crown you with the incorruptible crown. "Wait on the Lord. Rejoice and do not despair and wait on the Lord." "The Light shall again and again rise for the righteous, and joy in the heart of the pious."[2] That applies to you. Hold fast to that. Do not deny the Word of God when it speaks to *you.* This much today in all haste. It is already late at night, and therefore I must now attempt to get some sleep.

Greet your dear daughter the bride, and assure her of my innermost wishes that the Lord would make her blessed and grant her salvation.

Your brother and fellow participant in the tribulation and in the kingdom and in the patience of Jesus Christ,

C. F. W. Walther

To Pastor J. G. Sauer

Concordia Seminary, St. Louis, Mo., June 19, 1881

My dear pastor,[1]

Several hours ago Professor Crull[2] and his family left here again for Ft. Wayne. Unfortunately his one surviving son was unable to find a cure for his illness here. The symptoms on the contrary became even more serious. His heavy speech, a result of nerve inflammation, became even heavier. Inability to focus the eyes, which is a frequent result of diphtheria, has also begun to afflict the boy. Professor Crull, for his part, instead of being able to recover and to recuperate here, rather became more run down than he was when he arrived.

These facts comprise the reason why I turn to you as a member and, if I am not mistaken, as the chairman of the [Ft. Wayne Concordia College] Board of Control. I must urgently beseech you as a matter of conscience that you and the other members of the Board of Control must object to the plan that Professor Crull should function till the close of the semester.

Our local Dr. Wislizency, an experienced and skilled physician, said that Professor Crull's son could only recover in a cooler climate, which is also the case in no less a way with the father. Now Pastor Adolph Biewend in Boston has a lovely little place on the seashore where Professor Crull would find everything necessary for himself and his family. I believe that the honorable Board of Control ought therefore to urge Professor Crull without delay to journey to Boston with his family to take advantage of this opportunity for recovery.

It would be irresponsible if the synod would not do everything which it could to save this lone surviving son for this faithful servant and that this faithful servant himself need not be offered up as a sacrifice. Of what benefit would it be for the synod if the professor would continue his classes till the middle of July if by doing this he would possibly go to ruin himself? What a burden rests on the heart of this poor man and how it gnaws on his vitality can well be imagined.

164

You will forgive my unsolicited imposition. But I know that you will forgive me, since you believe with me that love is the supreme commandment.

This matter now rests in your hands and in the hands of the whole Board of Control. And there it rests well. Do not let the excessive zeal of our precious Crull cause you to delay giving him a written prescription for this rest period.

Again, with a thousand thanks to you and your honored wife for the love you have shown me, and also for sending me the garment which I carelessly left behind at your place.

With heartfelt greetings to you and your wife,

Yours thankfully,
C. F. W. Walther

Notes

Walther in His Personal Letters

August 1833

1. Walther's older brother, Otto Hermann, was at that time serving as a private tutor in Kloesterlein, Germany. This is the oldest letter of Walther's extant. It was first put into English by the translator of this volume some years ago. This translation appeared in the CHI *Quarterly,* Winter 1957, pp. 178—80. Most of the original German can be found in Guenther, pp. 13—15, as can some other very early letters, on nearby pages.
2. Wilhelm may have been E. G. Wilhelm Keyl (1804—72), who was serving a congregation at Niederfrohna, Saxony, near the village where O. H. Walther was serving as tutor. He came to America in the Saxon emigration (1839) and was pastor in Missouri, Wisconsin, Maryland, and Ohio.
3. This name is illegible in the original, but seems to be Keyl. So Guenther reads it.

Aug. 10, 1841

1. This letter has been published in translation by W. G. Polack, *The Story of C. F. W. Walther* (St. Louis: Concordia Publishing House, 1947), pp. 138—42, and Carl S. Meyer, *Letters of C. F. W. Walther* (Philadelphia: Fortress Press, 1969), pp. 53—57. The earliest published translation was by the present translator, and appeared in *Alma Mater,* Feb. 10, 1943, p. 91. For Emilie Buenger's reply to Walther, see the translation by the translator of this volume, in CHI *Quarterly,* XVII (Jan. 1945) 106—107, or the translation in Polack's book, pp. 142—45.
2. (Christine) Emilie Buenger (1812—85) was the daughter of Rev. Jakob F. Buenger and his wife Christiane. The widowed Christiane Buenger and eight of her children emigrated in 1839, she and two of them landing in New York, while the other six, of whom Emilie was the oldest, went with the majority of the emigrants by way of New Orleans. At least one other child remained in Germany (see note 12 under Oct. 11, 1851, p. 168). For more on all this see Walter O. Forster, *Zion on the Mississippi* (St. Louis: Concordia Publishing House, 1953).
3. (Johann) Friedrich Buenger (1810—82), Emilie's older brother (who came via New York; see previous note), was a close friend of Walther already in their student days at the University of Leipzig. Buenger took an active part in building the log cabin seminary in Perry County, and in 1841 he came to St. Louis to assist his friend Walther by teaching in the parish school of Trinity Church. In 1844 Buenger was made assistant pastor, and in 1847 he took over the pastorate at one of Trinity's branches, Immanuel congregation. He was president of the Western District of the Missouri Synod 1863—75, was influential in beginning the Synodical Conference Negro missions, and founded Lutheran Hospital and the Orphans Home in St. Louis.
4. Emilie Buenger had been in Perry County during the first difficult years, when Walther and the other pastors and candidates struggled with their theology and with their consciences on the question of church and ministry. She also knew about the severe illness which afflicted Walther at that time.
5. Mrs. Christiane Buenger was living in St. Louis.
6. Walther is referring to Abraham's servant, who was sent to Nahor in Mesopotamia to negotiate for a wife for Isaac, and secured Rebekah, daughter of Bethuel. See Genesis 24.

7. Ernst Gerhard Wilhelm Keyl was married to Walther's sister Amalie Ernestine.
8. It was a carefully observed tradition in Lutheran churches to announce the marriage banns on several Sundays before the planned wedding.
9. Dr. Ernst Buenger was a younger brother of Emilie. Since he was not married at that time, Emilie kept house for him.
10. This was a younger sister of Emilie, who was also living with her brother.

Aug. 25, 1841

1. Although Emilie was now his fiancee, Walther throughout this letter addresses her with the formal "Sie."
2. Clementine Buenger was a younger sister of Emilie. She married a man named Neumueller.
3. Pastor E. G. W. Keyl in Frohna, Mo. On him see note 2 under August 1833, p. 167.
4. It is not known why the church in Frohna could not be considered. The Altenburg Debate had been held in the seminary building (the college) in April of that year, and the unpleasant memory of the sharp confrontation with Marbach and Vehse on the question of the church is what Walther is referring to.
5. Mr. Schubert was the courier for Walther, to deliver this letter to his fiancee.
6. Dr. Ernst Buenger, brother of Emilie. Lydia was still another sister of Emilie and Ernst.

Oct. 11, 1851

1. In 1851 Walther undertook his first trip back to Germany. The chief purpose of the journey was to try to reach doctrinal agreement with Pastor Wm. Loehe of Neuendettelsau, Bavaria. See note 8 below.
2. Franz Delitzsch (1813—90), famous Old Testament scholar, who was at this time a professor at the University of Erlangen.
3. Walther was traveling with Wyneken.
4. Heinrich Ernst Ferdinand Guericke (1803—78), confessional Lutheran pastor and theologian. In 1835 he was deposed from his professorship at Halle because he opposed the Prussian Union, but in 1840 was reinstated.
5. Mr. Rudloff has not been identified.
6. Francis Adolph Marbach (1798—1860), an attorney and lay leader of the Saxon immigration, had been Walther's chief opponent in the first period after the deposition of Stephan and in the Altenburg Debate. Marbach then returned to Germany.
7. Schneider has not been further identified. Karl Friedrich August Kahnis (1814—88) was a prominent Lutheran theologian and professor at Leipzig. Gerhard von Zezschwitz (1825—86) was a conservative Lutheran professor in later life. At the time Walther met him he was in his mid-twenties.
8. (Johann Konrad) Wilhelm Loehe (1808—72) was instrumental in sending many church workers to America. He held a more Romanizing view on the doctrine of the church than the Saxons did. Loehe was somewhere between Grabau and Walther on this doctrine.
9. The Doederleins were probably members of the church in St. Louis.
10. This is the town where Walther was born.
11. Walther's sister Constantine was married to an Engel.
12. Who these pastors were has not been further ascertained. Mrs. Walther's sister Emma Buenger, who did not come to America with the rest of that large family, was engaged to a Fuellkruss, probably the brother of the Rev. Fuellkruss mentioned below.
13. Walther uses the word *Vetter*, cousin. Actually this man was the brother of Walther's future brother-in-law.
14. Emma Buenger. See note 12 above.
15. Walther is referring to the Awakening of the 1830s there.
16. Another sister of Mrs. Walther. She had come to America and married Walther's brother Otto Hermann. After the latter's death she married Ottomar Fuerbringer.
17. Probably Constantine. See note 11 above.
18. Hermann Hasse has not been identified.

19. This book was *Die Stimme unserer Kirche in der Frage von Kirche und Amt. Eine Sammlung von Zeugnissen ueber diese Frage aus den Bekenntniszschriften der Evangelisch-lutherischen Kirche und aus den Privatschriften rechtglaeubiger Lehrer derselben. Von der deutschen evan.-luth. Synode von Missouri, Ohio und anderen Staaten als ein Zeugnisz ihres Glaubens, zur Abwehr der Angriffe des Herrn P. Grabau in Buffalo, New York, vorgelegt durch C. F. W. Walther,* Erlangen, 1852. See our volume *Walther on the Church.*
20. The University of Erlangen faculty is meant. In mid-century it was developing a mediating position in theology.
21. Theodor Brohm (1808—81), pastor in New York City at the time. See note 6 under May 2, 1860, p. 170.
22. It is possible this may have been the maid in the Walther household.

July 1, 1853

1. Franz Adolf Marbach (1798—1860), Saxon lawyer and government official, was one of the lay leaders of the Saxon immigration. He had been Walther's chief opponent in the Altenburg Debate, April 1841. He returned to Germany later in 1841.

Feb. 24, 1860

1. Walther was on his way to Europe for rest and recuperation from illness.
2. Johannes Walther (1840—97), the son of C. F. W. Walther's older deceased brother, O. H. Walther. O. H. Walther's widow married Ottomar Fuerbringer. Johannes Walther prepared for the ministry, and served congregations in Wyandotte, Mich., Johannisburg, N. Y., and others. He had chronic health problems, had to resign parishes several times on this account, and died at the age of 57.
3. Friedrich Schiller (1759—1805), the great German poet.
4. Friedrich Richter (1763—1825), known in history as Jean Paul, devoted his life to literature. He was called the poet of the poor and the author of the lowly.
5. Wandsbeck was a part of the city of Hamburg in Germany. From 1771 to 1775 Matthias Claudius (1740—1815) edited a newspaper owned by J. J. Ch. Bode there. Later Claudius, an author and literary figure in the *Sturm und Drang* period, came to be known as the "Wandsbecker Bote."
6. Johann Georg Hamann (1730—88), German writer whose works marked the transition into the romanticist period of German literature, the period of *Sturm und Drang.*
7. Johann Gottfried Herder (1744—1803), the romanticist German poet and scholar.

March 8, 1860

1. Friedrich Wyneken was president of Synod at the time.
2. Christoph Carl Metz (1831—68) was pastor at St. John congregation, New Orleans.
3. Albert Friedrich Hoppe (1828—1911), one of the leading Luther scholars in the Missouri Synod, and later the editor of the St. Louis Edition of Luther's works.
4. Walther had been very ill, and for this reason Friedrich Wyneken and Wilhelm Sihler intervened and arranged for Walther's congregation in St. Louis to give him time off to recuperate in Germany.
5. One can speculate that in addition to the reasons of health adduced by Walther, Wyneken refused a letter of introduction in his capacity of president of the Missouri Synod because the Prussian General Synod was not considered confessional enough by the Missouri Synod.
6. Stroebel has not been further identified.
7. Stephanus Keyl, Walther's nephew, worked for Walther while he was a seminary student. It had been decided that he would go along on the trip to Germany to look after his sick uncle. For more on Stephanus Keyl, see note 1 under Aug. 30, 1885, p. 173.
8. August Craemer (1812—91), president of the Ft. Wayne seminary. See also note 13 under May 10, 1849, p. 179.

9. Walther refers to the special meeting when Wyneken and Sihler, who was then president of Synod's Central District, came to St. Louis to discuss with Walther what to do about Walther's health.
10. Genesis 15:1 KJV.
11. These were three of the 13 Wyneken children. Henry and Martin were twins, born Dec. 15, 1844. Both entered the ministry, Martin becoming the first Lutheran pastor to work in Arkansas. He later was pastor in Cincinnati. Henry became a professor at the Springfield seminary. Martin died at age 39, and Henry at age 54.
12. See Psalm 128:3.
13. Gerhard Heinrich Jaebker (1821—77), whom Wyneken began to train for the ministry when he was pastor in Ft. Wayne before the mid-1840s.

May 2, 1860

1. Walther's son, 13 years of age at that time (born Feb. 23, 1847).
2. Constantin was Walther's other son, Ferdinand's twin brother.
3. Adolph Fr. Th. Biewend (1816—58), a professor in the preparatory department of the seminary in St. Louis, till his untimely death at age of 41.
4. This person has not been identified.
5. Robert Engel was Walther's nephew, the son of his sister Constantine. Engel was later a professor at the Ft. Wayne preparatory school.
6. Theodor Julius Brohm (1808—81), one of the original Saxon pastors. He helped found the Altenburg school in 1839. His first parish in America was Trinity, New York City. In 1858 he accepted a call to Holy Cross, St. Louis. He also helped teach at the seminary.
7. Heinicke was evidently a member of the St. Louis congregation.
8. Lenchen was Walther's oldest child, at that time 17 years of age.

May 17, 1864

1. Konrad Ludwig Moll (1839—97) was a Franconian from the Loehe colonies in Michigan. He was an 1864 seminary graduate, serving his first charge in Calumet, Cook County, Ill. Later he was called to the newly organized Immanuel Church on Detroit's west side, and by the time he ended his ministry there, a veritable cluster of new congregations had grown out of his work, Zion (founded 1882), Bethlehem (founded 1887), and Emmaus (founded 1889). Moll did win the hand of Fuerbringer's daughter Renata.
2. Mrs. Agnes Fuerbringer, nee Buenger. She was the sister of Walther's wife. She had previously been married to O. H. Walther, C. F. W. Walther's older brother, who died at an early age.
3. On Friedrich Brunn see note 1 under Feb. 21, 1872, p. 187.

Jan. 8, 1866

1. Julie was Walther's younger daughter, 16 years old at this time. She was apparently visiting her sister Magdalene and the latter's husband, Rev. Stephanus Keyl, who were then living in Philadelphia, Pa.
2. Emilie and Teddy were Keyl children.
3. Walther no doubt refers to the "theoretical" department of the seminary in St. Louis.
4. August C. Crull (1845—1923), graduate of the St. Louis seminary, was ordained and installed as Friedrich Lochner's assistant at Trinity, Milwaukee, in 1865, but he had a chronic throat ailment which forced him to resign in less than a year. Later he served with some distinction—though not without tensions—at Concordia College, Ft. Wayne, Ind.
5. Johann Georg Birkmann (1819—65) had served Holy Cross Church, Waterloo, Monroe County, Ill., since 1848.
6. Walther's older daughter, Magdalene.

Sept. 27, 1866

1. On Johannes Walther see note 1 under Feb. 24, 1860, p. 169.

2. Walther refers to the deep remorse which some of the Saxon immigrants felt after the deposition of Bishop Stephan, when they began to doubt the validity of their emigration. O. H. Walther was said to have labored under an especially heavy feeling of guilt.
3. The father of Johannes Walther, Otto Hermann Walther, had died in 1841. The widow married Ottomar Fuerbringer, to whom Walther makes reference here. On Ottomar Fuerbringer see note 2 under May 1841, p. 173.

April 18, 1867

1. Walther's daughter Magdalene was married to Stephanus Keyl, pastor of St. John's Church in Philadelphia, later immigrant missionary in New York. He was Walther's nephew, the son of Walther's sister. So Magdalene and Stephanus were first cousins.
2. The deletions are in the copy of the letter which was available to Ludwig Fuerbringer when he edited *Briefe von C. F. W. Walther* (St. Louis: Concordia Publishing House, 1915—16). This copy is the only version of this letter in the Walther file at Concordia Historical Institute. It is therefore impossible to check what has been omitted.

May 24, 1870

1. On Johannes Walther see note 2 under Feb. 24, 1860, p. 169.
2. It is not clear whether it was Kurt Heinrich Sprengeler, pastor of Immanuel, Carver Co., Minn., or his son, Heinrich F. Sprengeler, pastor in Elysian, Minn.
3. San Salvador church, Venedy, Ill., was the first Missouri Synod church in Washington County.
4. His actual father was long deceased. Walther here refers to Ottomar Fuerbringer, his stepfather.
5. Wilhelm Georg Carl Hattstaedt (1811—84) was pastor at Monroe, Mich. The son to whom Walther refers to was probably Freidrich Wilhelm (1849—73), who was then 20 years old.

Aug. 21, 1871

1. Stephanus Keyl, Walther's nephew and son-in-law, living in Port Richmond, Staten Island, N. Y. For more on him see note 1 under April 18, 1867, p. 171.
2. It has not been ascertained who Mr. Birkner or Mr. Saxer were. Friedrich Traugott Koerner (1845—1905) was a pastor in Brooklyn and was married to Marie Keyl, the sister of Stephanus.
3. On Friedrich Brunn see note 1 under Feb. 21, 1872, p. 187.
4. Magdalene, Walther's daughter, married to Stephanus Keyl.
5. Emma Mathilde was the Keyl baby, Walther's granddaughter. For her death see the letter of May 22, 1872.
6. This refers to Stephanus Keyl's parents, Rev. E. G. W. Keyl and his wife, who lived in Willshire, Van Wert Co., Ohio. See note 2 under August 1833, p. 167.
7. Ferdinand Walther in Brunswick, Mo., Walther's son. See the letter to him, p. 51.
8. Julie Niemann, Walther's younger daughter. See the letter to her, p. 37.
9. These were all people of the seminary and the church community. On Th. Brohm see note 6 under May 2, 1860, p. 170. Louis Lange was a well-known layman and publisher in St. Louis; Ernst August Brauer was professor at the seminary. For Eduard Preuss see note 2 under June 30, 1869, p. 187.

Dec. 13, 1871

1. Isaiah 1:18.
2. *The Lutheran Hymnal*, 347:6.
3. Martin Guenther (1831—93) came to America with the Saxon immigrants; he had become pastor in Saginaw, Mich., in 1860, and in 1872 he took the call to St. Matthew's in Chicago. In 1873 he became a professor at the St. Louis seminary.
4. Julie was Walther's younger daughter. The unsuccessful suitor referred to here has not been identified.

5. Julie married Rev. Johann Heinrich Niemann (1848—1910). He was pastor in Little Rock, Ark., and, beginning in 1876, in Cleveland, Ohio. He served as president of the Central District of the Missouri Synod 1880—1909.
6. F. A. Schmidt, see note 1, Jan. 9, 1866, p. 181.
7. Brunswick, Mo., was where Walther's son Ferdinand was pastor.

May 22, 1872

1. Pastor Keyl was scheduled to attend the synodical convention in St. Louis beginning April 26. See p. 127 of this volume. His family apparently stayed on in St. Louis after he returned to New York.
2. See Isaiah 55:8-9.
3. Acts 14:22.
4. Genesis 22:1-14.
5. *The Lutheran Hymnal,* 406:1.
6. Job 1:21.
7. John 14:27.

Jan. 15, 1873

1. Ferdinand, Walther's son in the ministry in Brunswick, Mo., was planning to marry Bertha Biltz, the daughter of Pastor and Mrs. Franz Julius Biltz, of Lafayette Co., Mo.
2. Constantin Walther was the twin brother of Ferdinand. He learned the milling trade.
3. Our placement of commas in this list is open to question. Most of these names have not been identified.
4. *The Lutheran Hymnal,* 261.
5. Carondelet, south of St. Louis, had developed as a separate municipality till it was incorporated with St. Louis in 1870. The seminary was in the 3600 block of South Jefferson Avenue, thus in the area which was being enhanced by this municipal growth.

Feb. 26, 1881

1. Ernst August Brauer (1819—96), pastor in Crete, Ill., at that time. In 1863 he had become the second professor at the St. Louis seminary. In 1878 he accepted a call to Trinity Church, Crete. This letter does not give the addressee, but the internal evidence shows that it is addressed to Rev. Brauer.
2. On Sept. 12, 1880, Walther had thanked him for a bottle of cherry wine. That letter is given in C. S. Meyer's *Walther Speaks to the Church,* p. 94.
3. Phrases like "evil matters," "miserable person sitting in shame," and "bitter life" probably refer to Walther's chagrin at being called a heretic during the predestinarian controversy, which was then at its height.
4. Walther gives this expression in both Latin and Greek, but not in German.
5. In Roman Catholic theology, under the topic of repentance and confession the subdivisions of *attritio, contritio,* and *satisfactio* are used. The words are used by Walther in Latin in this letter. The first word refers to the fear of God's punishment for sin, the second word refers to the sorrow of the sinner for having offended God, and the third word refers to the satisfaction which the sinner does to show his true repentance.
6. Walther gives this saying only in Latin.
7. Pastor Friedrich Pfotenhauer (1859—1939), who served as president of The Lutheran Church—Missouri Synod 1911—35, married Helene Brauer. See CHI *Quarterly,* X (April 1940), 10—11.
8. Rev. Wilhelm Huebner was pastor at St. Trinitatis Church, Dresden, Saxony, Germany.
9. Ludwig Fuerbringer, in annotating Walther's letters, supplied the information that this was Rev. Hein.
10. During the predestinarian controversy, then raging, F. A. Schmidt of the Norwegian Synod in America was a caustic critic of Walther.
11. *Lehre und Wehre,* Vol. XVIII (1872), had been running an article by Walther on the question whether it was really Lutheran doctrine that the salvation of man in the final

172

analysis was his own decision. The article had six installments, in the later part of the year.

April 9, 1884

1. Walther's son Ferdinand was married to the daughter of Pastor Julius Biltz.
2. Julie and Magdalene were Walther's two daughters.

Aug. 30, 1885

1. Stephanus Keyl was married to Magdalene, Walther's older daughter. He was immigrant missionary in New York. Another translation of this letter is found in C. S. Meyer's *Letters of C. F. W. Walther: A Selection*, pp. 139—43.
2. Walther's son Ferdinand was pastor in Brunswick, Benton County, Mo.
3. It is not certain who this Mrs. Lange was, possibly the wife of Louis Lange the publisher.
4. Mrs. Tschirpe was the widow of August B. Tschirpe, who had been a druggist in St. Louis and a member of the Board of Control of the seminary from 1849 till his death in 1861.
5. The widow of J. F. Buenger was Johanna Sophie nee Reiszner. Buenger, who had died on Jan. 23, 1882, was Mrs. Walther's brother.
6. The maid in the Walther household.
7. Georg Stoeckhardt (1842—1913) was at that time pastor of Holy Cross congregation, St. Louis. He later became a professor at Concordia Seminary.
8. Walther's younger daughter, married to Rev. J. H. Niemann, at this time pastor in Cleveland, Ohio, and president of the Central District of the Missouri Synod.
9. Ferdinand and Constantin were the two Walther sons.
10. Magdalene, Walther's older daughter, married to the addressee of this letter.

Walther as *Seelsorger,* Pastor of Congregations

[May 1841]

1. Friedrich Sproede was a lay leader with the Saxon immigration. In the first year or two after the settlement in Perry County, he and C. F. W. Walther had some sharp clashes. In the Wadewitz transcriptions, this letter is bound with other letters of Walther which are dated from the 1870s. The internal evidence indicates that this letter was written sometime in late April or May 1841, since Walther says he had been in St. Louis "a few weeks." He went to St. Louis soon after the Altenburg Debate, which concluded on April 21, 1841.
2. Ottomar Fuerbringer (1810—92) was a candidate of theology when the Saxons came to Missouri, helped found the log cabin seminary in Perry County, and in 1840 became pastor of San Salvador congregation, Venedy, Ill. Beginning in 1851 he was pastor in Freistadt and Kirchhayn, Wis., and from 1858 to 1892 in Frankenmuth, Mich. He was president of the Northern District of the Missouri Synod 1854—72 and 1875—82. He married Agnes nee Buenger, the widow of Walther's older brother Otto Hermann.
3. Gottlieb Kluegel was a candidate of theology who had come to Missouri with the Saxons.
4. When C. F. W. Walther's older brother, Otto Hermann Walther, pastor of Trinity congregation, St. Louis, died in Jan. 1841, the congregation called C. F. W. Walther to become their pastor.
5. On Friedrich Buenger see note 3 under Aug. 10, 1841, p. 167.

Aug. 20, 1842

1. Wege is usually called by the honorific *Magister* (Master) Wege, which is the reason for the "M" here. Emil Julius Moritz Wege (1801—70) was from Silesia, became the pioneer missionary pastor in Benton, Morgan, and Pettis Counties, Mo. German families, mostly from Hanover, had settled there. Wege's work centered on Cole Camp. After about 14 years there, he accepted a new challenge in Cole County and around Jefferson City. He had major disappointments there.
2. This contains a section on the call of God as it comes through men, in a sermon which

Luther preached in the 1520s on Exodus. Walther used the Walch edition, edited by Johann Georg Walch in the mid-18th century.
3. This contains Luther's *Die Deutsche Messe,* Walch edition.
4. This is E. G. W. Keyl, at that time still in Perry County. On him see note 2 under August 1833, p. 167. Wege was there at the time, assisting with the teaching in the parish school in Frohna.
5. Graf Detlev von Einsiedel, royal counsel in Saxony.
6. Georg Albert Schieferdecker (1815—91), one of the candidates of theology who had come with the Saxons. In 1841 he founded St. Paul's congregation, Columbia, Ill.
7. Andreas Gottlob Rudelbach (1792—1862), confessional German Lutheran theologian, opponent of the Union of Lutheran and Reformed in the various provinces and kingdoms of Germany. He was critical of state churchism, a man of vast erudition and a very successful preacher.
8. The original manuscript is illegible here.

Aug. 30, 1842
1. This letter, according to internal evidence is addressed to people in Benton County, Mo., who had requested a pastor.
2. On Wege, see note 1 under Aug. 20, 1842, p. 173.

Jan. 19, 1846
1. The internal evidence indicates that this letter may well have been written to Rev. Leberecht Friedrich Ehregott Krause and his congregation in Wisconsin. See note 23 under Jan. 2, 1845, p. 178.
2. Pietism was a movement in Lutheranism, beginning with the publication of Spener's (see note 14 below) *Pia Desideria* in 1657. It stressed a conversion experience, heartfelt religion, and the shunning of worldly amusements.
3. Johann Arndt (1555—1621), known as the forerunner of German pietism, famous for his devotional writings in a mystical vein. Walther consistently left off the final "t" in the name.
4. Heinrich Mueller (1631—75), German devotional writer and hymnodist.
5. Christian Scriver (1629—93), German Lutheran pastor, preacher, and hymn writer.
6. Karl Heinrich von Bogatzki (1690—1774) lived in Halle, where he wrote devotional literature and hymns. "Awake, Thou Spirit Who Didst Fire" (*The Lutheran Hymnal,* 494) is by him.
7. Johann Anastasius Freylinghausen (1670—1739), German theologian who succeeded Francke as superintendent of the academy in Halle in 1727. He was one of the best-known hymnodists of pietism.
8. Johann Porst (1668—1728), pietist hymn writer.
9. Johann Caspar Schade (1666—98), pietist who worked with Spener in Berlin.
10. Joachim Lange (1670—1744), professor at Halle, prolific pietist author, one of the active polemicists against the theologians of Lutheran orthodoxy.
11. It is not clear whether Walther is referring to Heinrich Nikolaus Gerber (1702—75), German Lutheran composer, or to his son Ernst Ludwig Gerber (1746—1819), musicologist.
12. Johann Philipp Fresenius (1705—61), Lutheran clergyman, well-known churchman in the moderate pietistic tradition.
13. In his student days Walther had come under strong pietist influence and had been very unsure of his salvation. He wrote for comfort to Martin Stephan (1777—1846), who later became the leader of the Saxon emigration. When Stephan's comforting letter arrived, Walther did not open it until he had prayed that the Lord would preserve him from "false comfort."
14. Philipp Jacob Spener (1635—1705), the "father of pietism." He helped establish the University of Halle, Germany, in 1694, which became a great center of pietism.
15. August Hermann Francke (1663—1727) was a professor at Halle. He established

charitable institutions there and was influential in sending out missionaries, particularly to India.

16. Watertown, Wis. A colony of Lutheran immigrants had settled there who had come to America in 1843 under Rev. Adolf Kindermann. He was not able to serve them, for it was about 40 miles from Kirchhayn, where his main congregation was located some 25 miles northwest of Milwaukee. Therefore the people in Watertown asked the Saxons in Missouri to send one of their unemployed candidates of theology. Thus Karl Ludwig Geyer (1812—92) became the pastor there, the first Saxon to work in Wisconsin.

March 19, 1849

1. This unidentified German churchman was probably someone associated with Loehe.
2. *Der Lutheraner* was the church paper which Walther began publishing in 1844. It appeared uninterruptedly until 1974, which may be a record among publications of any sort.
3. This man has not been identified.
4. Friedrich Hecker (1811—81), a German politician and statesman who had been the leader of the 1848 revolution in Baden. With many other so-called '48ers he came to America when the revolution failed. In Belleville, St. Clair County, Ill., there was a settlement of these German political activists, including such well-known men as Gustav Koerner. In 1849 Hecker joined them. He was also very much the political activist, running on the same Republican ticket in 1856 with Abraham Lincoln. There was no love lost between confessional Lutherans such as Walther and the '48ers. Wadewitz read "Hoper" here, but it should obviously be "Hecker."
5. Walther was at the time president of Synod, president of Concordia Seminary, and pastor of Trinity Church in St. Louis.

April 19, 1849

1. Wilhelm Sihler was pastor in Ft. Wayne, Ind. and vice-president of Synod. From 1854 to 1860 he was president of Synod's Central District. He also served as president and professor of the "practical seminary" in Ft. Wayne.
2. This is the Belleville area, where a considerable settlement of Germans was developing.
3. *Lichtfreunde* is the term applied to an association of "enlightened" Germans who were rationalistic in religion and activistic to the point of being revolutionary in politics. Many of them were disappointed revolutionaries from the 1848 uprising in Europe.
4. F. W. Poeschke was received into the Missouri Synod and its ministry at the first convention of 1847. Because of conduct unbefitting to a pastor, Walther, president of Synod, suspended him the next year. Synod confirmed the action in the 1849 convention.
5. Adolf Kindermann was pastor of the Buffalo Synod congregation in Kirchhayn, Wis.
6. Where Sihler's article appeared is not clear. It does not seem to have been published in *Der Lutheraner.*
7. August Wolter was a professor at the Ft. Wayne seminary. He died Aug. 31, 1849 of cholera. His article appeared in *Der Lutheraner,* V (Nov. 14, 1848), 41—44, and was entitled *Luegenhaftigkeit der kathol. Kirchen Zeitung in Baltimore.*

Feb. 11, 1856

1. The addressee is not stated. The "far north" may well have been Canada. Ludwig Fuerbringer added the note on the manuscript that this letter is from the papers of C. A. Mennicke.
2. Hugo Hanser, who graduated from the St. Louis seminary that year, was posted to a congregation in Canada upon graduation, then served in Johannisburg, N. Y., and later in Baltimore.

Sept. 30, 1860

1. Jacob Matthias Buehler (1837—1901), the first Missouri Synod pastor in California, began his ministry in San Francisco in 1860.

2. *The Lutheran Hymnal,* 520:5.
3. *The Lutheran Hymnal,* 385:1.
4. Here again, Walther quotes a hymn verse.
5. Psalm 77:10 KJV.
6. Walther has just returned from his trip to Germany to recuperate from illness.

Sept. 16, 1861

1. Kaspar Schwenkfeld, contemporary of Martin Luther and a leader of the radical reformation.
2. C. A. T. Selle, pastor in Crete, Will County, Ill., had obviously evaluated the work of F. A. Ahner (1835—1907), who had finished the St. Louis seminary in 1856 and then served in Rock Island for five years before he was called to Grafton and Cedarburg, Wis., in 1863.

July 26, 1867

1. Johann List (1836—1915), had begun his ministry in New Orleans in 1860, but became ill there. He then accepted a parish in Town Sherman, Sheboygan County, Wis.
2. Private confession for Communion is to be distinguished from Communion announcements. Confessional Lutherans attempted to reinstitute the use of private confession, an old salutary custom which had largely died out in Germany. Many parishioners therefore were not used to it, or they considered it as being too Roman Catholic. Thus there was a great amount of resistance to the reintroduction of this usage.
3. This was in a continued series which Walther had been running in *Lehre und Wehre,* entitled "Materialien zur Pastoral Theologie," XII (Oct. 1866), 288—97, continued (Nov. and Dec.), 321—24.
4. Theodor Gustav Adolph Krumsieg (1836—1900) was pastor at St. Johannis congregation, Town Auburn, Fond du Lac Co., Wis., at the time.

Dec. 11, 1867

1. On Johannes Walther, see note 2 under Feb. 24, 1860, p. 169.
2. Johannisburg, N. Y., near Buffalo.
3. It is not certain whether Walther is referring to C. J. Otto Hanser or to his brother Hugo Hanser.
4. F. Theodore Miessler (1841—1928), younger brother of the missionary Ernst Gustav Herman Miessler, and twin brother of Bruno Ernst Miessler, was pastor in Cole Camp, Benton Co., Mo.
5. Wyandotte, Mich., where Johannes Walther was pastor.
6. Carl Gross (1834—1906) served his first charge in Richmond, Va., and in 1867, just before Walther wrote this letter, accepted a call to Trinity, Buffalo, N.Y.
7. Wadewitz reads Weimach here, but I believe Weinbach is the correct reading. Johannes Wilhelm Weinbach was a former Buffalo Synod pastor and the stepson of Christian Hochstetter. After the 1866 colloquy Weinbach was deposed by his Buffalo Synod congregation in New Wallmow, whereupon he accepted the charge in Bergholz, not far from there.

April 10, 1868

1. The Canada Synod had been organized in 1861, the first elements of it consisting of Lutherans who had moved into Canada from upper New York State. Walther here is referring to the church polity by which synods tried to tie congregations to themselves by having the synod hold church property deeds.

July 21, 1876

1. Kirchhayn, Wis., was the place where a second large group of German Lutheran immigrants had settled in 1843, almost four years after the earlier settlement at Freistadt. It is about four miles northwest of Freistadt. At first the people in Kirchhayn were unified

176

in one congregation belonging to the Buffalo Synod, but when the tensions with Krause developed a few years after Kirchhayn had been founded, they spilled over to those people also. The congregation split into three parts. The Buffalo Synod congregation was St. John's. The smallest part in the split was comprised of the people who joined the Missouri Synod. This congregation is Immanuel. The largest part of the immigrants formed David Star Church, which eventually joined the Wisconsin Synod. The Missouri Synod congregation was beset by many problems, and synodical officials were quite frustrated with the intransigent members there. The pastor at the time was Johann Heinrich Meyer. He held the pastorate there from 1872 to 1876.

2. Sihler found out for himself how bad the situation was. After the visitation he remarked that he had never seen such belligerent Lutherans. One member of the church had called a nonmember a *Hurenbok*, a fornicator. The whole congregation was up in arms as to whether this was not unchristian. The issue was not whether the labeling of the nonmember was accurate or not. The issue was litigated up to the district president, who ruled that it was not improper for a church member to call a nonmember who was a fornicator such a name.

Jan. 13, 1878

1. Article VIII of the Augsburg Confession states that the official acts of an unworthy pastor are nevertheless valid.

Walther as Churchman: Administration of Synod and Interchurch Relationships

Jan. 2, 1845

1. On Sihler see note 1 under April 19, 1849, p. 175. Large sections of this letter can be found in translation in C. S. Meyer's *Walther Speaks to the Church*, pp. 15—17.
2. Adam Ernst, one of the two first missionaries sent by Wilhelm Loehe to work in America, arriving in 1842. He first taught school in Columbus, Ohio, but in the summer of 1843 took a pastorate in Marysville, Union Co, Ohio, 30 miles northwest of Columbus. Ernst called the town Neuendettelsau after Loehe's hometown in Bavaria.
3. (Johann) Friedrich Buenger, the older brother of Walther's wife, one of the Saxon candidates of theology, who was helping Walther in St. Louis both by teaching school and in the parish ministry. For more on him see note 3 under Aug. 10, 1841, p. 167.
4. Wittenberg, Perry Co., Mo., is the town on the river where the Saxons first landed.
5. Altenburg and Frohna were Saxon settlements in Perry County which flourished and developed vigorous churches. Dresden did not flourish, and before long was remembered only as a name.
6. Gotthold Heinrich Loeber (1797—1849) was the oldest of the Saxon pastors.
7. J. F. Winter was a teacher.
8. Ernst Moritz Buerger was one of the Saxon candidates of theology. When he wanted to return to Germany because he was convinced the church did not exist among the Saxons after Bishop Stephan's dismissal, he traveled to Buffalo, N. Y., to see some relatives. Just at that time some of Rev. J. A. A. Grabau's people were forming a new congregation there in protest against Grabau's authoritarian ministry, and Buerger was persuaded to remain in America and take over that congregation. In the tensions with Grabau and the Buffalo Synod, Buerger's name therefore comes up frequently.
9. Johannes Andreas August Grabau (1804—79) led a group of Prussian Lutherans to America in 1839. He founded the Buffalo Synod, with which the Missouri Synod had a long controversy, principally over the matter of clerical domination. Grabau feared "mob rule" if the laity were given a strong voice in church government.
10. The congregation which Buerger pastored in Buffalo was Trinity.
11. E. G. W. Keyl was one of the Saxon pastors. For more on him see note 2 under August 1833, p. 167.

12. Theodor Carl Friedrich Gruber was one of the Saxon pastors.
13. Those Saxons who settled in St. Louis founded Old Trinity, of which O. H. Walther, older brother of C. F. W. Walther, was pastor till his death in 1841. Thereupon the congregation called the younger of the brothers, who then served them till his death in 1887.
14. Theodor Ernst Buenger, a younger brother of Walther's wife. He was an accomplished musician and teacher. See note 1 under May 7, 1861, p. 190.
15. The school which now Concordia Seminary, St. Louis, was founded in 1839 in Perry County.
16. Johann Jacob Goenner was one of the Saxon candidates.
17. On Ottomar Fuerbringer see note 2 under May 1841, p. 173.
18. Georg Albert Schieferdecker (1815--91), one of the Saxon candidates, at that time pastor of the congregations in Columbia and Waterloo, Ill. He later had to leave the Missouri Synod because of his millennialism but eventually renounced millennialism and returned to the Missouri Synod.
19. Ottomar Fuerbringer, was pastor of the congregation at Elkhorn Prairie (now Venedy), Washington County, Ill.
20. Emil Julius Moritz Wege, usually called *Magister* (Master) Wege, Saxon candidate who took over a mission field on the frontier in Benton Co., Mo.
21. Ludwig Geyer, one of the Saxon candidates, was the first of their number to serve in Wisconsin. When Pastor Adolf Kindermann arrived in Wisconsin from Germany in 1843, a substantial portion of his members settled in Kirchhayn. Kindermann suggested that possibly one of the Saxons could serve the Watertown group, and thus Geyer became pastor there.
22. The *Hirtenbrief* was a pastoral letter which Rev. J. A. A. Grabau had written in 1840 to hold those people, especially in Wisconsin, in check who, because they had no ordained pastor in their settlements, were going to have laymen administer church rites and sacraments. Critiques and counter critiques of this letter, with the original document, were published by the Saxons in Missouri as *Der Hirtenbrief des Herrn Pastors Grabau zu Buffalo vom Jahre 1840, nebst den zwischen ihm und mehreren lutherischen Pastoren von Missouri gewechselten Schriften.* New York: H. Ludwig & Co., 1849.
23. Heinrich Karl Georg von Rohr, military officer who had come with the Prussian immigration, was at first the lay leader of the group which went to Wisconsin in 1839. Before long he took up theological studies at Martin Luther Seminary, Buffalo, N.Y., which J. A. A. Grabau had founded, and became a pastor in the Buffalo Synod, founded 1845. Leberecht Friedrich Ehregott Krause was a Silesian, and the first Lutheran pastor to work in Wisconsin. He was affiliated with Grabau in the Buffalo Synod. The Buffalo Synod, in fact, was founded in his parish in Freistadt and Milwaukee, Wis. Before long, however, Krause was to have a falling out with Grabau. For Kindermann see note 21 above.
24. By Evangelicals are meant those German Protestants who did not have the high level of confessional Lutheranism that others like the Saxons had who had come through the anti-rationalistic Awakening in Germany. Without strong confessional consciousness, many German Protestants were willing to gloss over the doctrinal distinctions between Lutheran and Reformed churches, and therefore they preferred the term *evangelisch*, or "evangelical," which in this context has a totally different meaning that it does in American church circles in the 20th century. Since the Evangelicals advocated union with the Reformed, they are also called *Unirte*, a word difficult to translate, but which must be rendered as "United" at times.
25. This refers to the projected conference which Grabau and his men were planning for 1845, which became the organizing convention of the Buffalo Synod.

May 10, 1849

1. On Wilhelm Sihler see note 1 under April 19, 1849, p. 175.

2. C. L. August Wolter (1818—49), who died about three months after Walther wrote this letter, a victim of cholera.
3. C. H. Siegmund Buttermann (1819—49), pastor in Chester, Randolph County, Ill., only a few months before he died of cholera. He had probably not even seen his article against Church Union in print, which came out in *Der Lutheraner*, V, 23 (issue of July 10, 1849), p. 182, since he died on July 12.
4. "Unionistic faith" refers to the attitude which accepted or at least tolerated the union of Lutherans and Reformed, such as was being enforced in the Prussian state church, for example. This movement preferred the term "evangelical" to "Lutheran," and in America was represented by a fairly strong and persistent tendency which produced several church bodies with the word "Evangelisch" prominent in the official name.
5. Carl J. A. Strasen, pastor in Collinsville at the time.
6. Carl Heinrich Gottlieb Schliepsick was posted to Neubielefeld, St. Charles County, Mo., at the end of 1848. By 1850 he was in Madison County, Ill.
7. Friedrich Lochner was pastor of Holy Cross, Collinsville, Madison County, Ill.
8. Town Eden, just outside Buffalo, N. Y., was an important out-post for the Missouri Synod at the time, since this was a point of confrontation with the Buffalo Synod. In 1849 the congregation there was received into synodical membership.
9. E. G. W. Keyl was pastor of the historic congregation in Milwaukee and Freistadt, Wis., at the time. For more on him see note 2 under August 1833, p. 167.
10. Heinrich Ludwig Dulitz had come from Germany in the summer of 1847. Walther's disappointment with Dulitz proved to be premature. Dulitz was at first taken aback by the coldness and contentiousness of the Lutherans in America, especially in Wisconsin. But he soon worked into the pastorate at St. John's congregation in Milwaukee, and later served in a very critical post in Buffalo, N. Y., with a very fine record.
11. Johann Nickolaus Volkert, trained by Loehe, had come to America in 1847, was examined and admitted to the ministry in 1849. His first charge was in Calumet, Wis. By 1860 he was out of the ministry because of personal moral deficiencies.
12. On Brohm see note 6 under May 2, 1860, p. 170.
13. August Craemer was the founding pastor of the church in Frankenmuth, Mich., and was soon to be called to the seminary in Ft. Wayne.
14. Ernst Moritz Buerger (1806—90), pastor in Buffalo, N. Y.
15. Friedrich Lochner, pastor in Collinsville, Madison County, Ill; C. J. Hermann Fick, pastor in Neu-Melle, St. Charles County, Mo.; Georg Schieferdecker, pastor in Centreville, St. Clair County, Ill.; F. J. Biltz, pastor in Dissen, Cape Girardeau County, Mo. On Strasen see note 5 above.
16. Ludwig Fuerbringer adds a note that Walther was, after all, able to come to the convention, although only from the fifth session on.

June 5, 1852

1. A good part of this letter can be found in C. S. Meyer's *Walther Speaks to the Church*, pp. 25—26. On Loehe see note 8 under Oct. 11, 1851, p. 168.
2. Friedrich Konrad Dietrich Wyneken (1810—76), German Lutheran missionary to America, who arrived in 1838. He was directly responsible for arousing the concern of Wilhelm Loehe of Bavaria about the needs of the German immigrants on the American frontier. He was a traveling missionary in Ohio and Indiana, pastor in Ft. Wayne, Baltimore, St. Louis, and Cleveland, and served as president of the Missouri Synod 1850—64.
3. Back in St. Louis. On Walther's trip to Germany see the letter on p. 18.
4. To achieve agreement with Loehe was the chief purpose of Walther's trip. Unfortunately, the understanding they reached did not last long.
5. The Ohio Synod was organized in 1818 by pastors who had migrated into Ohio from Pennsylvania. Some of the Loehe missionaries first were associated with this synod, but they soon severed their connections to begin negotiations with the Saxons in Missouri for

a new more German and more confessional synod, which led to the organizing of the Missouri Synod in 1847. By the latter 1860s the two synods drew very close together, but the predestinarian controversy of the early 1880s split them apart again.

6. Columbus, Ohio, was the location of the Ohio Synod seminary.
7. J. A. A. Grabau; see note 9 under Jan. 2, 1845, p. 177, also notes 22 and 23 under the same date.
8. Wilhelm Loehe had plans to establish a normal school for training parochial school teachers somewhere in Michigan.
9. Johann Michael Gottlieb Schaller (1819—87), graduate of the University of Leipzig in theology and a Loehe missionary, came to America in 1848, joined the Missouri Synod the next year. He held important pastorates in Detroit and St. Louis, and from 1872 to 1886 was professor at Concordia Seminary, St. Louis.
10. This is a reference to the Loehe colonies in Michigan, the first of which was Frankenmuth.
11. It is not known what happened to Siekelmann.
12. Philip Fleischmann (1815—68), a Loehe missionary who was to work in California missions in 1853. But, for reasons unknown, he was diverted from this and worked in New York, Milwaukee, and Kendallville, Ind. It is not known what happened to Pruotti.
13. The reference is probably to Christian Frederick von Boeckh (1795—1875), pastor in Nuernberg.
14. Walther is referring to the north wing of the seminary, built in 1852.
15. These men have not been identified.
16. On Brohm see note 6 under May 2, 1860, p. 170.

June 10, 1852

1. Ottomar Fuerbringer, pastor of Trinity, Freistadt, Wis., north of Milwaukee, had married the widow of Walther's brother. For more on him see note 2 under May 1841, p. 173.

March 17, 1855

1. This letter is apparently addressed to one of the Wends in Texas, possibly Pastor Johann Kilian (1811—84), who led a group of Wends to Texas in 1854.
2. Those who favor church union without doctrinal agreement, especially between Lutherans and Reformed.
3. Followers of the Swedish scientist, philosopher, and mystic Emanuel Swedenborg (1688—1772), the Church of the New Jerusalem.
4. *Lehre und Wehre,* the German theological journal launched by Walther in 1855.
5. Johann Friedrich Buenger (1810—82) was the older brother of Walther's wife. For more on him see note 3 under Aug. 10, 1841, p. 167.
6. This would no doubt include the *Hirtenbrief,* see note 22 under Jan. 2, 1845, p. 178.
7. This is the report of the Buffalo Synod convention of 1848.
8. Walther refers to orders of worship or liturgical forms as well as organizational documents such as constitutions which reflect the polity of a church.
9. Walther was president of Concordia Seminary besides serving as pastor of Trinity, St. Louis.
10. Christoph Carl Metz (1831—86), pastor in New Orleans 1854—67.
11. Wilhelm August Fick (1825—55), who died of yellow fever about five months after Walther wrote this letter. His brothers Hermann and Carl also were pastors in the LCMS.
12. The University of Goettingen, Germany, was considered by conservative Lutherans in America as being decidedly liberal in theology, although at the very time Walther was making this comment the faculty at Goettingen was making a public attempt to prove its orthodoxy in a defense drawn up by Isaac Dorner. But Johann David Michaelis, Johann Gottfried Eichhorn, and other higher critical theologians had been professors there, which

went far in persuading the confessional Lutherans that Goettingen theology was decidedly left of center.

Jan. 25, 1861

1. Friedrich Wilhelm Tobias Steimle (1827—80), born in Wuerttemberg, prepard for mission work in the Basel mission seminary. In 1851 he arrived in New York. He became a member of the New York Ministerium, the second-oldest Lutheran synod founded in America, dating back to 1786. Theological tensions dealing with the inadequate confessional position of the General Synod, of which the New York Ministerium was a member, disturbed a number of pastors, leading in 1866 to the formation of the German New York Synod, of which Steimle served as president. This movement combined a return to confessionalism with a strong tendency to authoritarian church polity and a preference for German culture in contrast to tolerating the gradual switch to English. After six years of existence, most of the members of the German New York Synod again rejoined the New York Ministerium, but not Steimle. It is worth noting that at least one of Steimle's associates joined the Buffalo Synod, which also had an authoritarian church polity.
2. Jeremiah 7:4.
3. The Roman Catholic doctrine that the sacraments confer grace by the act itself, apart from faith.
4. Cf. Nehemiah 4:16-18.

July 8, 1865

1. On Ottomar Fuerbringer see note 2 under May 1841, p. 173.
2. Fuerbringer had been an instructor in an institute for boys in Eichenberg, Germany, 1831—38.

July 17, 1865

1. Friedrich Dietz had been a pastor near Ft. Wayne but accepted an offer to join the Iowa Synod in 1856 and took the pastorate in St. Sebald, Iowa. Soon he was transferred to St. John's Church in Dubuque, where he served seven years.
2. Walther probably had the brothers Siegmund and Gottfried Fritschel in mind, both professors at the Iowa Synod seminary in Dubuque.
3. Paul Bredow had succeeded Dietz as pastor of St. John's Church in Dubuque in 1864.

Jan. 9, 1866

1. This letter was very likely written to Friedrich August Schmidt (1837—1928), who was professor at the Norwegian Synod's Luther College, Decorah, Iowa, 1861—72 and was one of the pioneers in promoting English work in the Missouri Synod. He later became one of Walther's chief opponents in the predestinarian controversy.
2. Lohmann has not been identified.
3. F. A. Schmidt had launched a modest English publishing project in a magazine he called *Lutheran Watchman.*
4. Walther is probably referring to Rev. H. Wetzel, who was at one time the pastor of Mt. Calvary, near Woodstock, Va., in the Ohio Synod, and served as the president of the Concordia English District.
5. Samuel Kistler Brobst (1822—76) was a pastor in the Pennsylvania Ministerium and the publisher of *Lutherischer Kalender.*
6. Johann Georg Birkmann (1819—65), pastor at Waterloo, Monroe County, Ill., died of tuberculosis on Dec. 28, 1865.
7. This man has not been identified.
8. The Wadewitz transcription reads Muckley. The original of this letter was not available, for the CHI Walther files contain only a copy which is written in English script. I conjecture that the person who copied the letter misread the name and it should read

Muckel. Leonhard Muckel (1835–70) was pastor at Staunton, Macoupin County, Ill., at this time.

9. Georg Reinsch was a Loehe missionary who worked for the Iowa Synod but in 1865 joined the Missouri Synod. He was sent to Milwaukee to work as assistant to Friedrich Lochner, who was pastor of Trinity. They were developing a new mission station which soon organized as Immanuel congregation, of which Reinsch then became pastor. August Crull, who preceded Reinsch as Lochner's assistant, developed throat trouble and needed to be relieved of official duties for a time. For more on Crull see note 4 under Jan. 8, 1866, p. 170.

10. Henry Craemer was the son of August Craemer, president of the practical seminary, at that time in St. Louis, later in Springfield, Ill.

11. Robert Engel was the son of Walther's sister Constantine.

12. Peter Laurentius Larsen (1833–1915), a Norwegian Synod professor, had taught at the St. Louis seminary 1859–61. When the Norwegian Synod opened Luther College in La Crosse County, Wis., in 1861, Larsen was posted there. F. A. Schmidt joined him there that year. In the following year that school was moved to Decorah, Iowa.

13. My conjecture is that Walther had in mind Nils Olsen Brandt (1824–1921), one of the first Norwegian Lutheran pastors in Wisconsin and Iowa. In 1851 he had come to America, held several pastorates in Norwegian congregations in Wisconsin, was a traveling missionary, and also a professor at Luther College.

14. Walther is probably referring to G. E. Chr. Ferdinand Sievers (1816–93), the father of missions in the Missouri Synod.

May 15, 1866

1. Heinrich Christian Schwan (1819–1905), pastor in Cleveland, was at this time president of the Central District of the Missouri Synod. He served as president of the whole synod from 1878 to 1899. In the early years of his ministry he became well known for popularizing the use of a Christmas tree in church. In his later years he prepared the well-known Schwan catechism.

2. Heinrich Craemer, the son of August Craemer, professor at the practical seminary.

3. Friedrich Buenger was president of the Western District, which at that time still included Illinois. For more on him see note 3 under Aug. 10, 1841, p. 167.

4. Walther's advice was followed, and the young Craemer remained in Cleveland.

5. For Wyneken see note 2 under June 5, 1852, p. 179.

6. Wilhelm H. Lothmann (1845–1931) was installed in his first charge in Valley City, also called Liverpool, Ohio, on Aug. 19, 1866.

7. Philip Fleischmann had been in charge of the teacher training program in Ft. Wayne till 1864, when J. C. W. Lindemann was called to head this program. Fleischmann had trouble with his eyes and for that reason had to get out of teaching. He took a call to Marion Township, Adams County, Ind.

8. Heinrich Moritz Hamann (1835–68), pastor in Carondelet, Mo., south of St. Louis, from Oct. 1862 on. He became very ill and decided to return to Germany, where he died.

9. Richard H. Biedermann (1837–1909) finished his studies at the practical seminary in 1862. Within a year he took his second parish, in New Wells, Cape Girardeau County, Mo, and in March 1866 he took the call to St. Jacobi congregation on the White Water, Cape Girardeau County, Mo. Before a summer was over, he was pastor in St. Clair, Mich., but in three years was back in his first charge at New Wells.

10. Ferdinand Doederlein (1834–1915) was a Loehe missionary who worked among the Indians in the northwestern states for a while, then located in southeastern Missouri. His friend Otto Hanser induced him to join the Missouri Synod. He was the father of Dr. Theodore Doederlein, Missouri Synod medical missionary to India.

11. Ludwig Fuerbringer, in editing Walther's letters for the two-volume edition published 1915–16, edited out the name here. What Walther wrote was "Fuerbringer," meaning Ottomar, the father of Ludwig. Ottomar Fuerbringer was a district president who did not like to travel or attend meetings.

182

12. Charles Porterfield Krauth (1823—83), well-known scholar, writer, pastor, and professor in the General Council.

Jan. 16, 1867

1. The preparatory department of the St. Louis seminary had been moved to Ft. Wayne in 1861, when the Ft. Wayne "Practical" seminary was moved to St. Louis.
2. F. A. Schmidt was a graduate of the St. Louis seminary, and was of German extraction, but he had learned Norwegian (as also English) and could preach and lecture in both of these languages. He was a professor at Luther College, a school of the Norwegian Synod.
3. The organizing meeting of the General Council had taken place Dec. 12-14, 1866 in Reading, Pa.
4. Walther had been in Buffalo, N.Y. for the colloquy with the Buffalo Synod in November, 1866.
5. Walther preferred more free conferences of all confessional Lutherans before any new organization or federation of synods be effected.
6. J. A. F. W. Mueller (1825-1900), the first graduate of the Log Cabin seminary, was pastor in Pittsburg and attended the Reading meeting as the representative of the Missouri Synod.
7. Walther has Gottfried and Siegmund Fritschel in mind, the two leading lights of the Iowa Synod.
8. See "Convention der ev.-lutherischen Synoden zu Reading, Pa., von 11. bis 13. December 1866," in *Der Lutheran* XIII (1867) pp. 15-20.
9. The Iowa Synod, though considered by Walther as being too lax confessionally, had raised concerns about some points of theology in the General Council.
10. These names cause us considerable difficulty because the original letter is not available. In the CHI a handwritten copy is available on the basis of which Wadewitz made his transcription. The person who copied the original had difficulty in reading the names, because some of them obviously are mutilated, which becomes evident when one compares this letter with the printed records of the Buffalo Synod. But the printed Buffalo Synod records provide no easy solutions either, since there were some pastors in the Buffalo Synod in the first half of the 1860s who came and went. In some cases there is no information where they came from or when they joined the Synod, and termination of membership is sometimes not clear. I have tried to correct the obvious mutilations in spelling by logical reasoning and by process of elimination. I believe that of the dozen errors occuring in the Wadewitz transcription (all but one of which were in the German long-hand copy which he was forced to use in the absence of the original) there can be any doubt in only 2 or 3 cases. The names of "Lowen" and "Lohe" caused me the most difficulty, the second and last ones on the list. But by process of elimination one can be reasonably certain about these also. It is reasonably certain that Walther wrote "Renold" and "Schroeer" originally.
11. Christian Hochstetter (1829-1905) from Wuerttemberg, came to America about 1850 or 1851, affiliated with the Ohio Synod, served a congregation in Ft. Wayne, Ind., which was in opposition to Wm. Sihler and St. Paul's congregation of the Missouri Synod. Hochstetter joined the Buffalo Synod in the 1850s, and became alarmed at J.A.A. Grabau's authoritarianism. He was a leader in the pro-Missouri movement in the mid-1860s, and joined the Missouri Synod in 1867.
12. Wadewitz reads "Lowen" here, but there is no such name in all the Buffalo Synod records. Ernst Denef, the Buffalo Synod historian, in his history of the Buffalo Synod published serially in *Die Wachende Kirche* (1923-1925) gives the name of a Pastor Renold who was pro-Missouri. However, this name does not seem to occur in any Buffalo Synod records. I am conjecturing that Denef is not likely to have made a mistake and that Renold is the name in the original. I have, however, not turned up one clue about him in the Missouri Synod.
13. Johannes Wilhelm Weinbach (1841-1913), born in Cleveland, Ohio, served in the Buffalo Synod ministry in New Wallmow, and Martinsville, N.Y. He favored the Missouri

Synod, was deposed by his congregation in 1867, and the following year joined the Missouri Synod, bringing the larger part of the Martinsville congregation with him. In the Missouri Synod he served as President of the Canada District and as editor of the paper called *Lutherische Volksblatt*. In his last years he served as pastor of the church in Little York, N.Y.

14. Franz Gottfried Zeumer, served the Ohio Synod in Pittsburg, Penn., then served at St. Peter's, New Wallmow, N. Y., of the Buffalo Synod. He was assistant professor at Martin Luther Seminary, Buffalo. In 1867 he joined the Missouri Synod while pastor in Rome, N.Y., (where he is listed as F. G. Zeumer), but the following year it is simply stated that he had left his congregation and the Missouri Synod. Further information on him was not available.

15. Edo Leemhuis (1807-1892) from Hanover, began his ministry in America in Lafayette, Ind., where he exerted a strong confessional influence. He served in the Buffalo Synod, but in 1867 was among those pastors who affiliated with the Missouri Synod. He served congregations in New York and Pennsylvania.

16. A. G. Doehler (? — 1896), came from Germany in Nov. 1857 when he heard of the Buffalo Synod's need for pastors. When there was a split in the Missouri Synod congregation in Pomeroy, Meigs Co., Ohio (founded by Wm. Sihler), and the discontented rump group applied to the Buffalo Synod, Doehler was sent there, to the distress of Paulus Heid, the LCMS pastor in Pomeroy. Before long, Doehler served a small off-shoot of an Iowa Synod congregation (Salem) in Toledo, after the congregation had split on the issue of chiliasm under the ministry of Johannes Doerfler. By 1861 he was in Buffalo as assistant to Grabau at the Buffalo Synod's Martin Luther Seminary. In two years he was at Wollcottsburg, N.Y. as pastor. In 1867 he joined the Missouri Synod with his congregation, but by 1871 he resigned from Synod because of his view on usury. Before long, however, he was back in the ministry in Door Co., Wis., and brought this congregation into the Missouri Synod. He died in Two Rivers, Wis.

17. A. Carl Christian Groszberger (1843-1898), born in Bavaria, student at Wartburg Seminary (Iowa Synod), Dubuque, Iowa, then switched to the Buffalo Synod, was given a post as teacher in Buffalo, and in a few years managed to pass the examinations for the ministry and in 1866 entered the ministry in Kewaskum, Wis. After the 1866 Colloquy he worked for the unity of Missouri and Buffalo Synod elements there, and he became pastor of the Missouri Synod congregation also. In 1869 he took over the pastorate at historic St. Andreas church in Buffalo, and later served other congregations in the east. He died in Worcester, Mass.

18. Hermann C. A. Kanold (1838-1909), born in Sachsen-Weimar, Germany; his family emigrated in 1850, settled in Johannisburg (near Buffalo) N.Y.; he attended the Buffalo Synod seminary and entered the ministry in 1861, serving several congregations in upper New York. After the Buffalo Colloquy of 1866, Kanold became pastor of the reunited congregation in Wolcottsville, N.Y.

19. Friedrich J. Mueller, long-time acquaintance of Heinrich von Rohr, the latter one of the leaders of the Prussian immigration in 1838-39, Mueller having been a musician in the military band in the outfit in which von Rohr served as captain. Mueller served as teacher in the Lutheran school in Buffalo, then studied theology in the first group of four students at Martin Luther Seminary, Buffalo. He served in the ministry in New York and Wisconsin. After the Buffalo Colloquy of 1866, his congregation in Freistadt, Wis., for the most part merged with the Missouri Synod congregation there, and Mueller was out of a job. He had broken both with the pro-Missouri majority, as well as with Grabau, and thus openings were few, but he served a small church in Wollcottsville, N.Y. for some years, even trying to conduct a small seminary program there, no doubt one of the most unimposing theological enterprises ever conducted in America. When Friedrich G. Maschop (see below), president or "Senior" of this little rump synod, resigned from this "synod" and from the ministry, and when von Rohr, his successor as president, died in 1874, Mueller even got to be president of this branch-off of the Buffalo Synod, but he

died soon thereafter. Nothing further is known about his son, who also served in the ministry of the Buffalo Synod.

20. Friedrich G. Maschop appears in the records first when it was announced that his New York Ministerium congregation in Newark, N.J., joined the Buffalo Synod in 1852. He gained in prominence in this organization, and was the focus of anti-Grabau sentiment, but he had no sympathy for the Missouri Synod position, and thus in 1866, at the time of the breakup of the Buffalo Synod, Maschop headed a small group which included von Rohr, Friedrich Mueller, and a few others. In 1870 he resigned, and disappears from history. The Buffalo Synod historian, Ernst Denef, could only report that he had heard that Maschop had died in Iowa at his daughter's home.

21. Karl Schadow (1815?-1887) was a graduate of the Gosner mission seminary in Berlin; he worked in Indiana for the Ohio Synod, and in 1863 came to Detroit and joined the Buffalo Synod. He soon became one of the sharpest critics of Grabau, but at the same time continued his hostility to the Missouri Synod. Schadow insisted Grabau be deposed, which was actually accomplished even before the Colloquy of 1866. He served congregations in upper New York, and remained affiliated with the Maschop-von Rohr split from the Buffalo Synod until this small group, after the deaths of Maschop and von Rohr, made overtures to join the Wisconsin Synod in 1877. Schadow accused them of unionism, and remained aloof with his church in Detroit. He died in Bergholz, N.Y., 1887.

22. Gustav Wollaeger was a Loehe missionary who was to work for the Iowa Synod when he came to America about 1858. In the Buffalo-Iowa discussions, he came to agree with Grabau against Iowa on the issue of chiliasm, and thus joined the Buffalo Synod. He was pastor of St. Paul's congregation, Milwaukee, the Buffalo Synod part of the first Lutheran church in Wisconsin. He was inclined to the Missouri Synod, but just before the 1866 Colloquy he perpetrated an indiscretion with a girl in his congregation. He bared his soul to his congregation, and was asked to remain as pastor. He consulted Walther, and was encouraged to remain, but the turmoil in the Buffalo Synod exacerbated the situation so that his congregation was broken into three parts. The Maschop-von Rohr group "confirmed" his resignation in 1867. When Grabau had been deposed, Wollaeger inherited the unenviable position of Senior Minister, but this did not preserve him from subsequent obscurity.

23. G. Meiszner was thought to have been a Loehe man by the Buffalo Synod historian, Ernst Denef. Grabau, in a history of the parish school in Buffalo, once remarked that Meiszner was from Schlesien, that he had been taken in with the Roggenbuck sect but had returned to the Buffalo Synod and taught school in Buffalo. Later he evidently became a pastor, and he served at St. Paul's, Milwaukee till 1858. He seems to have become a member of the Indianapolis Synod, and subsequently is lost in obscurity.

24. George P. Runkel (1833-1905), was born in Hessen-Darmstadt, Germany, but when and where he entered the ministry is not known. He served congregations in Aurora, Ind., and in 1867 joined the Missouri Synod. In 1883 he accepted a call to Los Angeles, and later served as president of the California-Nevada District.

25. A. Christian Bauer (1833-1916), born in Bavaria, was partially trained for the ministry by Loehe and arrived in America in 1853. He was to work in the Iowa Synod but felt uncomfortable there. In 1860 he threw in his lot with Buffalo. He served congregations in Michigan and Ohio. In 1867 he joined the Missouri Synod. He resigned from the ministry about 1894.

26. Friedrich Eppling, from Elsass, trained in Neuendettelsau under Loehe and then studied at the Ft. Wayne seminary 1848-9. He served in Indiana but felt the Missouri Synod had not been dealing uprightly with the Buffalo Synod, so he joined the latter. He served various congregations in the Buffalo Synod, but the Buffalo Colloquy in 1866 froze him out. He could not stay in the Buffalo Synod, but neither could he return to Missouri, so he joined the Ohio Synod. During this time he pastored historic David Star congregation, Kirchhayn, Wis., which was then unaffiliated. In the election controversy, Eppling felt

185

uncomfortable in the Ohio Synod, thus joined Wisconsin. He died in retirement in 1897.

27. Friedrich Winkler was one of the earliest confessional Lutherans from Germany who came to America to plant the church, having arrived early in the 1830s. He served famous St. John's in Newark, N.J. for most of that decade. It is interesting to note that he was succeeded there by Maschop (see above), when he left to go to Columbus to work in the Ohio Synod seminary. Winkler has not been credited for his significant input among the Loehe men, and his leadership of the German confessional block at the Columbus seminary. When the Loehe men disassociated themselves from the Ohio Synod, Winkler was the chairman of their continuation committee before they began to negotiate with the Saxons in Missouri. The German Lutherans in Chicago asked Winkler to come as their pastor. He felt he had to decline, but recommended C. A. T. Selle, who became the famous Chicago pioneer pastor then. Winkler, however, accepted a call to Detroit, becoming the first resident Lutheran pastor there, and when he was caught in the bind between the Missouri and the Buffalo Synods, he threw in his lot with Buffalo. He left the pastorate at historic St. Matthew's in Detroit to become a professor at Martin Luther Seminary, Buffalo in 1856. From there on, his life was one increasing swirl of tragedy. He died in 1878.

28. Karl Gram (1834-1913) born in Magdeburg, Germany of a knightly family, was one of the original Grabau immigration to Buffalo, studied in the Buffalo seminary, and from 1858 served a number of congregations in upper New York. In the Buffalo Synod tensions of 1866, he resigned his ministry in Johannisburg, and sided with Grabau. He reentered the ministry later, and for many years, after the dust had settled, he served at St. Paul's Church, Milwaukee.

29. Georg Tuerk, a man partially trained by Loehe, was in America by the time the Missouri Synod was organized in 1847. It seems that he was supposed to receive more training before trying to launch out into the ministry, but he found a ready opening in Marion, Ohio, and established himself as pastor there. When the Missouri Synod declined to recognize him, referring to his many deficiencies, he joined the Buffalo Synod. He was catapulted into an important charge at St. Paul's, Milwaukee, but soon went east, serving in New York and New Jersey. He seems to have joined several different synods, including the Michigan Synod. He died in Lansing, Mich., in 1904.

30. Gottlob W. R. Graetz (1821—92) from Berlin, Germany, studied theology in Columbus, Ohio, was a member of the Buffalo Synod, possibly coming to the Buffalo Synod thru the influence of Winkler. He served as an important pioneer in Wisconsin for the Buffalo Synod when he was pastor in Cedarburg, from whence he reached out to many other places. He could not maintain himself in the Buffalo Synod in 1866, so he rejoined the Ohio Synod.

March 25, 1867

1. Christoph Heinrich Loeber came to America as a child in the Saxon emigration. He was an early graduate of Concordia Seminary. From 1862 to 1869 he was pastor at Thornton (also known as Coopers Grove), Cook County, Ill. In 1869 he accepted a call to Milwaukee, Wis., and from 1885 to 1893 he was director of the Missouri Synod college there. Ludwig Fuerbringer gives Loeber's address as "Milwaukee, Wis.," but he was still in Thornton at the time this letter was written.

2. Walther is referring to the Buffalo Colloquy, held in Dec. 1866, in which representatives of the Buffalo Synod and of the Missouri Synod discussed points of theological difference. The result was that a majority of the pastors of the Buffalo Synod were convinced their former position was untenable and then joined the Missouri Synod.

3. Gotthold Loeber had been pastor in Perry County, Mo., and had died Aug. 19, 1849.

4. The Pastor Hahn referred to here must be J. G. Hahn, who was pastor at Brady's Bend, Armstrong County, Pa., in the 1850s. Karl Gram was one of the faithful adherents of Grabau, serving congregations in Johannisburg and Martinsville, N. Y., and for many years as pastor of St. Paul's, Milwaukee. For his autobiography see *Die Wachende Kirche,* Vol. 47 (Sept. 1, 1913), p. 133. He died in 1913.

5. On Heinrich von Rohr see note 23 under Jan. 2, 1845, p. 178. His son Philip Andreas (1843—1908) joined the Wisconsin Synod in 1877 and was its president 1889—1908.

June 30, 1869

1. Walther, president of Synod, was in Ft. Wayne at the time, and Sihler was vice-president. Rev. W. Stubnatzi was Sihler's assistant in Ft. Wayne. On H. C. Schwan see note 1 under May 15, 1866, p. 182.
2. Eduard Preuss, a well-trained German scholar, was being engaged by the Missouri Synod to teach in St. Louis. Two and a half years later he joined the Roman Catholic Church.
3. In the 1850s and 1860s the Missouri Synod was exploring the plan of having exchange professors from other Lutheran synods teach at synodical schools.
4. The General Council was a new federation of relatively conservative English-speaking Lutheran synods organized in 1866. Some of the more confessional synods, like Missouri, Wisconsin, Ohio, and the Norwegians, joined and left, or refrained from joining. Early in the 1870s these latter synods tried to find a way of amalgamating their seminary programs as well as amalgamating their congregations into state synods.
5. August Craemer, head of the practical seminary in St. Louis at that time.
6. For Herman Baumstarck, who (like Preuss) joined the Roman Catholic Church, see note 10 under May 21, 1861, p. 190.

Nov. 1, 1870

1. The Ohio Synod took the initiative in negotiations which led to the formation of the Synodical Conference in 1872. One of the objectives was to have the participating synods pool their resources for ministerial training, and another was to effect an amalgamation of synods in a more orderly fashion, which was later called the state synod plan. On this see note 2 under Dec. 7, 1876, p. 188.

Feb. 21, 1872

1. Friedrich Brunn of Steeden, Germany, was operating a recruitment program for church workers for the Missouri Synod at that time. He gave young men some preliminary training, then sent them to America, where they were further educated in either theology or teaching.
2. John 9:4.
3. In spite of Walther's pleading, Fuerbringer did not come.

July 11, 1873

1. Walther was president of the Synodical Conference, which was just about to convene its second convention, July 16 — 22, in Ft. Wayne. Sihler was not an officer, Prof. W. F. Lehmann of the Ohio Synod being the vice-president.
2. It is not quite clear either from Walther's letter or from the minutes of the Synodical Conference convention what the division of labor was on the first of the theological essays presented there, "Thesen ueber Kirchengemeinschaft" ["Theses on Church Fellowship"], *Verhandlungen der zweiten Versammlung der Evang.-Luth. Synodal-Conferenz von Nord-America* [*Proceedings of the Second Convention of the Ev.-Luth Synodical Conference of North America*] *zu Fort Wayne, Ind., vom 16 biz zum 22. Juli 1873.* (Columbus, Ohio: Druck von John J. Gaszmann, 1873), pp. 5—20. The minutes give no clue as to who delivered the essay or who led the discussions. It may have been planned to have a cooperative presentation by both Walther and Sihler.
3. Prof. E. A. Brauer, professor in St. Louis to 1872, and at the time of this writing pastor of Trinity, St. Louis.
4. Walther evidently prepared the material for the second theological presentation at the 1873 convention of the Synodical Conference. The topic was "Thesen ueber das Jus Parochiale" ["Theses on Parochial Rights"], ibid., pp. 20—26, in which the matter of

orderly arrangement of parish boundaries was discussed. This is one of the classics in Lutheran theology.

Feb. 20, 1875

1. Carl Manthey-Zorn (1846—1928) was a missionary of the Leipzig Mission Society in India. A year after Walther wrote this letter, Zorn and three other Leipzig missionaries left that society on doctrinal grounds, and several of them became pastors in the Missouri Synod.
2. John Frederick Zucker (1842—1927), also a missionary of the Leipzig Mission Society in India, see note above. Zucker also became a pastor in the Missouri Synod.

Aug. 8, 1876

1. Johann Christoph Wilhelm Lindemann was director of the synod's normal school in Addison, Ill. See note under Aug. 7, 1878, p. 192.
2. Hugo Hanser was pastor in Baltimore, Md.
3. The practical seminary, formerly in Ft. Wayne, was to be moved to Springfield, Ill.

Nov. 22, 1876

1. On Ottomar Fuerbringer see note 2 under May 1841, p. 173.
2. Carl Manthey-Zorn (1846—1928), former Leipzig Mission Society missionary in India, 1876—81 pastor in Sheboygan, Wis., and 1881—1911 in Cleveland. For more on Zorn see Feb. 20, 1875, note 1, p. 188.
3. Heinrich A. Ph. Kleinhans of St. Paul's, Herman, Sheboygan Co., Wis., a Hermannsburger missionary in the Wisconsin Synod.
4. A. Daniel Stecher, sent by the Dresden Verein to America, became a missionary in Wisconsin and founded several congregations in the Sheboygan area. He was pastor at Trinity, Sheboygan, at the time of this letter. It may not be insignificant that he had serious tensions with his members, resigned his ministry a year after this letter was written, and left behind him a split congregation.

Dec. 7, 1876

1. This letter is obviously written to one of the district presidents of the Missouri Synod, but not to Wunder or Strasen, since they are mentioned in the letter itself. It could be H. C. Schwan of the Central District, or C. Gross of the Eastern District, or O. Fuerbringer of the Northern District or J. F. Biltz of the Western District.
2. The plan which Walther mentions, of demarcating the synods, was called the state synod plan. It basically involved having all Missouri Synod congregations, for example, which were in Ohio, join the Ohio Synod, having all Missouri Synod and all Ohio Synod congregations in Illinois join a new synod whose boundaries would be coterminous with the boundaries of the state, and so on. These different synods then were to comprise the Synodical Conference. See also note 1 under Nov. 1, 1870, p. 187.
3. Heinrich Wunder (1830—1913) was president of the Illinois District. He served as pastor of St. Paul's Church, Chicago, for 62 years.
4. Karl J. A. Strasen (1827—1909), president of the Northwestern District, was for 41 years pastor of St. John's Church, Watertown, Wis.
5. Matthias Loy (1828—1915), president of the Ohio Synod.

Nov. 25, 1877

1. Among Lutherans in Saxony there had been a concerned caucus of people who were finding it more and more uncomfortable to remain in the state church. When the government consistory no longer required pastors to pledge themselves to the Lutheran Confessions, two small congregations, in Dresden and in Nieder-Planitz, left the state church and in 1872 called Friedrich Carl Theodor Ruhland (1836—79) as pastor. In June 1877 the Saxon Free Church was organized. See *Verhandlungen der ersten*

Jahresversammlung der Synode der evang.-luth. Freikirche in Sachsen u. a. St. [*Proceedings of the First Annual Convention of the Synod of the Evangelical Lutheran Free Church in Saxony and Other States*], Anno Domini 1877 (Zwickau i. S.: Druck and Verlag von Johannes Herrmann), held June 20—26, 1877.

2. A. Hoerger had gathered an independent congregation in Memmingen, Bavaria. In the 1870s he had association with the Saxon Lutherans who organized the Saxon Free Church. But he was caustic in his criticism and soon alienated most people, including Walther. It is not certain who the Krauss is to whom Walther makes reference here. Wagner was evidently a German churchman who had left the state church, but his name does not appear on the roster of the free churches.

3. Walther may be referring to Valentin Curtius (1493—1573), one of the earliest adherents of Luther and leader of the Reformation in Rostock and Luebeck.

4. Friedrich Brunn in Steeden, in western Germany, had separated from the state church already in 1846 and was active in the free church movement. See note 1 under Feb. 21, 1872, p. 187.

5. On Schwan see note 1 under May 15, 1866, p. 182. Henry August Allwardt (1840—1910) was a Missouri Synod pastor who later opposed Walther in the predestinarian controversy and joined the Ohio Synod. On Sihler see note 1 under April 19, 1849, p. 175. Wolfgang Simon Stubnatzy (1829—80) was a Bavarian trained by Loehe for the ministry and was pastor of the congregation in Thornton (also known as Coopers Grove), Cook County, Ill., 1849—62, then called to St. Paul's, Ft. Wayne, as Sihler's assistant. Walther spells the name with an "i" at the end.

6. *Luther's Works,* American Edition, 7, trans. Paul D. Pahl (St. Louis: Concordia Publishing House, 1965), 64.

March 23, 1881

1. Johann Georg Sauer (1814—85) had been serving as the associate of Dr. Wm. Sihler at St. Paul's Church, Ft. Wayne, Ind., since 1876.

2. Walther is no doubt referring to Stephanus Keyl, who was immigrant missionary in New York for the Missouri Synod.

3. Heinrich Christian Schwan was president of Synod.

4. Frederick William Stellhorn (1841—1919), Missouri Synod pastor and at that time professor at the college in Ft. Wayne, Ind. Although Walther evidently was relieved at some news from him, before long Stellhorn left the Missouri Synod and joined the Ohio Synod.

5. The headquarters of the Ohio Synod was located in Columbus, Ohio.

6. Matthias Loy (1828—1915) was president of the Ohio Synod.

Walther the Schoolman

Aug. 1, 1855

1. Goettingen University, founded in 1737, came to rank as one of the outstanding universities in the world. Johann David Michaelis (1717—91) and his pupil Johann Gottfried Eichhorn (1752—1827) had advanced the cause of higher-critical theology, which was unpalatable to confessional scholars like Walther.

Dec. 29, 1855

1. Gustavus Seyffarth (1797—1885), professor at the University of Leipzig and noted Egyptologist. He held two earned doctorates. When he was pensioned by his university, Walther was very anxious to secure his services for the seminary in St. Louis. Seyffarth differed with Walther on the slavery issue and very likely found his continuing service uncomfortable. He taught at the St. Louis seminary 1856—59.

2. Adolf Biewend (1816—58), a gifted young scholar whose career was cut short by an untimely death.
3. Gottlieb Christoph Adolf von Harless (1806—78), a Bavarian churchman, professor at Erlangen and other universities.

March 25, 1856

1. On Seyffarth see note 1 under Dec. 29, 1855, p. 189.
2. Conrad Diehlmann of Rainham, Canada, was the man whose services Walther secured to publish the *St. Louiser Volksblatt.*

May 7, 1861

1. Theodor Ernst Buenger (1821—76), a younger brother of Walther's wife and of Pastor Johann Friedrich Buenger (see note 14 under Jan. 2, 1845, p. 178) was teacher at Immanuel, Chicago.
2. Walther gives the address of Kerckkoff or Kerkkof as: Kerkkofs Farm, Sand Creek, Hillsboro, Jefferson Co., Mo.
3. Heinrich Boernstein was a prominent German in St. Louis, and was editor of *Westliche Post,* a German newspaper. He was named as commander of the Second Regiment of German volunteers in the hectic days of spring and early summer 1861, when the Germans rallied in St. Louis to the cause of the Union, to prevent the Federal arsenal from falling into the hands of Governor Jackson.
4. It has not been ascertained who the Muellers were. Heinrich Wunder (1830—1913) became pastor of St. Paul's, Chicago, in 1851. Georg Schick (1831—1915) had been pastor at Immanuel, Chicago, but was at the time on the faculty of the preparatory department of the St. Louis seminary. He must have been in Chicago at this time.

May 21, 1861

1. Jacob M. Buehler (1837—1901) the pioneer Missouri Synod pastor in California. See the letter of Sept. 30, 1860, p. 69 of this volume.
2. Claiborne F. Jackson was governor of Missouri from the time of his inauguration, Jan. 4, 1861, till the Provisional State Convention removed him at the end of July 1861.
3. On Heinrich Boernstein see note 3 under May 7, 1861, p. 190.
4. Frank Blair Jr. (Walther uses the original German spelling, "Blaer") was a leading figure in the pro-Lincoln political life in St. Louis in 1861. He was elected to Congress, and in the crucial days in May and June, when it looked as if the governor of the state, Claiborne F. Jackson, would be able to swing all of Missouri to the Confederate cause, it was largely due to Blair's leadership that the young Germans were organized into a military troop which soon gained official status in the Union forces, Blair himself receiving a commission. He eventually rose to the rank of a brigadier general.
5. Johann Jacob Goenner was rector. Georg Schick was conrector.
6. The Voigt family has not been identified, but presumably they lived in Jefferson County.
7. Ch. A. Mennicke (1834—1909) had just graduated from the seminary in 1861. He was posted to Rock Island, Ill. See the letters to him in this volume.
8. C. August T. Selle (1819—98) had left the parish in Crete, Ill. in 1858 and was now serving at Immanuel, Rock Island.
9. E. L. Mangelsdorf (1837—1908), a son of Trinity, St. Louis, finished the seminary course in 1861 and was sent to Belleville, Ill.
10. Hermann Baumstarck (Walther seems to have spelled it "Baumstark") had studied at the universities of Heidelberg and Leipzig, took a finishing course at the St. Louis seminary, and was ordained June 9, 1861, at St. John's, Quincy. Two years later he was called to Aurora, Ill., and soon after that was appointed as instructor at the St. Louis seminary. Before the end of the decade he defected to the Roman Catholic Church.
11. J. Leonhard Mueckel (1835—70) was posted to Trinity, West Seneca, N. Y. when he had finished the seminary.

12. The "conditional Union people" were those who believed that the Union should be preserved if at all possible, but without war.
13. Cf. Romans 13:1.
14. This may have been Rev. Heinrich Steger (1836—1906), who was pastor of the congregations in Cumberland, Md., and Pine Hill, Pa., at the time.
15. Wilhelm Bartling (1838—98) had vicared in Pittsburgh for E. A. Brauer, then was posted to Elk Grove, Ill. He was married to Minna Brackmann.
16. Friedrich August Schmidt (1837—1928) was a gifted seminary graduate of 1857 who was working in Baltimore. He was trying to get an English congregation going for the Missouri Synod. The whole enterprise collapsed in a year or two. For more on him see notes 1 and 2 under Jan. 9, 1866, p. 181.
17. These men have not been further identified, but from Walther's letters they appear to have been members and mainstays of F. A. Schmidt's English congregation in Baltimore.

Aug. 11, 1862
1. On Johannes Walther see note 2 under Feb. 24, 1860, p. 169.

May 16, 1866
1. Christian Diez was a music teacher in Milwaukee, but also taught in St. John's parochial school in that city. He was received as an advisory member of Synod in 1853, but seems to have prospered more as a private music teacher.
2. Karl Brauer (1831—1907) had come to America in 1850 and taught in various parochial schools in Synod. He served as professor of music at the Teachers Seminary in Addison, Ill., from 1866 to 1897. In 1888 he published his famous *Choralbuch*. He contributed many articles on music and on organs in the teachers' journal of the Missouri Synod, the *Evangelisch-Lutherisches Schulblatt*.

July 10, 1871
1. The Wisconsin Synod's college at which students received their pretheological training was located in Watertown, Wis.
2. Obviously by "superior officer" Walther, the president of Synod, was meant.
3. Walther quotes the English directly from the periodical.
4. W. Achenbach (1831—99), conrektor of the college in Ft. Wayne, received a call to Venedy, Washington Co., Ill., and was installed there Sept. 3, 1871.
5. Walther quotes the English directly from the periodical.
6. Georg Schick (1831—1915) had come to America in 1854, took a position as pastor of Immanuel, Chicago, and in less than two years was called to the preparatory department at St. Louis. He moved to Ft. Wayne with the preparatory department and was rector of the prep school in Ft. Wayne for some decades then. Obviously he suffered under the difficulties the school encountered there and repeatedly submitted his resignation.
7. As president of Synod, Walter was required to make regular visitations at synodical schools to assess their function.
8. G. Alexander Saxer was director of the preparatory department in St. Louis and, like Schick, moved to Ft. Wayne when this department was established as a separate preparatory school in 1861. Very little is known about him. He was in charge of this school for 14 difficult years. There were serious health problems at the school in Ft. Wayne, and serious administrative problems, some of them disciplinary in nature.
9. Rudolf Lange was a professor in the preparatory department in St. Louis and also was moved to Ft. Wayne.
10. Here again Walther uses the English.
11. Again Walther uses the English.

Dec. 14, 1871
1. Gottlieb Sihler was the second son of Wilhelm Sihler and was usually known as Ernst G. He did not go into the ministry but became a professor of classical languages.

191

2. On Eduard Preuss see note 2 under June 30, 1869, p. 187.
3. See "Einige Gedanken ueber die Gefahren Deutschlands in der Gegenwart und Zukunft," by Sihler, in *Lehre und Wehre*, XVIII (Jan. 1872) pp. 9-16.
4. Georg Schick was pastor of Immanuel church, Chicago, and in 1856 he became professor at the preparatory department of the St. Louis seminary.
5. C. H. Rudolf Lange had taught in the preparatory department 1858–1861.
6. On Theodor Brohm see note 6 under May 2, 1860, p. 170.
7. There were two Stubnatzi's in the Missouri Synod ministry at the time, Ernst (1843–86) and Wolfgang S. (1829–80). On the latter see note 5 under Nov. 25, 1877, p. 189. It is not clear which of the two Walther had in mind.

May 30, 1872

1. Hugo Hanser (1831–85) had just been elected to a special committee to investigate the unsatisfactory condition at the Ft. Wayne college.
2. The preparatory department of the St. Louis seminary had been moved to Ft. Wayne, Ind., in 1861. When students graduated there, they entered the seminary in St. Louis.
3. The sense of this sentence does not seem to agree with that of the following ones, but we checked Walther's original letter and found that he wrote "nichts weniger als," which seems to make our translation imperative. Perhaps Walther meant to write "etwas weniger als," "something less than."
4. On Lindemann see note 1 under Aug. 7, 1878, p. 192.
5. Friedrich Wyneken was president of the Missouri Synod at the time.
6. H. C. Schwan was president of the Central District at this time.

Jan. 6, 1873

1. Ferdinand Sievers (1816–93), the man who really espoused the cause of missions in the Missouri Synod.
2. A. F. Brackmann was a teacher from Baltimore who was engaged by an association of Lutherans in St. Louis to conduct what Walther calls a "Buergerschule." This word, precisely translated, is "citizens' school." August C. Stellhorn, *Schools of The Lutheran Church—Missouri Synod* (St. Louis: Concordia Publishing House, 1963), pp. 165 f., takes this as the first attempt at a Lutheran high school in St. Louis. From a letter of Walther dated Dec. 4, 1869, it is evident that the enterprise was not going well.
3. Edmund R. Baierlein had been one of the missionaries working among Indians in Michigan before the Missouri Synod was organized. He had been trained by the Leipzig Mission Society but sent by Loehe. In 1853 the Leipzig Society wanted their man back in order to send him to India. Since Baierlein had been a member of Synod and knew the pastors, he served as a natural bridge between the Missouri Synod and the Leipzig Mission Society's work in India.
4. The two sons must have been Frederick, born 1852, and Bernhard, born 1853.
5. For the letters from Neustadt see "Nachrichten aus und ueber die bairische Landeskirche, aus zwei Privatbriefen," in *Der Lutheraner*, XXIX, 66–68.

Aug. 7, 1878

1. This letter to J. C. W. Lindemann (1827–79), since 1864 director of the teachers seminary in Addison, Ill. (today Concordia Teachers College, River Forest, Ill.), reflects some of the problems this man had. He was a gifted individual but had received little formal education. It is obvious that he felt inferior. He died less than half a year after Walther wrote him this letter.
2. This is probably a combination of Psalms 62:5; 37:9; 49:3; 112:4.

June 19, 1881

1. On Johann Georg Sauer see note 1 under March 23, 1881, page 189.
2. On August Crull see note 4 under Jan. 8, 1866, p. 170.